Phone Losers of America

Phone Losers of America

by Brad Carter

Big Beef Bueno Books
PO Box 465, Albany, OR 97321

Copyright (c) 2010 by Brad Carter
First printing, November 2010

This book is a work of fiction. Names, characters, credit card numbers, places and incidents are either the product of the author's imagination or are used fictitiously, and any resemblance to actual persons, living or dead or undead, business establishments, events, uprisings or locales is entirely coincidental. Except for that thing at Fred Meyer, we totally did that.

ISBN 1452876169
EAN-13 9781452876160

No part of this publication may be reproduced, stored in or introduced into a retrieval system, or transmitted, in any form, or by any means (electronic, mechanical, morse code, photocopying, recording, smoke signals, artsy reenactments, reading stories to your friend on the phone, or otherwise), without the prior written permission of both the copyright owner and the above publisher of this book.

The scanning, uploading, and distribution of this book via the Internet or via any other means without the permission of the publisher is illegal and punishable by law. Furthermore, after you read the stories in this book you'll want to think twice before you go and put this book up on a torrent since Brad is the kind of guy that would use your IP address to track you down and harass you mercilessly for years on end.

Please purchase only authorized electronic editions, and do not participate in or encourage electronic piracy of copyrighted materials, unless Sammy Davis Jr. comes to you in a dream and tells you it's okay. Your support of the author's rights is appreciated.

When you think about the proportion of the volume of ink compared to the volume of blank space on a page, it's kind of like you just paid for a giant, empty notepad. Suckers!

Illustrations provided by Rob Vincent (Page 3, 73, 291), Shane Lawson (Page 77), Quinbus (Page 92), Brad Carter (Page 152, 252), Napalmoliv (Page 158), Sakerobot (Page 168, 270), Aftershocks (Page 236)

For Roy

TABLE OF CONTENTS

Leaving..1
Dino and his Cordless Phone........................9
Fun With Call Forwarding..........................27
Remote Overhead Paging............................39
Credit Card Fraud.......................................49
Automated Harassment..............................61
History Lesson..67
Listening to Cordless Phones.....................97
Homelessness 111
Wacky Morning DJ 119
7-Eleven Looting.......................................139
Red Boxing...147
Taking Revenge Too Far............................159
Big Larry..173
eBay Feedback..179
McDonald's Sign Prank.............................197
Boulder News Frenzy................................213
Cactus 233
Beige Boxing Celina..................................237
Finding a Job...255
Curtis the Superhacker.............................267
The Yellow Pages Prank............................275
Back...281

Foreword by Rob Vincent

"I'm amazed at the accomplishments of PLA. Reading or hearing about different entities and organizations getting exploited with a hilarious twist is my idea of the perfect read." -beerfuck

It was a late summer night, sometime in the mid 1990s. Dressed in dark clothes, backpack slung over my shoulder, I snuck out the window of my bedroom. From my back yard I headed across town to my favorite rooftop, the high one with easy access to a building's worth of telephone lines belonging to businesses which had closed and emptied for the day. There was a convenient fire escape reaching from the ground straight up to the roof, and no nosy neighbors anywhere within view. I reached the roof, hooked my cheap plastic phone up by starlight, and dialed a string of digits I knew by heart.

The phone ringing soothed me until it ended in a clumsy analog clatter. A gruff voice I'd come to know well mumbled a sleepy, "Hello?"

"Cactus?" I responded cheerily, in a voice the called party had grown to know equally well. Their resulting string of swear words was *awesome*.

I'd first come across the Phone Losers of America in text files on BBSes a year or so earlier. In the mid '90s, the BBS scene was still desperately trying to be all cool and underground and exclusive. Countless text files which mostly looked and sounded alike, wrapped what actual information they had in an air of forced mystery, all "we are super-elite and we grace you with this meager info because we are *so* much smarter and cooler than you."

Smarter I could have believed. I was a total newbie and knew it, but I also knew I definitely *wasn't* cooler than very many people. I was the quiet, brooding, artsy, fat, nerdy kid with social anxieties in the back of the classroom who read *2600* and listened to *Off the Hook*. "Cool" was something that happened to other people, most of whom enjoyed kicking the crap out of me for being different, so why would my fellow nerds waste our time pretending otherwise in what was entirely our own world? That whole act struck me as really dull, stupid, and unconvincing.

Every so often, though, I'd find a file with a sense of humor. Something that spoke *my* language. Instead of forcing an unconvincing Disney villain act, the author was obviously having some damned *fun* for a change, and his life seemed to be an endless quest to amuse himself and others. These were the files I'd save to disk, maybe print out to hard copy, and reread often. It didn't take me too long to recognize that most of these really cool files were from a 'zine called "Phone Losers of America." They actually labeled *themselves* "losers," *celebrated* it even! How great was *that*? To a loser like me, *pretty freaking great!*

The writer, RedBoxChiliPepper, didn't just focus on phreak and hacker tricks. The PLA zine was a jolly mix of jokes, pranks, insane adventures, endless non-sequiturs involving some guy named Roy and a certain breed of thorny desert plant, and guides to the exact sorts of irresponsible hobbies I'd taken up to preserve what passed for my boyhood sanity. RBCP celebrated

Foreword by Rob Vincent

the angry and absurd right alongside my own twisted sense of humor, and taught stupid tech tricks while he was at it.

By day I might have been too much of a loser to stop the "cool" kids from making my life hell, but by night I was just enough of a loser to make sure their phones kept mysteriously ringing nonstop, their mailbox was overstuffed with magazine subscriptions, or their cable bill was loaded with expensive pornography for their troubles.

When you're a miserable kid who feels like nothing makes sense and the entire world is against you, your first instinct is usually to lash out and break some shit in retaliation. Using my growing skill set to accomplish the petty acts of destructive revenge every oppressed teenager dreams about, I was able to have the last laugh in my own aching head. It was more than that, though... lying on that rooftop, looking up at the stars, with endless possibilities at my fingertips as my nerdy skills, explorations, and pursuits became things I could actually make work *for* me, I felt like I was finally part of a world which could be a fun and entertaining place, and in which my taking part made some damn *sense*.

Eventually, I grew up a little. School ended, I became prosecutable as an adult and a lot less willing to pursue a life of petty crime. Without my former peers to worry about, I had a chance to finally live life on my own terms and develop my own opinions of what was "cool." For example, I rediscovered how fascinating the tech and telecom worlds were in their own right, when I wasn't just focusing on what I could use from them toward irresponsible ends. No longer out to make a pain in the ass or a criminal of myself, I realized I'd always be a hacker.

Fast-forward 15 years or so. Things have certainly changed around here. Through growing up with the PLA I built up the courage to get out of the damn house and start attending 2600 meetings. Finding crowds in which I truly belonged led me to finally figure out how to deal with other people, a skill which I hadn't had cause or ability to develop before. Taking an active role in hacker culture and meeting like-minded gecks has led to my greatest friendships, as well as my involvement with hacker conferences and *Off the Hook*. Helping newbies find their niche in the ever-evolving hacker community has become one of the driving forces in my life. Against everything I ever expected, my creative pursuits have actual audiences! I'm living the sort of life I've always wanted to, surrounded by a far better crowd of wonderful people than I ever could have asked for. My world is still an amazingly fun place, and I don't see how any of this would have happened were it not for what those crazy text files and their nerdy shits and giggles did for me half my lifetime ago.

These are the tales you now find yourself holding in the form of a book by my brilliant friend Brad Carter, RBCP himself.

Nowadays, those expensive phone calls I was going to such risk and trouble to steal range from dirt-cheap to free. I've matured into something like a reasonably responsible adult, far more interested in learning, teaching, and getting a laugh than randomly breaking stuff. But if sometime today, tomorrow, or far into the mysterious future you find yourself with access to a certain stream of telecommunications data, don't be *too* surprised if it decodes to a voice not unlike my own, still cheerfully asking some unsuspecting human the eternal question...

"Cactus?"

Rob T Firefly
Rob Vincent
New York, USA, September 2010

Leaving

"One Saturday morning I started browsing the PLA forums on my laptop. Within two minutes, I was connected to the speakerphone inside an elevator in a Las Vegas casino, yelling at the occupants to stop farting in the elevator... all the way from Australia. If that's not cool, then I don't know what is! Thanks PLA!" -Tim

    My life abruptly changed the night I let my best friend die in a gruesome phone phreaking accident. The accident wasn't exactly my fault, but I kind of assumed that the whole thing would be blamed on me since I was there and did nothing about it. So I panicked and I ran away. Looking back, I realize I could have handled it differently, but this is what I did instead.

    It began in the Spring of 1990 in Edwardsville, Illinois. It was around 3 o'clock in the morning and I sat upon a hill in a stranger's back yard, overlooking the back of the phone company building. My job was to keep a lookout as my partner in crime, Doug, rummaged around in a dumpster next to the building. We were behind the Illinois Bell building where they parked all the phone company vans and stored a few old broken phone booths. It wasn't a fenced-in area but it should have been. It's a wonder that any phone company would leave their dumpster wide open like they did. Phone phreaks had been using the "trash" found in dumpsters for decades to acquire confidential information from the phone companies, yet very few bother locking their dumpsters even today.

Sometimes we would both climb into the dumpster, grab a few bags and throw them in my car. Then we could take the loot home and sort through it for anything valuable. Doug liked to find passwords and phone numbers to modems so he could log in and attempt to gain access to Illinois Bell's computers. I was more into just the coolness of having secret phone company memos and other papers.

Employee time sheets and records were boring, but they were useful when we wanted to call Illinois Bell and impersonate an employee there. Since we had their employee number or technician ID code, they had little reason to doubt our lies.

Sometimes we would find huge printouts full of customers' voicemail passwords and phone numbers. The fun never ended with those; we could set up our own private mailboxes, we could completely take over someone else's box by changing their password and locking them out, or we could silently watch a box, checking a person's messages and never letting ourselves be known to them.

Tonight we were doing things a little differently. Doug was sitting in the dumpster, sorting through papers and looking for anything good while I sat under a tree, keeping an eye out for anyone who might interfere. Police would sometimes circle the parking lot and nighttime employees would occasionally venture outside for a cigarette break, so it was good to know when to keep still and wait for them to leave. We kept in touch with a couple of Radio Shack walkie talkies. I was tired and was only half listening as I cranked up Love and Rockets on my Sony walkman.

"Alex, are you there?" I heard Doug ask through the walkie talkie.

"Yeah, I'm here. Are you almost done? I've been sitting here for almost an hour."

"Five minutes tops. I've found something here that you'll like," he replied. "Keep a lookout when I get out."

"Gotcha," I said as I turned my walkman back up and lay down in the grass, staring at the full moon and the clouds rushing past it. Once the song ended I would sit back up and give Doug the all-clear to climb out. Right about that time must have been when the garbage truck started rolling up.

By the time I sat up, I was horrified to see it holding the dumpster in the air with its giant metal hooks, shaking the dumpster violently. I stood up and screamed for the driver to stop, but he didn't hear me. From my walkie talkie I could hear Doug yelling my name. As the garbage fell out of the dumpster and into the back of the truck his voice turned into static.

I threw down my walkman and walkie talkie and began rushing down the hill and towards the truck, hoping that I could stop them from crushing Doug alive, but by the time I jumped down onto the pavement, the garbage truck was already pulling away, out into the street.

"WAIT! STOP!" I screamed as loud as I could but the driver didn't hear me. I ran down the street and after the truck for several blocks hoping to catch up to it and jump on, but I never made it.

Any moron would know to immediately call the police. The police could have stopped the truck wherever it went and gotten to Doug. But how would that conversation go?

"Yes, officer, me and my friend were working together to steal phone company secrets when out of nowhere this garbage truck shows up..."

The problem with getting the police involved was that Doug and I had caused so many problems in the past with our phone antics that the police were sure to piece it all together if they knew what we were up to. The police had been called because of our activities so many times over the past couple of years, yet they'd never managed to figure out that a couple of innocent-looking, nerdy high school kids were responsible. In my panic, I was only thinking of myself and the trouble I would be in. I chose my own freedom over Doug's life.

Doug was surely dead by now anyway. The crushing mechanism would have gone to work immediately after the trash was dumped, right? I had to face it, Doug was dead and I was solely to blame for it. My whole future was completely screwed if I told anyone. And what if I didn't tell anyone? Would they ever find his body? Surely it would come back on me somehow. We were best friends after all. How could I look anybody in the eye and tell them I didn't know where he was?

So I ran. I ran back to the Illinois Bell building and up the hill to gather my backpack and my walkman. I eyed my walkie talkie, which was still lying on the ground. Should I even try? It was a 5 watt CB walkie talkie so if Doug was still alive he would still be in range.

"Doug?" I said nervously into the walkie talkie. "Are you there, Doug?"

Nothing but static. I felt tears coming on as I began to realize the severity of the situation and that I would never talk to

Doug again. I threw the walkie talkie against the side of a garage and watched it break into several pieces. A kitchen light turned on in the owner's house so I quickly grabbed my backpack and headed towards my car, which was parked a few blocks away.

If the police stopped me on the way to the car I wouldn't have been capable of lying to them. I'd confess everything. I'd tell them that we'd been stealing phone company trash and I watched my best friend get crushed to death and I did nothing to prevent it. That we'd been tapping into various neighbor's phone lines for years to avoid long distance charges to computer bulletin board systems. That our troublemaking had been featured in the paper so many times that Doug began keeping a scrapbook of the articles. But I wasn't stopped by anyone. I climbed into my car and began to drive towards my home in nearby Alton.

A million thoughts and questions raced through my head during the 30 minute drive. Should I just go home and sleep as if nothing happened? Should I go to school in the morning? How long would it take before authorities or parents or teachers came to me asking about Doug? What were the chances of his body even being found? Wouldn't they just dump all the trash into some big pit and nobody would ever see it? What would happen if I just confessed to everything? I'd end up in jail for sure. If not for Doug's death, they'd link our being at the phone company dumpster somehow with all the other things that we'd done over the past several years.

Breaking into voicemail boxes was nothing compared to all the chaos we'd caused since we started playing around with the phone company. There were too many newspaper articles to count that we'd been responsible for. And both of us stupidly kept clippings of every one of them. How was I supposed to get those articles out of Doug's room? Once they decided that Doug was really missing they would find a notebook full of headlines reading things like, "Local Resident Hit With $50,000 Phone Bill" and "Pay Phone Stuffing Scammers At Large" and my personal favorite, "Vandals Opening Phone Boxes, Ringing Up

Big Charges." That was just the stuff that actually made the papers. There were countless incidents that had to have been investigated at some point.

As I got within a few blocks of my home I switched off the ignition and headlights of my '79 Dodge Colt, coasting down the street and through a few stop signs. This was to avoid waking my parents with my loud engine or the backfiring that sometimes occurred when I switched it off. I rolled to a stop in front of my house and headed for the basement window, which I'd left unlocked. My parents weren't too crazy about me leaving the house so late into the night so I'd found it easiest just to come and go quietly through the windows.

By the time I'd gotten home I decided that I would leave. Not only leave the town, but the state. I could write a short note for my parents telling them I had run away and everyone would just assume that Doug came with me. Doug absolutely hated his parents and fought with them constantly whenever I visited his house. In a way I was saving his family a lot of grief, I reasoned. They'd be much better off thinking Doug had run away with me rather than knowing he was rotting away at the bottom of a nearby landfill.

Running away was something I had wanted to do for a long time. Not to run away from any problems really, but just to get out and see some more of the world and have a little more freedom. Aside from a few out of state camping trips as a kid, I really hadn't seen much of the world and I wanted to experience more. I wasn't too terribly close with my parents, I was doing horrible in school and my best friend was now dead. So what was left to stay for?

Earlier in the year my girlfriend and I had been making plans to drive a U-haul down to Texas and live. She was set on moving to an island called Galveston, which wasn't too far from Houston. I'm not sure if we would have really gone through with it or not, but we spent a lot of time planning it. Our year-long relationship ended just a few months before, so maybe I could just make the trip there myself. I had no idea what Texas had to offer but it had to be at least a little cooler than Alton, Illinois. So I figured I'd head south and see what happened.

I wanted to travel as light as possible, but ended up making about twenty trips to my car, filling it with all kinds items I thought would come in handy. I had hundreds of cassette tapes and if I had to drive for a few days then I may as well have my music. I ended up bringing about half of my clothes, my laptop computer with about 100 floppy disks, phone equipment, photos, a travel atlas, binders full of hand written information and printouts on the phone companies that I'd collected over the years. And, of course, I gathered up all the newspaper articles related to our activities, just to make sure that nobody else would find them.

I jotted a quick note on the kitchen table which simply said, "Mom & Dad, moving south. Be in touch someday. -Alex" I was careful to leave out the word "I" so they could take the note to mean "Doug and I are moving south" whenever Doug turned up missing. I wondered if they'd even notice the note sitting on the table covered with old mail, newspapers and napkins. It could be days before they even noticed I was gone since I wasn't home that often.

I stopped by a 24 hour grocery store to cash my paycheck from the movie theater I worked at. I didn't want my manager telling my parents or the authorities that I cashed my last check in Texas. After that I was off. It was 5 a.m. and the sky was just beginning to light up. I had no idea how I was going to drive all day since I hadn't slept the night before, but somehow I managed to go on until the next evening. I spent most of the day driving and finally stopped at a rest stop somewhere in Mississippi, parking my car and almost immediately falling asleep in the front seat.

I ended up arriving in Galveston, Texas early the next day. I'd slept off a good 4 hours or so at the rest stop and spent a few more hours just hanging out, eating and relaxing before hitting the road again. I was dead tired when I got into Galveston, but still managed to drive myself around the island for most of the day, checking out the sites and learning where everything was. Spending my entire life in a small Midwestern community really made me appreciate a place like Galveston. Seeing all the beaches, surf shops and palm trees was quite a culture shock for me.

Around 8:00 p.m. that night, as it started to get dark, I pulled my car into a grocery store parking lot, reclined my seat and went into a deep, dreamless sleep. I worried that the police would notice me there, find out that I was only 17-years-old and then send me back to Illinois. I couldn't afford to sleep in a motel, though. As I woke up later during the night I noticed there were several other cars, vans and RVs parked around the same, quiet end of the parking lot. I later learned that they were also sleeping in their cars every night, so I decided to keep sleeping there until I secured some income.

You'd think this story would continue in a strict, chronological format, telling you exactly what happened after I covered up the death of my best friend. But no. Instead I'm going to tell you all about the Phone Losers of America, better known as the PLA, in a completely haphazard fashion. Those of you who know about the PLA will recognize the themes and stories in this book. Those of you who are new should prepare to enter the bizarre world of the PLA, where you'll find your outlook on life severely altered and you'll never look at a telephone the same way again. Just keep reading and it will all make sense to you eventually.

Dino and his Cordless Phone

> "*This made me laugh until I was crying. I hope all is well in Dino's life and I hope he wins the lottery. He deserves something good to happen. Wherever you are Dino, I hope you are drinking a beer and chillin'.*" -Sam in Nebraska

In early 1995, after living for a month in Austin so that I could attend a hacker conference called HoHoCon, I took a train up to Illinois to visit my parents for a few weeks. I hadn't seen them in over a year at that point, and had a good time catching up with them and seeing some old friends. I'd taken up residence in their attic, and I spent most of my evenings calling up computer bulletin board systems and watching television, just killing time and chatting with friends before I headed back to Texas.

On the evening that this story took place, I was scanning local cordless phone channels on my new Bearcat scanner that I'd just purchased a few weeks earlier in Austin. Throughout the 1990s, it was easy to pick up cordless phone conversations from several blocks away with just about any police scanner.

After buying the scanner, my friend Zak, who was in Austin with me for the conference, spent hours listening to a teenage girl talk on her cordless phone and interfered with her conversations by calling up her friends and saying crazy things to them. To us it seemed like a huge leap forward in prank calling since we could listen to the cordless phone user call up everyone and flip out over the crazy pranks they were receiving.

As I sat on the couch, watching television and scanning the cordless phone channels, I suddenly heard a dial tone on my scanner and someone slowly pushing touch tones. I turned the TV down and the scanner up. The signal was coming in really loud and clear, which meant that the caller was very close to me. A girl answered the phone with the name of a local hospital, then said, "This is Sharon, may I help you?"

The man on the cordless phone didn't seem to really need anything from Sharon, but just wanted to chat. After listening to the conversation for a few minutes, I heard Sharon refer to him as Dino and it seemed that they were a married couple. Sharon seemed like a normal enough person, but Dino was extremely amusing in the way that he spoke and the bizarre things he said.

It didn't take long for me to notice that Dino wasn't very bright. He was always smoking a Marlboro and cursed nonstop, whether he needed to or not. He was always upset about trivial things and never seemed to be happy. All he did was complain to Sharon as she tried her best to console him. It was easy to come up with a mental picture of a slack-jawed Dino wearing an old flannel shirt and covering his greasy, stringy, shoulder-length hair with a Nascar cap.

As the conversation wore on, he began yelling at Sharon, telling her that something was wrong with the television and that there was nothing good to eat in the house. Meanwhile, I was thumbing through the phone book, looking for the phone number of the hospital that Sharon worked at. I found it just as Dino was making a comment about wanting to beat Sharon's ass when she got home from work, but then told her that he was just kidding. I quickly dialed the hospital and heard Sharon's phone ringing in the background as Dino continued to rant at her.

"Hold on, Dino, I've got another phone call." She put him on hold and switched over to me.

"Hey, Sharon," I said to her. "You better be careful. I think he's lying to you and he might actually beat you tonight."

Before I could even hang up on her, she clicked back over to Dino and said, "Dino, I just got the weirdest phone call..." She told him about my call and they tried to figure out how that could have happened. I felt like I'd done them a huge favor since they were now working on a problem as a team instead of yelling at each other. My single phone call had been more effective than any marriage counselor could have been. In the end, they concluded that some guy named Matt must be responsible. Not wanting to get this Matt character in trouble, I immediately called the hospital back and told Sharon that I definitely wasn't Matt.

"Dino, hang up! Somebody's listening to our conversation! It was that guy and he said that he's not Matt!"

"Huh?" Dino replied.

"The guy that we've been talking about just now." She sounded as if she were explaining to a small child. "He just called me back and told me that he's not Matt. That means that he must be listening to our conversation somehow."

"Hey, if there's some dickhead out there listening, why don't you call *me*, you chickenshit bastard! 555-3466, you little fuck," Dino yelled blindly into the phone, hoping that whoever was listening would hear him.

I could tell that this was going to be even more fun than the girl we bothered in Austin, so I called up Zak, who had the luxury of three-way calling on his line. I explained to him what was happening and that Dino had just given me his phone number, so we called him up and we both gave him a piece of our minds.

"Listen here, you little pricks," Dino yelled. "I'll give you a hundred dollars if you come over here and show your faces instead of hiding behind your fuckin' phones!"

"Would that be cash or food stamps, sir?" was Zak's hilarious reply.

"Hey, fuck you! Come on over here and show your face!"

"If we come over will you give us a beer?" I asked Dino.

"Yeah, I'll give you a beer. Come over and we can all drink a beer."

"But then you'll kick my ass."

"No, I won't kick your ass. Just come on over here and show your face."

As crafty as Dino was being, we didn't fall for his ruse and Zak finally hung up the phone on him so we could listen to him call up Sharon to yell at her about us. He called up several of his friends afterwards, telling them about our phone calls and asking if they had any idea who it could be. We wanted to make things a little more exciting for Dino, so we decided to send the police to his house. I had a cellular phone that wasn't registered to anyone's name, so I could dial 911 and they would have no idea where the call was coming from.

"911, what's your emergency?"

"Yeah, I'm over here parked on the side of the street in my car and I'm watching these kids break into some guy's house here. They're all going into the basement window and they've got flashlights."

"Alright, what address is being broken into?" the 911 operator asked and I gave him Dino's address, which Dino had given to us so that we could come over to collect our $100 and drink a beer with him. He lived across the street from my parents and I had a perfect view of his house from one of the attic windows.

I turned off the attic light and crouched by the window, waiting for the excitement to begin. Luckily, Dino lived just down the street from the neighborhood donut shop, so three police cars were there in a matter of minutes. Two of them began shining their spotlights all over his house. While all of this was happening, we were listening to Dino talk to some guy on his phone about us. Suddenly he noticed the spotlights shining into the windows and exclaimed, "Fuck! Hold on a minute!" as he ran outside to talk to the police.

Zak and I spent the next hour just listening to all the phone calls that Dino made. He called his wife at work and told her about everything that had happened with the police. Then he called up a friend and told him the same story, only this time making things up so that it was even more interesting. He asked his friend if he could borrow his caller ID box so that he could see who's calling him and the friend had to explain to him that it doesn't work like that and Dino would have to subscribe to the caller ID service with the phone company. This wouldn't do him much good anyway, given Zak's unconscious habit of always blocking his number with *67 before dialing anything.

As things became boring and repetitive in the Dino household, I once again whipped out my Motorola flip phone and made a collect call to Dino's house. When Dino answered, the operator said to him, "This is the Ameritech Cellular operator. I have a collect call from a Roy Gerbil. The charges are approximately $1.95 per minute. Will you accept the charges?"

For some reason, the idea of having to pay for harassing phone calls to himself upset Dino and he refused the charges by yelling obscenities at the operator until she hung up. Then Dino immediately clicked back over to his friend to tell him what had just happened. It was such a bonus to prank calling, getting to hear, in great detail, exactly how upset we were making our victim.

Zak picked a random name out of his telephone book and dialed the number for me, which happened to belong to a man named David Vaughn. By this time, it was past midnight.

"Hello?" a sleepy Mr. Vaughn answered.

"Hi, this is the Ameritech Messaging Service," I said. "I have an emergency message for you. Do you have a pen or pencil?"

"Uh, hold on a second," he said. "Okay, go ahead."

"Is it a pen or is it a pencil you have?" I asked.

"What?"

"Never mind. The message says that you need to call this phone number. It's 555-3466. And that it's an emergency and you need to call him as soon as possible."

"Okay. Thank you," Mr. Vaughn replied.

"Thank you for using Ameritech!"

Less than a minute later, Dino's cordless phone began ringing on my scanner. He sounded extremely pissed off when he picked up the phone and screamed, "*What!?*" at Mr. Vaughn.

"Uhhhh, someone just called here saying that I need to call you," Mr. Vaughn explained. Surprisingly, Dino actually believed what Mr. Vaughn was telling him, so he explained the entire situation to Mr. Vaughn in great detail. It was obvious that Mr. Vaughn just wanted to hang up the phone and go back to sleep. It drug on and on with Dino asking him all kinds of questions.

"Do you have a cordless phone?" Dino asked him.

"No," Mr. Vaughn replied.

"Do you have Caller I.D.?"

"No."

"Okay. Do you have a cellular phone?" Dino was unable to pronounce the word cellular correctly and it came out more like cellayer. Zak and I would burst into laugher each time he attempted the word.

"No. Whoever called me was some guy from Ameritech. It wasn't a kid."

"Did he say anything about Roy?" Dino asked.

"Uh...no, he said he was from the Ameritech Message Service and he had a message for me."

"Do you live here in Alton?"

"No, I'm in Wood River. I don't know where they got my number."

"Well, my number's in the phone book. They call me and all they can do is sit there and play little games with me. And I told 'em, hey, come down here and I'll give you a hundred dollars to see your face. I just wanna see who the hell you are. They say that they live here and his name is Chris something but I don't even know if that's true or not."

Zak and I continued to laugh hysterically together at all of Dino's silly questions and at poor Mr. Vaughn who was too polite to just hang up on Dino and go back to sleep. We repeated the same trick several times, introducing ourselves as various messaging services with names like the Goo Goo Relay Message Company. Dino, apparently starved for companionship, would keep them on the phone as long as he could, telling them all about us and the crazy night of prank calls that he was having. And he always asked them if they had caller ID, hoping that maybe they'd caught our phone number. This gave us a great idea, so Zak called Dino's house.

"Hello?" he said to me.

"Uh, yeah, I just got a call from something called the Kick Ass Relay Service and I'm supposed to call you or something?" I said in a confused voice.

"Okay, let me explain to you what's going on. There's these kids..." And Dino gave me a lengthy rant about the problems he'd been dealing with. When he asked if I had caller ID, I told him that I did, which really excited him. Caller ID was a relatively new technology in 1995 and not too many people had it yet. Dino thought he'd finally lucked out, finding someone who actually had caller ID and could reveal the identity of the pranksters once and for all. So he asked if I could check the caller ID box to see who called me.

"Okay, hold on, let me get up," I said. "Alright, you want the number that's on here?"

"Yeah!" Dino could barely contain his excitement.

"It's 618-555-0537."

He thanked me and we both hung up. He immediately called the number I gave him, not realizing it was the number of some guy Zak and I had been screwing with for the past year named Chris McCall. Chris' dad answered, "Hello?" in a sleepy voice and Dino yelled at him, "I got your number, you mother fucker!"

Chris' dad just sat there silently, not really knowing what to think as Dino continued to yell at him. After about a minute, he finally hung up on Dino. And before Dino clicked his cordless phone off, we could hear him happily *singing*, "Ha ha, you little pricks, I know who you aaaare!"

As soon as he hung up, Zak called Dino's home.

"Hello?"

"I don't think you're gonna get a record contract anytime soon with that voice," Zak told him.

"Hey, wait a minute! Hey, don't have fucking people calling my fucking house, you little fucking jack off. What's your number, man?"

"555-0537"

"Are you sure?" Dino asked playfully.

"No, I'm telling you a big fucking joke."

"Well, I imagine you would because that's all you've been doing all fucking night long is playing a fucking joke. Let me tell you something else. Every fucking call you make at my wife's fucking work number is being recorded, but I know you don't care."

"Will your wife sell me the tapes because I've said some pretty funny things tonight."

"Hey, lemme tell you something, boy, you fuck with my wife, you're fucking with your own life."

"I already have. She's not that good."

"Oh, yeah, right."

"And she gave me herpes. Well, I gotta go now." Zak was obviously bored with Dino.

"Hey, wait a minute, man, let me get a pen. I wanna call you. What's your name?"

"I'm G Homey Roy! Who you down with?"

"Fuck you!" Dino yelled.

"Okay. Bye."

"Later on, dickhead!"

Dino sure knew how to get the last word in. A few more people called Dino and told him the Huge Relay Service left his number for them and Dino went through the whole spiel of keeping them on the phone and asking them questions for as long as he could with each of them. A friend had told Dino earlier that he needed to dial *69 to get our number after we called, but Dino couldn't remember this complex string of digits and repeatedly referred to it as *32 to everyone else, which made both of us laugh every time.

After talking to Zak for awhile, rewinding the cassette tapes that I'd made of his ranting and giggling over it, we started to get bored again so we called Dino. It was now approaching 1:00 a.m.

"Hi, Dino," I said to him in a deadpan voice. "I just wanted you to know that I'm monitoring all of your phone calls."

"Yeah, I know you are, dickface," he replied.

"You know the grey box on the side of your house that says Telephone Network Interface on it? Well, I've plugged my phone into that and I have complete control over your lines. Resistance is futile."

"Yeah, you're full of shit, you little fucker! Why don't you tell me where you are?"

"Okay. We're parked across the street by the church in a blue van. There's a satellite beamed at your house so we hear everything you say even when you're not on the phone."

"Bullshit, that's the church's van. It's always parked there."

"Of course it's always parked there. We always watch you. There's a camera over there on your bookshelf."

"Listen, you little dickweeds. I'm gonna find out who you are."

"Hey, Dino," Zak said. "Exactly what year of grade school did you drop out of?"

After Zak hung up the phone, Dino called his wife at work and began telling her everything I said in a panicked voice. He'd apparently taken everything I told him seriously.

"What's wrong with you?" Sharon asked him.

"Man, these guys have got something huge going on. They've got a big setup somewhere and they said there's some kind of grey box on the outside of the house. I'm walking around the house right now looking for it."

I jumped up off of the couch and ran to the window. I looked across the street for Dino, but I must have just missed him. A second later he told his wife that he was back inside and couldn't find any grey box, but that we'd tapped his phones and that we were watching their house.

"Dino, they're probably lying and they're just listening to the cordless phone." This was the first time we'd heard them guess that it was their cordless phone's fault. If they knew we were listening to the cordless phone, then why did Dino continue to use it?

I could just imagine the dramatic spy music playing in his head as he peered out the windows at the church's van and ransacked his bookshelf, looking for hidden cameras. As tough as he acted with us on the phone, he sounded on the verge of tears while talking to his wife.

I picked up my cellular phone again and placed a call to a random number in Los Angeles, telling the roaming operator that I wanted to bill it to my home phone. The roaming operator asked for my home phone number and I gave him Dino's number.

"Okay, I'm going to have to verify charges. Could I have your name?" she asked.

"Yeah, my name is Sharon," I replied.

"Sharon?"

"Are you making fun of me?"

"Uh, no. Hold just a minute, please."

After a few rings, Dino hung up on his wife and answered his phone.

"Hello?" At this point he sounded exhausted.

"Hi, this is Ameritech Roaming operator #1753. I have a Sharon placing a call to California from her cell phone and wants to bill the charges to you. The charges are approximately $1.95 a minute. Will you accept the charges?"

"Is this really the cellayer operator?" Dino asked.

"Yeah..." she responded slowly.

"Well, I'm talking to Sharon on the other line. Is there any way you can trace that call?"

"No, I can't trace the call but I can put a block on the phone so they won't be able to bother you any more."

"Okay, could you do that?"

The cellular operator arranged to have all attempts to bill calls to his house denied. This meant that anyone wanting to make a legitimate collect or third-party call to Dino from a cellular phone on that carrier wouldn't be able to. Of course, that was just on a cellular phone, but he seemed to think this meant that there was absolutely no way that we'd be able to call him on any phone ever again.

Dino called Sharon back and explained to her that everything was taken care of and that he'd just fixed things with the operator so that we'd never be able to call them again. As he was finishing up telling her how the long nightmare was finally over and they could rest easy again, Zak called him to let him know that he was completely wrong.

I couldn't believe how much Dino and Sharon talked on the phone together. You might think that since they were a possibly a newly married couple, maybe they just enjoyed hearing each other's voices, but it wasn't like that at all. They were mostly fighting about ridiculous things or talking about the prank calls and they seemed to completely despise each other. Zak kept calling Dino during their conversation, but he refused to click over once he figured out that it was us.

After a while, they hung up with each other and Dino dialed zero and asked the operator to connect him with the local police. He told the policeman the entire story of his crazy night, oblivious to the fact that the policeman was treating him like a complete idiot. The policeman told him that there was nothing they could do about harassing calls and he should try calling the phone company. So Dino looked in the front of the phone book and found the number for Ameritech customer service. Lucky for him, the phone company's billing office was open 24 hours a day.

"You have reached the Ameritech Customer Billing Office for residential accounts. All representatives are currently busy. For faster service, please call us Tuesday through Friday during the daytime. Your call will be answered by the next available representative. Your approximate wait time is greater than ten minutes..."

Dino sat on the phone, listing to phone company hold music for more than fifteen minutes. Zak constantly interrupted the phone company's hold music with call waiting beeps, but Dino wouldn't click over and talk to us. Finally he got through and told the Ameritech representative his life story and she told him that she could change his phone number or sign him up with the caller ID service. It would cost $80 to have his number changed. She also told him that there was no such thing as a cellular operator. After spending about 10 minutes on the phone with her, he told her he wasn't ready to change his number or sign up for anything and they hung up.

He began thumbing through the yellow pages and he called up every cellular network number, only to find that they all seemed to be closed at 2:00 in the morning. Then he happened upon the number to the Illinois Relay Service and called them. He began explaining everything that had happened to him to the lady who answered, and she interrupted him by saying, "Sir, this is the Illinois Relay Service for deaf people. I have no idea what you're saying."

Soon after this, Zak hung up with me and I sat alone for several more hours, listening to Dino try to solve the mystery by calling up even more random businesses out of the phone book. I couldn't understand some of the connections he was trying to make with the places he was calling, but most places were obviously closed at that hour.

He called his wife many more times throughout the night, yelling at her and complaining about miscellaneous things and finally got her permission to change their phone number so that we could never call again. He was put on hold for another ten minutes and then arranged to have his phone number changed to an unlisted number. Fortunately for him, they decided not to charge him $80 for the change, but just $1.85 per month to keep the number unlisted. The operator gave Dino his new unlisted number as I wrote it down.

At about 4:15 a.m., he was talking to his wife at work again and they were still trying to figure out everything that happened and who could be responsible.

"Well, I'm wondering about this one house across the street, on the next block over. The whole time all this was happening the light upstairs was on and now they're not calling anymore and his light is turned off."

"Which house is it exactly?" Sharon asked.

"There's the yellow house, a blue house and then a white house and *that's* the fucking one I'm talking about."

I reached up and turned on my light.

"There his light just went on again!" Dino exclaimed.

"I know who lives there," Sharon exclaimed. "It's Alex Carbon! I went to school with him. He knows all about computers and phones and stuff. He was like a total weirdo in grade school. I bet it's him!"

Meanwhile, I'm frantically thinking, "Shit, shit, shit, shit, shit, shit, shit, shit! I've been found out!" I suddenly realized that Sharon's voice sounded familiar because I knew exactly who she was. She used to date my brother in Junior High. In fact, I used to make prank calls to Sharon all the time when we were in third grade together. She always knew it was me and would yell at me about it in school the next day. This was a semi-regular routine for Sharon and I back then. I had never heard of anyone named Dino, but I was beginning to think that it would be a good idea to cut my vacation short and head back to Texas.

Soon after this, Sharon had instructed Dino to find her high school yearbook so he could see a picture of me. Clearly unfamiliar with the concept of a book, Dino was having a tough time locating me.

"I can't find it anywhere," he complained.

"It's in the Juniors section." Sharon had reverted to her talking-to-a-child voice.

"There isn't a Junior section. It goes Senior, Sophomore, Freshman. I think they forgot to put Junior in here."

"Nooo...Look right after the Senior section, it should be there." This went on for minutes. He finally figured out the yearbook and found the right class, but then had to deal with the complex task of how to spell Carbon, which had him flipping all over the Junior class pages, even though I was on the very first page. When he finally found my picture, he said, "Yeeeah, he *looks* like someone that would do something like this."

Since Sharon worked at the hospital, she was able to access patient files on her computer and found my parents phone number, which she gave to Dino. I was becoming more nervous as their conversation continued about me and my family. After they hung up, I knew that Dino would probably try to call me since he seemed completely oblivious to the fact that most people were asleep in the middle of the night. I dialed a phone company test loop number and listened to the silence so a ringing phone wouldn't wake my parents downstairs. When his call beeped in, I answered in a deep, sleepy voice that I hoped Dino wouldn't recognize.

"Hello?"

"Yes, could I speak to an Alex Carbon?"

"He doesn't live here anymore," I replied, trying my best to sound annoyed.

"Well, I think he's been calling my house tonight."

"Do you have any idea what time it is?" I asked him. Dino ignored the question and went into the same rant that I'd heard many times before that night, telling the entire story of a couple of pranksters that had been harassing him.

"Well, Alex hasn't lived here for more than two years now. If he's calling you, he's calling you from Texas and it has nothing to do with us."

"Okay, thank you," he replied and hung up.

To my relief, Dino immediately called back his wife and assured her that he talked to my father and it wasn't me after all. He told her that I was going to college in Texas (College, what?) and that I hadn't lived in the area for awhile.

"All I know is that he was really strange in grade school and junior high," Sharon told him. "He had a cellular phone back then and all this electronic stuff and he knew how to take a phone apart and tap it..."

Sharon continued to tell Dino all about me and the amazing things that I knew how to do. I don't know where she was coming up with all of it, but most of it was either exaggerated or not true at all. It made me wonder what kind of crazy rumors must have gone on about me back then. Sure, I was a complete weirdo in school, but Sharon was making my weirdness sound epic.

This was in 1986 when *nobody* had cellular phones, let alone kids in Junior High, but I did remember one incident where I brought my cordless phone to school so a friend and I could make calls from a nearby cordless phone line. We'd been doing this all week during lunch, and one morning, during band practice, I was horrified to hear the cordless phone ringing from my backpack. Most likely it was the ringing from the same guy's cordless line that we'd been stealing phone calls from. The band instructor stopped our practicing and asked what the noise was and after a few seconds of praying that it would just stop, I said, "Oh, uh, let me get that." The entire class watched as I walked across the room to switch it off.

I guess Dino fell asleep soon after this conversation since my scanner went silent after that phone call ended. I fell asleep too, but was woken at 10:00 a.m. by the sound of Sharon dialing a number on her cordless phone. I had left my scanner on all night so I could listen to things if they developed any further. I also left my speaker phone on the silent test loop number all night, just in case Dino decided to call back and grill my father any further, which he never did. My eyes were still closed as I reached over to shut off my speaker phone and listened to Sharon's phone call.

Sharon called her mother, told her about everything that had happened that night and gave her mom the new phone number. Then she called her sister and did the same thing. I couldn't understand why they would continue using the cordless phone when they knew that somebody was listening to their conversations on it. Sharon called several more people that morning, telling everyone what had happened and making up new details as she went along. Both her and Dino seemed unsatisfied with a true story and had to exaggerate or make up details to make it even more interesting.

That morning marked the end of our adventures with Dino, for more or less the rest of that decade. Later that day, I typed the entire story out on my laptop computer, turned it into an issue of the newly formed PLA 'zine and uploaded it to a few computer bulletin board systems so that other people could have a laugh at it all, just as Zak and I had.

I left town a couple of days later, taking an Amtrak back to Texas. Although I held on to Dino's new phone number, Zak and I only called him back once or twice more over the next few years and nothing too interesting ever came out of the calls, other than a lot of swearing and threats from Dino. It just wasn't as fun, though, without being able to hear Dino's frantic calls to his wife after the prank calls.

A few years later, in 1997, I passed through town to visit my parents again, and I was surprised to hear Dino and Sharon having a fight on the phone when I turned on my scanner. Sharon was at home on the cordless phone and Dino was at a friend's house. She'd called to yell at him because he always spent all of their money by cashing checks at the grocery store. She asked what the hell he wrote a check for $15.00 for and he claimed it was for a gallon of antifreeze, which costs $3.99 for most people.

The argument climaxed and right around the end Sharon said, "Dino, I need to know where you and me stand...I need you to meet me half way here..." There was complete silence from Dino. "Dino?"

Dino replied to her, and I swear I'm not making this up, "Hold on, I gotta find my cigarettes." It was classic Dino. The conversation ended abruptly after that.

In 2004, Dino found out from a relative that he was an internet celebrity and that hundreds of people were commenting on the story about him. An uncle of his stumbled across the story and recognized Dino's name, so he printed out the entire page and gave it to him. This didn't appear to set well with Dino because he showed up at my parent's door one night around 10:00 p.m., printout in hand and extremely angry. I got a breakdown of the story from my dad the next day. He said that Dino claimed that my phone calls were the reason he divorced Sharon and that he would be serving papers to have me sued soon. My dad explained to Dino that I was 30 years old and hadn't lived at that address in over a decade.

I'd never told my dad about the Dino incident, so after he told me about his Dino encounter I let him in on what Zak and I did to him that night, nearly ten years earlier. My dad said he remembered Dino from when he lived by the church and that he was always yelling at his wife outside and speeding off in his car. Yet somehow, Dino wanted to blame a single night of prank calls for the demise of his marriage.

Obviously, the lawsuit never happened. At that point, I had been living back in Alton for several years and I expected Dino to show up at my door soon since I had a listed phone number and address in the phone book. I had a security camera on my front porch and I really hoped to videotape a confrontation with Dino, but he never showed up. A video of me getting my ass kicked by Dino would have made an excellent addition to my Dino page on the internet.

During the few years that my wife and I lived in Illinois, we made it a yearly tradition each Halloween to take our daughter trick-or-treating in Dino's neighborhood, just so we could cower back in the shadows as our daughter knocked on Dino's door and accepted candy from him. It was amusing to see Dino up close and to hear him talk to the kids coming up to his door. To us it was like visiting a celebrity.

Fun With Call Forwarding

"From the start, Phone Losers of America seemed different from most other hacking groups. PLA offered no high-minded justifications for its illegal activities and no ideological bullshit (which most hacking groups had in spades). PLA was less about technical wizardry and more about practical applications. PLA was all about pranks and somewhat malicious activities, goofy stunts, over-the top revenge schemes and simple technical tricks intended to drive a mark completely batty. The best thing about PLA, in my opinion, was the much greater emphasis on humor. PLA was the Three Stooges of the hacking community." -Colonel Panic

"What have you done with the phones?" my mother asked as I walked through the door. I'd been in school all day and had no idea what she was talking about.

"The phone company has been calling me all day," she said, "trying to figure out what you've done to your phone number. They think your line is a pay phone."

I had my own private phone number in my room. Normally my answering machine picked up my calls, but sometimes for fun I would forward my number to other numbers, such as Dial-

A-Story, Time and Temperature or miscellaneous pay phones. Recently I had started forwarding my line to various phone company test numbers. These were special phone numbers, set up by the phone company, that had all kinds of error recordings and other fun things on them that phone company technicians used for testing purposes.

The first one I'd ever called was the sweep tone. A friend of mine gave this number to me years earlier, telling me that it was a number to detect phone taps on your line. This, of course, wasn't true, but it was still a cool number which made a bizarre noise.

Years after that, my friend Shonna introduced me to loops. There were two phone company numbers that connected to each other, so one person called one line and another person called the other, then they could talk to each other. Before I had my own phone line, I used these to talk to girls from school late at night. Since most teenagers weren't allowed to receive late-night phone calls, myself included, we'd arrange to call each other at predetermined times on the loop numbers.

The sweep tone ended with the digits 9998, and the loop numbers ended with 9991 and 9992. Immediately after learning about the loops, I knew there must be other interesting things buried in that particular phone exchange. So I called every number from 9900 to 9999 in that exchange and found dozens of interesting phone company recordings. Most were various error recordings and one played the really loud off-hook signal. Another number seemed to be a room monitor for what I assumed was the phone company central office, a few miles away from us. I could hear machinery running inside and, occasionally, I would hear an employee in the room. Those numbers were cool, but my favorite was the one that said, "The call you have made requires a 25 cent deposit. Please hang up, deposit 25 cents, and try your call again."

This is apparently what had the phone company stumped all day; the simple act of using call forwarding to send my calls to the pay phone recording. Some lady had called my phone number earlier in the day in response to an ad I had in the paper. Hearing the recording asking her to deposit 25 cents made her think that something was wrong with her phone line so she called Illinois Bell to report the problem. A technician checked her lines to determine that everything was okay. Then she called my phone number for the technician. According to my mother and the one flustered Illinois Bell lady I spoke to, this threw the phone company into complete turmoil for most of the day.

As hard as they tried, they couldn't understand how my line could possibly cause that recording to play. They thought my line had somehow been turned into an actual pay phone line and they couldn't figure out why they weren't able to switch it back to a regular line. Since I wasn't sure I was even allowed to call that number in the first place, I lied to the lady at Illinois Bell and said I just had the "Please deposit 25 cents" recording on my answering machine. I promised her that I would change my message since it was causing so much confusion there.

She said she would have the guy in charge of my case call me back the next day, but he never did. He probably felt pretty foolish, spending so much time and energy on something that turned out to be an answering machine message. My mother, who normally didn't care too much for my telephone antics, actually seemed amused by the whole incident.

Throughout the years following this incident, I continued to find call forwarding extremely useful and entertaining not just by forwarding my own line, but by forwarding other people's lines as well. I first started doing this while attempting to wire myself large amounts of cash via Western Union, using stolen credit card numbers. I ordered call forwarding for a person's number, and then I would call that person and talk them into dialing the codes that forwarded their phone line to a pay phone I was standing at. Any calls they received would go straight to my pay phone, so I was able to answer the verification call from Western Union.

The first time I put call forwarding to any kind of fun use was in 1993. At the time I lived in Indianapolis and worked at a movie theater. I decided one day that it'd be fun to screw with customers that called into the movie announcement line. Instead of the customers hearing a recording with movie times, they could talk to me. Rather than get myself fired by answering the phone at the theater I worked at, I picked some other random movie theater to pull this prank on. I settled on a place several hundred miles away in another state.

After ordering call forwarding for the theater's line, I just had to call the theater's manager and talk him into dialing the proper numbers. I did this by impersonating a phone company repair technician. I explained that we'd been having problems with their line and that I needed him to dial a number that would run a complete test on their line. The manager was happy to help out, and as soon as he did, the pay phone next to me rang. I picked it up and informed the manager that the test was in progress and we'd call him back if there were any further issues.

As the evening approached, I started receiving calls from customers. I spent the next several hours making up fictional movie titles and claiming to have sequels that didn't exist yet. I told some customers that the theater had been destroyed by a meteor the previous night, I yelled at others for bothering me while I was trying to sell tickets and I shocked a lot of them with made up insane policies and movie prices.

"We're the only movie theater in town, ma'am, so it's not like you can go to the competitor."

The call forwarding on this theater's line lasted until late in the night. The theater employees had no idea that anything was amiss until angry customers started showing up at the theater demanding to know which of their employees had been so rude to them. It took another hour after this for them to notice that their phone line was being picked up by someone else. It then took even longer for the phone company to understand how it was happening and turn off the call forwarding. I know all of this because I called the theater the next day pretending to be with the phone company and asking the manager to tell me everything that had happened.

Fun With Call Forwarding - 31

At some point during my stay in Indianapolis, I discovered the phone company's newest feature: remote access call forwarding. It worked just like regular call forwarding, but it allowed me to forward the lines on my own. Instead of relying on the owner of a phone number to do it for me, all it required was a four digit pin code that the phone company allowed me to pick myself, over the phone, as I was setting up the feature. I would explain that I wanted the same pin number that was on my calling card and they would be more than happy to accommodate me. How could they possibly have expected something like this *not* to be abused?

When you called a forwarded phone number, the original number would ring a half-ring, then it would forward to whatever line it was programmed to ring. This is so that whoever was present at the original number would know that their calls were being forwarded somewhere. At least, that was the idea. Most people didn't know what to think when their phone would half-ring and nobody was ever there when they picked up. Most Americans don't use call forwarding.

While working at the Lafayette Square Mall's movie theater, I came up with a plan that seemed really interesting at the time, though I couldn't get any of my coworkers to share my enthusiasm for it. I wanted to order remote access call forwarding for all of the businesses in the mall that were visible from the movie theater's concession stand. My plan was to initiate a chain of call forwarded numbers, causing every phone within earshot to do a half-ring, one after the other. I would forward the clothing store line to the pretzel place, the pretzel place to Orange Julius, Orange Julius to the shoe store, and so on. I would make a complete call forwarding circle which would perpetually half-ring every phone in our wing of the mall.

It almost worked. Making a complete chain of numbers just gave me a busy signal, so I had to break the chain by removing the forward on the last number. Each phone would only ring once, but they wouldn't continue ringing forever like I'd hoped. When I called the first number, it started working just like I'd planned. Each number gave a half-ring until the forward reached the last number, where someone answered the phone. I hung up and did it several times, instructing my coworkers at the theater to keep calling it while I stood at various places in the mall, listening for the ring to happen at each store.

Ultimately, the results were pretty disappointing. The problem was that most of the stores' phones just weren't very loud. Not to mention that my hopes for creating the perpetual half-ringing didn't work at all. If it had, I'd planned to forward every single number in the mall, making every store's phone ring with just one phone call.

It's too bad that the phone company wouldn't let me forward pay phone lines. I could have created quite a show with the large banks of pay phones at the Indianapolis airport.

Regardless of my recent disappointment, I still occasionally found ways to keep myself entertained with call forwarding. There were two major theater chains in Indianapolis: Act III and Lowes. I worked for Act III. My manager once told me a story about him and some employees writing, "LOWES SUCKS" on Act III's giant marquee next to a major highway. They only did it so they could snap a quick picture of it and then take it down. It was this story that inspired me to play my own prank on Lowes, thinking my manager would find it just as hilarious as I did. Man, was I wrong.

There were four Lowes theaters in Indianapolis and I ordered remote access call forwarding for all of them. I then forwarded all of their movie announcement lines to Mann's Chinese Theater in Hollywood, California. Anyone trying to call the Lowes theaters for show times would end up hearing the times for Mann's instead. The recording clearly stated that it was the historic theater in Hollywood. With Mann's higher prices and address on Hollywood Boulevard, this prank was sure to confuse any Lowes customers that called in to see what was playing in Indianapolis.

Fun With Call Forwarding - 33

After the forwarding was working on all four theaters, I went up to my manager's office and tossed a phone book onto his desk, opened to the page of theater listings.

"Call Lowes!" I said with a smile.

"Why should I do that?" he replied slowly.

"Just call one of their numbers and see what you get!"

He dialed the number, not sure what to expect. His face shifted from curiosity to confusion and finally to complete shock.

"How did you change their greeting?" he asked me, obviously a little panicked.

When I explained to him that I didn't change their greeting, I simply forwarded their phone lines across the country, he was horrified. Above all things, he was worried he was going to be charged for the long distance calls to California. I assured him that Lowes was picking up the long distance tab for everyone who called the theater that night.

Even so, he was still upset. He couldn't believe what I had done and he demanded that I fix it immediately. His next concern was that what I did would be traced back to his theater and that he would end up getting fired for it. No matter how much I reassured him, he just didn't see the humor in what I'd done. I went out to a pay phone to fix it and he settled down, but since I already had call forwarding set up on Lowes numbers, I sure had fun with them over the following weeks, answering calls for their customers.

I didn't realize it at the time, but my manager's concerns over the long distance charges being passed through the call forwarding weren't completely unwarranted. A couple years later I began call forwarding numbers to 1-900 numbers so that I could dial a local number and be connected to a psychic or a phone sex line for free. Or so I thought.

It turned out that some of these places could see what number we were calling from, even when we were dialing through the forwarded number. Most 1-900 lines would bill the number that we forwarded, but occasionally one would manage to bill our number *and* the forwarded number at the same time.

This caused the 1-900 service to be paid twice for our call, and it caused major confusion with the phone company.

I had a 1-900 block on my home phone, which prevented me from making calls to 1-900 numbers, but since I was calling a local number to reach these 1-900 services, the block didn't matter. That is, until some of these 1-900 services began billing me for the calls. Once again, call forwarding confused the hell out of the phone company, which couldn't understand how 1-900 charges could show up on my bill when I had a 1-900 block on my line. As far as they were concerned, this was impossible.

One morning, an employee from Southwestern Bell called me up and he stuttered the whole time because he was so confused about the charges and didn't seem to know exactly how to ask me what was going on. I played dumb with him and claimed that I would never have a reason to call 1-900 numbers since I was a devout Christian. They agreed to remove the charges from my bill since I obviously had the 1-900 block on my line, but they called me several times after that to question me further, even though they never accused me of doing it myself. They just didn't understand how it could be happening and were hoping for some kind of an answer.

We just had to learn which 1-900 services would pass along our number and which ones wouldn't. This ended up being determined by which long distance carrier the 1-900 company was using. We had a lot of fun bridging phone sex operators on the line and trying to get them to talk to each other. We also used 3-way calling to give all of our friends free psychic readings. It's funny how those psychics never seemed to use their psychic powers to figure out that we were committing phone fraud. It's when I found the number for BBS900 that things started to really get out of control.

BBS900 was a service for owners of computer bulletin board systems who wanted to charge a membership fee to their users. They would instruct their users to call a certain 1-900 number which would charge $25.00 to the user's phone bill. This charge would pay for the user's access to the bulletin board service. And each month, the owner of the bulletin board would receive a check from BBS900 for all the money he'd earned from the 1-900 charges.

I signed up for it as soon as I found it. I ran a computer bulletin board, but I had no intentions of trying to charge my users a fee. Instead, I was going to use call forwarding to make myself rich. From each call to my 1-900 number, I would earn $20.00 of the $25.00 fee. In the first month, I made four fraudulent calls to it, just to test it out. Slightly over a month later, I received a check for $80.00.

I took the check to the bank, cashed it, and asked for two rolls of quarters. Throughout the week, I stopped by every pay phone I encountered, making several calls to a local phone number which forwarded to my 1-900 number. I had 80 quarters on me and I used all of them to make 80 calls to my number. It seemed like a foolproof way to make $1,600 in one week. I planned to wait until I received my $1,600 check before pouring any more money into it, just to make sure it worked. No reason to get greedy with it, right?

Once again, mass confusion ensued at the phone company and I never received my money. A month after making those 80 calls, I called BBS900 to ask why I hadn't received my check yet and they told me that the phone company had been calling them all month wanting to know how someone could possibly be calling their 1-900 number from a bunch of pay phones. From what the lady told me, the phone company had no clue at all how it could be happening which put an abrupt end to my dreams of building a massive fortune from my very own 1-900 number.

Besides getting free phone sex and psychic calls, I used call forwarding to get free long distance too. While working as a telemarketer at a portrait studio in Texas, I began forwarding their dozens of phone lines to out-of-state numbers that I commonly called. The portrait studio's lines were only used for outgoing calls, so they didn't notice there was a problem until they received the next phone bill. I forwarded some lines to computer bulletin board systems and others were sent to chat lines or 1-900 numbers. Whenever I wanted to call one of those numbers, I would just call the corresponding telemarketer line to connect me. A few weeks after quitting that job, the forwarding disappeared. I could still forward numbers remotely, but that was a hassle considering the amount of different phone calls I made each day and I would have to change the forwarding number before every call.

It was around this time that I found out I could forward a local business number to AT&T's calling card access number, which could then be used to make free calls with my calling cards and credit cards. Of course, these were cards that I'd either ordered for other people or numbers that I took from my various jobs. Since the calls were technically made from the forwarded line, I never ended up getting charged back for them. Instead, the business line that I forwarded would have to deal with it.

I usually picked a secondary phone number at a business that never received calls, such as its credit card machine line. The line would remain forwarded to AT&T's calling card number usually for a few weeks until the owner of the store noticed the extra charges on their bill and had it removed. This worked great for about a year, until I was arrested for it.

Looking back, you'd think that something like this would be simple for the phone company to figure out. A bunch of fraudulent calls turn up on a subscriber's line right around the same time that someone mysteriously ordered call forwarding for them. It was obvious what was going on, right? But call forwarding never failed to perplex a phone company employee.

While living in Albany, Oregon in 1996, a cop and a detective appeared at the door, demanding to search my room. After having half of my room packed into the police car, I went to the police station to talk to the detective about the $10,000 in fraudulent calls that they'd traced to me. I was cooperative with the detective and he was nice enough to tell me exactly how they tracked me down and how completely unhelpful the phone company was.

It turned out that many of the local people who were finding unauthorized charges on their credit cards for phone calls that they didn't make were calling the police and filing reports about it. The police started investigating the charges and everything seemed to point to the number that they thought the calls were coming from, which was a local business. When diverting my calls through AT&T, they always had to ask which number I was calling from. I gave them the same number every time, which turned out to be a local company. I only picked the number because the last four digits spelled out my name.

The police and the company launched an investigation into the employees that worked there. After determining that none of the employees were responsible, the phone company suggested that somebody was probably hooking up a phone to the phone box outside of their business. I imagined the police staking out the business for days, keeping an eye on the business' phone box and hoping to catch the elusive phone fraudster. They finally ruled out that possibility and came to the conclusion that they were dealing with a big-time hacker who was using a computer to hack into the phone company's switches so that they couldn't be traced.

The detective, determined to figure out who it was, resorted to calling every single phone number that was showing up on the credit card bills. Mostly these were calls to a public party line for hackers called the Defcon Voice Bridge and a lot of computer bulletin board systems, which were all dead ends for the detective.

Finally, the detective noticed a few calls to Target's public relations office in Minnesota. I worked at Target at the time and had called them on several occasions. The detective called Target's office and asked the lady who had called them from the Albany area on a certain date. The lady was nice enough to give him my name and address.

I didn't end up with any jail time, but I was fined $250 as a punishment for the estimated $10,000 in fraudulent phone calls I'd made. After it was all over, they returned all of my confiscated property. That officially ended my fraudulent credit card habit, my 1-900 calls, and most of my call forwarding experiments.

Remote Overhead Paging

"Reading tons of uninformative and useless PLA articles while listening to RBCP ramble on about irrelevant topics on The Phone Show has wasted my life. I have gained over 270 pounds while sitting here at the computer, but I must admit that I owe it all to the PLA." -Phish-Phreak

In 1994, while living in Portland, Oregon, I regularly shopped at a large chain of stores known as Fred Meyer. If you don't live in the Northwest, you may have never heard of them, but they're about the equivalent of a Super Wal-Mart. It was primarily a department and grocery store and there wasn't much you couldn't find at a Fred Meyer. I shopped there often and it was a nice chain of stores, but that didn't stop what I did to them.

During the time this incident happened, all of the employees at Fred Meyer were on some kind of union strike so there were temporary employees working in the stores while the strikers lounged around in front of the store, holding signs and trying to get cars to honk at them. The fact that none of the regular employees were working just added to the chaos which made it even more fun for me. We always hoped that everyone would speculate that the strikers were somehow responsible for what happened.

My girlfriend and I were walking around the Fred Meyer located at the Gateway Shopping Center and eventually got separated, as she went off to find something she needed. After walking around for 20 minutes and finding no sign of her, I decided to pick up one of the store phones and just page her to where I was waiting. The store phones were located on posts every few aisles for employees to use. I found a phone in the toy department and looked at the huge list of all different departments they had to choose from, finally finding one for the All Store Page listed at 1800, so I dialed 1800 and heard a loud click throughout the store, then I announced, "Colleen Card to the toy aisle. Colleen Card to the toy aisle."

While I was waiting for her to arrive, I examined the phone and noticed that all the department numbers were in the same format as the store paging number - they were all 4 digits and most of them started with the number 1. Electronics was 1296, Hardware was 1693, etc. So I wrote down the two phone numbers listed on the front of that phone and a few department numbers and the paging extension before Colleen and I went to Burger King for a tasty meal of Whoppers.

By the time we finished eating, I'd come up with this really great plan that I was pretty sure wouldn't work but I knew I wouldn't rest until I tried it. The next morning while Colleen was at school I went back to the same Gateway Fred Meyer to test out my idea. I went to one of the pay phones that were located in the store's entrance and made a call to the inside of the store.

"Fred Meyer customer service, may I help you?"

"Yeah, this is Dave in electronics," I said. "Could you transfer me to extension 1800? I can't get it to work from here."

"Okay, just a minute, please!"

For just a second, I heard the funky Fred Meyer hold music, and then total silence. I wasn't sure if I was on their overhead paging system or not, so I hit the star button and I heard it echo inside the store. I was expecting complete failure with this idea and couldn't believe that it worked! I took a look around the entrance and there were a few people inside with me so I couldn't really say anything loud, for fear of them figuring out what I was up to. So I began playing Help Me Rhonda on the touch tone keypad (#636,##636), something I'd learned to do from watching the movie Short Circuit 2, and I listened as my musical masterpiece echoed throughout the entire store.

I couldn't wait any longer for the people in there to leave so I turned my back to them and in a low voice I said into the phone, "Fuck you alllll...You're all going to hell. I will kill yooooooou, I am Satannnnn..." and other various, childish things. Now you'll have to excuse the complete lack of creativity with my first Fred Meyer speech and I realize that a grade schooler could come up with something better than that. I just didn't have anything planned and I couldn't speak very loud and I felt I *had* to say something that would hopefully shock or offend the people inside, just so I could witness the reactions.

I hung up the phone and quickly walked into the store. Passing by the photo section I heard a customer exclaim to an employee, "Did you hear that crazy guy?" But the employee wasn't too talkative so that didn't go anywhere. When I got to the Deli, things were considerably more active there. A guy in a suit, possibly a manager, was talking to another important looking guy and the suit was pissed!

I went over to the Deli and pretended to look at the menus so I could listen. I was thrilled to hear them talking about me. I heard a few things to the effect of, "Well, Dan's looking around for him right now." and "If I catch the little fucker..." They thought someone in the store had just picked up a paging phone and done it all from inside. Looking past these men, I noticed a few guys patrolling the aisles with 2-way radios on their belts. Once things settled down at the store, I got bored and went back home, waiting for Colleen to return from school.

That afternoon, I excitedly told Colleen that I'd succeeded and wanted to try it again. So we picked up the phone in her room and called the same Fred Meyer. Again, I got the service desk and asked to be transferred to extension 1800. We heard hold music for a second and then dead silence.

The first thing I yelled into the phone was, "DON'T SHOP FRED MEYER!" That was the slogan that the on-strike employees were using on their signs and shouting at cars, so I thought that would liven up the whole strike thing and if nothing else, maybe make the local papers. I blasted my Good Morning Vietnam CD into the phone which starts out with Robin Williams screaming, "Goooooood morning, Vietnam!" and plays the clips of all his best radio stuff, including all the foul language and bad jokes. Then we played a few good clips from The Jerky Boy's first cassette and started making random silly pages to different departments of the store. After about twenty minutes I hung up the phone so I could call back and make sure I was really on the paging system and not just talking to myself like an idiot for the past twenty minutes.

"Fred Meyer customer service. May I help you?"

"Could I have the shoe department, please?" I asked.

"Please hold," she replied. A few seconds later, Kate from the shoe department picked up her phone.

"Hi, Kate. This is Dan from store security. Someone told us that they saw someone playing on your phone there and that they were saying vulgar things on the overhead paging system."

"Oh no, sir! That wasn't from this phone. They think it was kids in the food aisle. The security guys are looking for them right now!"

I thanked her and hung up. Now we knew we were getting through, so I called them back and once again asked customer service to connect me to extension 1800. By this time I guess she had figured out what I was up to because she refused to connect me. I hung up and called back, asking her to connect me to Lawn & Garden. When an employee there answered, I used the usual ruse and had them connect me to 1800 with no problems.

Over the next 2 hours, Colleen and I broadcasted whatever we felt like to an audience of probably 100 or so shoppers and employees. We cursed, we told jokes, we made fun of race and

Remote Overhead Paging - 43

religion, we ordered price checks on sexual items and paged people to departments that didn't exist. We announced 90% off sales, on real and fictitious items. We read children's books, but changed the wording around to make them as demented and disgusting as possible. We read phone sex ads, poetry, played the harmonica and sang songs.

Around the end of our broadcast, I made a special announcement. "Ladies and Gentlemen, may I have your attention please. At this moment I'd like you all to direct your attention to the individual working in Lawn & Garden. She is the very person who screwed up and allowed us to take over your paging system! Not that bright of an employee if you ask me, but hey, we're dealing with Fred Meyer, right? So ma'am, if you haven't been fired yet, thank you very much!"

Can you imagine the chaos and confusion caused by this? For a full two hours, we had complete control of their paging system. For some reason, they couldn't turn it off. They couldn't even turn the volume down. Maybe they just didn't know how. They were probably searching the store the entire time for somebody using one of their phones, oblivious to the idea that somebody could be doing it from miles away. The managers must have been horrified and frantic during those hours, trying to figure out what to do while dealing with confused employees and angry customers.

For a few days after this, broadcasting silly messages to all the Fred Meyer stores around Portland became our favorite activity, but it didn't take long for Fred Meyer to figure out how we were getting in. They tried to put a stop to it by alerting all of the employees never to transfer a call to the overhead paging extension. It got harder and harder to get transferred, and finally impossible. Some of the employees told us they knew what we were doing and said that it could never happen again. That sounded like a challenge.

So Colleen and I went to Gateway Fred Meyer again and wrote down the extension of a phone in the middle of a grocery department aisle. I hung out next to that phone while Colleen went to a pay phone at the entrance and had herself transferred to that extension. I picked up the ringing phone and transferred her to 1800 and went back to the pay phone to join her. We said a few assorted things into the phone such as, "Ha, ha! We got through! Nyah nyah nyah nyah nyah nyah!"

Soon after that we left. But it *worked*! A few days later we called from home and asked to be transferred to that same extension in the grocery department. A stock boy picked up the phone and we told him exactly what to press and we were broadcasting once again. Apparently he didn't get the memo.

After that night we became rather bored with the whole idea of taking over their paging system, mostly because we'd run out of material to yell at all the customers. And I was a little bummed that none of this ever made the newspapers, which I was sure would happen. Not receiving any press for it didn't give me much motivation to continue.

Weeks later, I was hanging around the Portland airport as I often did, talking on the pay phones and using my laptop to dial into bulletin board systems. As I was sitting at a pay phone, talking to my friend Zak, I noticed some grey phone wiring hanging down, next to my phone. Reaching up under the privacy wall, I found several phone lines which I correctly assumed went to the other pay phones next to me.

We decided to cut into the lines and make some 3-way phone calls to Fred Meyer stores. Since I didn't have anything to cut with, I walked over to an airport gift shop and stole a pair of fingernail clippers. Back at the phone, I used them to splice open the wires of the phone next to me. I accidentally ended up cutting one of the wires completely in half, which caused the Japanese girl at the phone next to me to look distressed, start yelling urgently into the phone and then hang up and walk away to find another phone. Whoops?

I left that side of the wire clipped so nobody could interrupt our phone calls. We ended up with access to another phone too, which I would bridge onto our line whenever somebody came to use it so we could silently listen to their conversation. Listening to a man enter his calling card number made me realize I'd found an awesome new way to steal calling card numbers.

After getting bored with eavesdropping, I used my extra line to call the Fred Meyer store in Beaverton. We had no problem getting into their overhead paging system and saying whatever we wanted to their employees and customers. We decided that it'd be funny to call store security for the Gateway Fred Meyer and laugh at him about our past exploits on their paging system, since that's where most of our antics had taken place. Keep in mind, we're brainstorming all of our wacky ideas and making plans while the audience at the Beaverton store listened to everything we said. I called up Gateway and asked to be transferred to security.

"Security, may I help you?"

"Yes, this is Roy Gerbil from the Oregonian Newspaper. I was calling concerning the problems that I've been hearing about with your paging system?"

"Well, sir, that's a problem that has been taken care of. What was happening is some kids were dialing in from the outside..."

The security guy rambled on for a while about the paging system problems at their store and how they had all been taken care of as I continued to ask him questions. Finally I decided to let him in on the joke.

"Sir, are you aware that you're participating in a four-way phone call and right now, as we speak, our voices are echoing throughout the bowels of Fred Meyer in Beaverton? Now, you say that you're security for Gateway Fred Meyer, correct?"

He went completely silent after that, then the line clicked and he'd hung up on us, probably frantically calling the Beaverton store to find out if he really did just conduct a live interview with the pranksters. I then made an announcement to the Beaverton shoppers, "Yes, shoppers of Fred Meyer, this is the kind of intelligent people that you're dealing with every day by shopping here!"

We hung up and immediately called the Beaverton Fred Meyer back to ask the customer service lady if we were really on their system. She verified that we were so we laughed at her and then asked to be transferred to extension 1800 again and she told us to please hold.

"Security, may I help you?" the voice asked us.

"No, she must have misunderstood us," Zak replied. "We didn't want security, we wanted extension 1800 so we can frolic around your paging system!"

"Well, sir, I don't think that's going to happen," security snapped back.

Weeks later, I was passing the time at a Clackamas Town Center Mall pay phone and for one reason or another, I ended up calling security at Gateway Fred Meyer again. A female security lady answered this time and we ended up having a long conversation together. I told her that I was the one responsible and she tried to scare me by saying, "I know you are, I have the same number on my caller I.D. here," as if she'd traced my phone call.

"Well, ma'am, did you think what I did was funny?"

"No, not at all, actually."

"I bet you smiled, though."

"Well, yeah, until you started getting vulgar. You really upset quite a few shoppers here."

Colleen, Zak and I continued to play on the paging systems of Fred Meyer for the rest of that year, until I moved to Texas where Fred Meyer didn't exist. No matter how hard they tried to train their employees, we still managed to slip through occasionally and say whatever we wanted to everyone in the store. We successfully broadcasted to every store in the Portland area several times and then started doing the same thing in other areas of Oregon and Washington. About a year later, I published this story as a PLA text file on the internet, and suddenly a *lot* of people were getting into Fred Meyer paging systems and writing to tell me about it.

In 1996, Colleen and I moved to Albany, Oregon and decided to try getting into the paging system there. It worked, it was fun, but then we never bothered to again. Months later, a friend of ours managed to get into the paging system in nearby Corvallis, Oregon. By the time we had moved out of Albany, they seemed to have closed the holes in the paging systems because we couldn't get on any of them, no matter how hard we tried. It took them 2 full years to finally prevent us from ever doing it again.

The only thing I could never figure out was why they couldn't somehow get rid of me when I was on their paging system. Why couldn't they shut off their all store paging system? Why couldn't they disconnect the speakers or at least turn them down? Why couldn't they pull the plugs on the phone for a second and then put them back in? Why couldn't they just hang up on line two? Many times we stayed on for an hour at a time, saying obscene and bizarre things to all the customers in the store and they appeared completely helpless to stop us. They had to know that we were calling in from the outside, especially after we'd been doing it for months, but we never got disconnected once we got in. We were on the air until *we* decided to hang up the phone. It seems like it would have been an easy thing to kick us off, but apparently it wasn't.

In 2001, EvilCal and I were bored and decided to call up Gateway Fred Meyer and try to get into the paging system again, just to see what would happen. The girl who answered the phone told us that there was no way to transfer to extension 1800 anymore. We told her that in 1994 we used to get on it all the time and asked her if she was working back then. She said no, but she'd heard about the incident. She seemed pretty amused that we were talking to her about it.

We transferred to security and asked him about the 1994 broadcasts. He knew exactly what we were talking about, but he wasn't amused at all. I can't remember exactly what he said to us, I just remember him not having a sense of humor. But it's good to know that we're remembered, all these years later.

Credit Card Fraud

"Hey, you know, the PLA, they called just the other day, tried to get me to switch from AT&T. Thought it was weird when they didn't need my credit card number, they already had it." -DejaOoze

My first act of credit card fraud was committed in 1991, when I was 17 years old. My then-girlfriend was in training to work for an airline and one day brought home a sheet of customer information she'd found in her school's computer, apparently belonging to someone who'd recently booked a flight. It included a customer's name, address, credit card number, and a lot of other information. We immediately put it to evil use by ordering sex items from the back of a Hustler magazine to the home of a mutual enemy of ours.

Soon after finding out that the mutual enemy actually received all the items we'd ordered for her, I decided to try and order something for myself. Thumbing through my collection of computer catalogs, I found the perfect item. A hand-held image scanner! It was a $250 item which scanned photographs into your computer. At the time, this was an item that very few people owned and it's something that I'd been wanting for a very long time. The idea of being able to import photographs into my home computer was beyond exciting for me.

So I placed the order and everything went perfectly. I called in the order from a pay phone and sent the scanner to my post office box. I reasoned to myself that the post office couldn't *prove* that I picked up the item. Less than a week later, I visited my box and found a yellow card inside, indicating that I had an oversized package waiting for me. I excitedly waited in line and approached the counter, not the least bit worried about the crime I was committing. The one thing I'd forgotten about was that I lived in a small town and the postal workers knew me.

"Hi, Alex!" the lady at the counter said, noticing the yellow slip in my hand. Without even going in the back room to check, she said, "I think something was sent to you by mistake! It's not in your name."

She left to retrieve it as my heart sank. My dreams were crushed. My hopes of running home and scanning my photos into my 286 PC were gone. I knew that if I took the package at that point, there's no way that she would forget that I'd picked it up. She came back to the counter with the package and asked if I recognized the name. I admitted that the name was unfamiliar to me and they must have written the wrong box number on it. I left the post office empty-handed, but the events of the past few weeks left me with some very valuable information – credit card fraud actually *worked*!

My first official success with credit card fraud happened almost exactly a year later. My parents were nice enough to fly my girlfriend, Sylvia, and I from Texas to Illinois to visit them. And I couldn't help but notice how easy the process was. My father simply called a travel agency in the city we were flying from, explained that he was flying his son out for a visit, and gave his credit card number to them. All of it was done over the phone. Then I just walked into the travel agency and picked up the tickets. They didn't even need to see my ID.

So a few months later, Sylvia and I decided that we'd really like to visit some of her family in Los Angeles. I called up a local travel agency and impersonated "a father" and set up a flight to Los Angeles for "my son and daughter" to "see their mother."

During our stay in Illinois, a good friend of mine had stolen a huge stack of carbon paper credit card receipts from his employer and given them to me. I used one of them to set up the flight, packed a few dozen of them in my duffle bag for the flight to Los Angeles, and stuffed the rest of them in a hiding place at my parents' house.

I was a little nervous, going into the travel agency to pick up my tickets, but the overly friendly woman at the travel agency immediately put me at ease. I told her that it was my first time ever flying and that I'd never been to Los Angeles before and that I hadn't seen my mother since their divorce. Everything went perfectly. I'd spent the morning memorizing my story, the details of my identity, and practicing the signature of my fake name, but they didn't even require me to sign anything. The travel agency woman just handed me the tickets, wished me a happy family reunion and told me to have a wonderful time in Hollywood.

Sylvia and I flew out of St. Louis the next morning. Back then, airlines didn't require any identification to fly, so we were able to fly under completely fictitious names. As long as we made it out of the airport in Los Angeles, there would be no chance of us being caught. And we weren't. It couldn't have possibly gone any more smoothly. You can't imagine, as a couple of teenagers, what a rush it was to get away with scamming a flight across the country. And the fact that we were going to live in Hollywood made it all the more exciting.

This one success inspired me to continue flying all over the country for the next four years. From Los Angeles to Houston to Miami, St. Louis, Seattle and Portland, I was able to fly pretty much anywhere I wanted to, on a whim, and I never had to pay for the travel expenses. During a Spring Break vacation with a friend of mine, we actually flew to 3 random locations all over the country, all within a week of each other. I almost always traveled by plane, but took an Amtrak a few times, just for the variety.

Of course, I was eventually busted. I'd successfully flown my then-girlfriend Colleen to Corpus Christi to visit me. But when I tried to fly her back to Oregon, we ran into problems. The credit card that I used to set up the flight ended up being declined, so when we stopped by to pick up the tickets, the travel agency lady told me that the credit card didn't go through. Since she thought my father was the one who called in and set up the flight, I pretended to call him but, not surprisingly, I couldn't get through. So I told her that I'd try to contact him and that I'll come back later once I've figured things out with him.

An hour or so later, I used an Office Depot pay phone to call the travel agency, pretending to be my father. I explained that I accidentally gave them my credit card that I'd maxed out with Christmas shopping and gave her another one. It didn't work either, so I tried "my" American Express card and that one worked just fine. Or so I thought.

A couple of hours later, we returned to the travel agency and they asked me to have a seat and they'd be with me in just a minute. As I was sitting there, I noticed that I was getting weird looks from the employees and that it was taking forever for them to help me. Just as I started to get worried that something fishy was going on, I got up to leave and a cop pulled up in front of the door. Another cop went to the pay phone outside to retrieve Colleen, who thought she was being busted for red boxing.

Since I was picking up the tickets under a false name, I made sure to leave my wallet and ID home just to avoid any accidents with my real name. When the cop asked for my name I gave him a fake name and he seemed to believe me. My hope was to be able to get away with spending a few days in jail under a false name, then once I was released I'd just never return. That plan might have worked, except that I'd picked up my mail on the way out of my apartment that day and it was in my backpack. And of course it was all addressed to my real name so, once again, he asked for my name and this time I gave it to him.

He emptied out the contents of my backpack onto the hood of his car and I just happened to have a red box, police scanner, camera, electronic organizer, PLA business cards and notebooks full of incriminating stuff. He and the other officer commented that I probably stole it all and said they wouldn't return any of it to me unless I could produce receipts for it all. I wasn't too happy about this since more or less all of it *was* purchased either with stolen credit cards or stolen money orders.

He was really curious about the PLA business cards and demanded to know what the phone numbers on the card belonged to. I told him they were voicemail numbers and he said I better not be lying because he'd be calling the numbers when we got to the police station. I don't know what he was expecting them to be, but luckily nothing came of that since one of the voicemail numbers was purchased with a stolen credit card number.

As he was driving me to the police station he kept trying to figure out how to work my Casio electronic organizer and as he kept looking back to ask me questions about it, he would swerve off the road while hitting buttons. We he first turned it on, the page it opened on in the "memo" section was a list of about a dozen credit card numbers which I had been using to buy the plane tickets a few hours earlier. He asked me how to delete the cards from there and I told him. He deleted that memo which seemed kind of stupid since you'd think that would be evidence. Luckily they didn't notice my paper notebook full of hand-written credit card numbers.

I ended up spending about a day and a half in a holding cell with a bunch of drunk guys, then they let me out and made me promise to come back for court. I spent a couple of months making bi-weekly trips to some probation guy to assure him that I hadn't left the city while I waited for a court date. They finally decided that I wasn't worth their time and the credit card fraud charges were dropped entirely. Not only that, but since I already had a warrant out for my arrest in Illinois and they refused to extradite me there, most of the charges against me in Illinois were also dropped. And they returned all of the contents of my back pack without asking for any receipts. All in all, it was a very productive arrest for me.

I didn't limit my experiments in credit card fraud to just jetting around the country, though. One constant obsession I had was trying to use Western Union to wire myself thousands of dollars with a credit card. I never succeeded at it but you can't say I didn't try extremely hard at it. I first started attempting this while living in Los Angeles. It seemed that Western Union's only security procedures were making sure that all of the information I gave them matched the credit card and calling me back on "my" home phone number to verify that I was the cardholder authorizing the transfer.

I tried it a few times with incorrect home phone numbers, just to see if they'd let it slip. I hung around Hollywood pay phones for hours, waiting for callbacks from Western Union. Some of them would call back and some wouldn't. But they never would transfer the money to me, most likely because I couldn't answer the cardholder's home telephone. Or could I?

I began trying to get customers to forward their phone numbers to a pay phone by calling them up and trying to talk them into dialing the proper numbers. I'd order call forwarding on their line, then call them and impersonate a phone company repair technician. This worked a few times, but there would always be some other problem with the transaction, such as their credit limit being too low.

While living in Illinois, I managed to acquire the credit card numbers of a few wealthy residents living in Edwardsville. I drove by their houses and I *knew* that they must have the credit limit that I was hoping for. So I called the telephone company and ordered call forwarding for both of the homes' phone lines. But as much as I tried, I was having absolutely no luck in persuading the homeowners to forward their phone numbers to my pay phone. Determined not to give up on these people, I decided that I'd just go to their houses and forward the lines myself.

Next thing I know, it's 1:30 in the morning and I'm driving my father's truck to this nice, suburban neighborhood. My plan was to sneak into their yards and open up the grey telephone box on the back of their houses. I'd plug my own telephone into it and dial the number needed to forward their phone lines to a nearby pay phone. I parked a few blocks away from one of the homes, thinking if I had to run away quickly I wouldn't want anyone to see what kind of vehicle I hopped into.

Armed with a jacket full of telephone equipment, screwdrivers, pliers and the phone number of a local pay phone, I began walking toward my first target. Looking back, I can't believe nobody happened to notice a scruffy-looking, big-haired stranger walking down the road in the middle of the night with his jacket bulging full of phone phreaking supplies. If a cop had happened to pass by, I'm sure he would have questioned me or at least parked somewhere and watched me.

My mission on this night was a complete failure. The first house I tried had lights all around it, and I noticed a dog house. I just didn't feel comfortable walking up to it. The second house had their telephone box too high up for me to reach, even when I stood on the rail of their deck. The whole thing was completely stupid and insane, walking around on some family's deck and snooping around their house at 2:30 in the morning. Their house was right on a lake, so after admitting defeat, I walked over to the lake and just sat in the grass for probably an hour before getting bored and going home. I'm amazed that I didn't get chased, shot, or arrested that night. It was this incident that caused me to finally give up on the dream of scamming thousands of dollars from Western Union.

During our stay in Highland, Illinois, I repeatedly tried to ship items to the vacant units in our apartment building. And I'd even tried shipping items to vacant houses, hanging out on strange porches for hours, waiting for a UPS truck that never arrived. At one home in Galveston, Texas, I even ripped the For Sale sign out of the ground the previous night to make the UPS driver less suspicious.

While walking through town in East Alton, Illinois one day, an election sign caught my eye. I knew I recognized the name that the sign was encouraging me to re-elect as the mayor. I later checked my list of credit card numbers and, sure enough, I had the credit card, home address and phone number for the Mayor of East Alton. Apparently he'd been in the 7-Eleven that I worked at and I'd written down his information, not realizing who he was. But even my attempt to order a laptop computer on the mayor's card failed. The only thing that seemed to work flawlessly was flying around the country on these cards. I never had a way to check the balances on the credit cards, so I think a lot of the cards were just dead or didn't have enough money on them for what I wanted to purchase.

My various convenience store jobs provided me with an unlimited supply of names and credit card numbers so I stopped relying on the old stack of carbon receipts that my friend had given me and I began using cards that I was given at work instead, paying special attention to the cards that were gold.

Around the end of my stay in Indianapolis I took a 2nd job at an Amoco station as a cashier. It was a combination service station and gas station, so we had people bringing their cars in all the time for repairs and sometimes the cars would sit in our garage all week while they were worked on. I began to think about cleaning out the whole place in the middle of the night and then stealing one of the cars to get away. Maybe I'd even drive the car across the country to whatever my next destination ended up being.

I started taking peoples' car keys home with me, making copies at the hardware store and then returning them. Then I'd write down the owner's home address and keep it with the keys. All this time I'm also taking rolls of cash register receipt journals home with me each night and writing down the credit card numbers, expiration dates and names, and looking in the phone book to get the cardholder's home address and phone number.

In the end, I decided against the idea of stealing a car and looting the Amoco, mostly because I liked the people I worked with at my other job and wanted to be able to visit them again someday, without the fear of being arrested. I left town quietly, but I still had a new list with hundreds of credit card numbers and names which funded my travels, phone calls and other shenanigans over the next few years.

Upon my arrival in Portland, Oregon, my luck with credit cards began to change drastically. After a successful credit card flight to Portland, I managed to check myself into a very nice downtown hotel for 3 days on a credit card number, by making the reservation over the phone. After that ended, I managed to do it again, in an even nicer hotel. And after that one expired, I spent a few nights living on the streets before booking myself back into the first hotel again for a few more days. During each of my hotel stays, I ordered plenty of room service and movies on demand. All by impersonating my father over the phone.

Committing credit card fraud became an every day event for me during most of my stay in Portland. My girlfriend Colleen and I spent much of our time going through catalogs and ordering items to our various post office boxes, which were all under fake names. Our daily trips to the post office were like Christmas. Colleen ordered massive amounts of clothing and various housewares for both of us, while I stuck to mostly computers and electronics. I ended up receiving a $1,300 laptop computer, more software than I could fit into it, a laptop printer, a ham radio, books, CDs, and so much more. We were selling a lot of the items for cash, giving some of it away and keeping the rest.

Not only were we doing great with the mail ordering, but I discovered that both Office Max and Office Depot would allow me to order items from their toll-free number and then pick them up in their stores. By posing as my father, as usual, I was able to order matching Sharp hand-held organizers for Colleen and I. They kept us busy on our carded vacation flight to Indianapolis and were the perfect place to store my extensive lists of credit card numbers. I even got a complete eye exam with a Portland eye doctor, and they charged my new glasses and contact lenses on my credit card. I chickened out on carding a dental checkup, worried that a deranged dentist would wait until he had a bunch of sharp objects in my mouth before confronting me about my fraud.

In 1994, it wasn't very common to see anyone with a cellular phone yet, but I started carrying one around with me all the time, using my massive collection of credit card numbers to make phone calls on it. The calls would run around $3.00 per *minute*, and I would spend hours at a time on my new NEC cellular phone. I wasn't able to receive calls on it, but I constantly checked the several voice mailboxes I had purchased from another company, using credit cards. Some of my voicemails were for friends to leave messages for me and others were for companies to contact me on if they had any problems with my fraudulent orders.

Using my new laptop computer and a program called Cmaster3, I was able to turn one single credit card number into hundreds. The computer program used an algorithm to generate hundreds of valid credit card numbers from just a single, 16-digit credit card number. I printed out huge lists of these numbers, always keeping them in my notebook to use for phone calls from pay phones and from my cellular phone.

Besides being able to collect credit card numbers from my places of employment, I began to discover new ways of obtaining card numbers. By calling up the employees of convenience stores and impersonating an employee of Visa or Mastercard, I could easily talk them out of several credit card numbers.

"Hi, this James from Mastercard," I'd say. "Were you having a problem with a transaction there? Our computer is showing some kind of a problem on your end."

"I don't think there's a problem," the clerk would say. "The last credit card went through just fine, I think."

"Hmmm. Well, it doesn't look like it completed on our end. Could you find the receipt for me and read me the information from it? Otherwise your drawer will end up short for the amount of the transaction."

Not wanting to get in trouble for missing money, most clerks were willing to give me all of the information from their last few credit card transactions. I became a regular caller at a few stores, convincing the employees that my frequent requests for credit card information were just a routine part of their job.

Eventually I began calling all kinds of businesses and talking them out of their credit card numbers. A few times, I'd reach them in mid-transaction with a customer and ended up talking directly to the customer, who would read me their credit card information and just about any other information that I requested. Since the phone was handed to them by an employee of a store they were doing business at, they had no reason to disbelieve me.

Another method I started to use was calling up people at their homes and impersonating the phone company. I'd tell them that I was a long distance operator and that a family member of theirs was trying to make a collect call to them. Once they authorized me to put the collect call through, that's when I talked them out of their credit card number.

"Okay, ma'am," I'd say. "I'll put the call right through. Thank for you using...oh wait. There's a problem here. You have a collect call block on your phone. I'm afraid I won't be able to put the call through after all. I'm sorry for the inconvenience."

"Oh," she'd say. "Well isn't there another way to bill the call?"

"Hmmm. Well, I could bill it to your calling card or a major credit card if you'd like."

Sometimes I'd get two cards from the person with one phone call, by telling them that their card was incompatible with our system and they needed to try another one. Once I had the card number, I would tell them that the calling party had hung up. Not surprisingly, these cards would end up being canceled within a day or two, probably after the victims discovered that the family member hadn't really been trying to reach them.

I was eventually arrested for making calls like this, and I was busted for some of the fraudulent calls that I'd made on credit cards. While the fines were never steep compared to the amount of damage I'd done, I'd still never recommend that anyone else try any of the activities that I've outlined in this chapter.

Keep in mind that, as of this writing, all of these events occurred more than 15 years ago. Most of the security issues written about were taken care of years ago. Today, flying around the country under a fictitious name would be nearly impossible with all the new security measures at airports, and they'd probably charge you with being a terrorist instead of fining you a few hundred bucks. You will be caught if you try these things, just as I was.

Automated Harassment

"The PLA taught me many skills that are thoroughly unimpressive to women. Thanks, PLA!" -DBK

Imagine one day your phone begins ringing. You pick it up and you're greeted with a fax machine beep, so you hang up. Several minutes later your phone rings again and you hear a recording of a voice announcing, "This is your free sample message!" and it goes into a big sales pitch. Even more minutes pass and your phone rings again, only this time it's a computerized voice saying, "ibaibaibaibaiba!"

Okay, so you're the victim of harassment. You're not too worried about it because you know that the guy doing it will get bored and it'll eventually stop. But it doesn't stop. It gets worse and worse, day after day, 24 hours a day, nonstop calls have completely put your phone out of commission and the only thing you can do about it is change your phone number and hope that it ends.

Right around the turn of the century, many companies were just beginning to integrate land line-based phone services with the internet. The big thing seemed to be fax-back services, which were web sites that let you choose from giant lists of documents that you could have faxed to yourself, all from the company's web site. It seems silly today in our world of printable PDF documents, but back then it made sense.

There were also a growing number of services that allowed you send phone-based messages to any number you chose. One company would let you phone reminders or wakeup calls to yourself at a future date and another would send personalized messages to people in a robotic voice, based on what you typed into a form. Most of these services allowed you to hear a free demonstration before paying money for their services.

While using automated phone systems to torture a person was nothing new, doing it via the world wide web felt quite revolutionary at the time. The problem with automated phone systems was that you usually had to invest just as much of your own time harassing a person as your victim did receiving it. But with all of these systems suddenly being available on the internet, this made it incredibly easy to completely automate the process.

All it took was some very basic knowledge of HTML to modify the forms on these websites and then place them on a public website for people to click on. By modifying the HTML code, I could turn the field to enter my phone number into a hidden field that only had my victim's phone number in it. Then I could turn the SUBMIT button into something a little more likely to be clicked, such as CLICK HERE FOR FREE NAKED PICTURES!

I set up fake porn sites like this that offered all kinds of saucy choices of free naked pictures. There was even one choice on the menu which claimed it was an archive of child pornography, but you were only allowed to view the pictures if you were under the age of eighteen. Because, of course, being an adult and looking at child pornography violates federal laws. I'm sure all the horny middle-aged men heeded that warning.

Of course there were no pornographic images of any kind on the sites I made since that would violate the terms of service on the free website services that I used. When a visitor clicked on an option, instead of seeing porn they would see confirmation messages such as, "Your fax has been sent!" or "Thank you for trying out our message service! Your phone will ring in just a minute..."

Sure, I could sit there and push the buttons I made over and over myself, but that would defeat the purpose of automating the harassment in the first place. I needed a way to trick lots of people into visiting my fake porn site so that the buttons would be clicked all day and night. So I turned to the popular chat service known as IRC.

I used a program called mIRC to write automated scripts that would automatically join pornographic chat rooms. Then the script would send private messages to each person who joined the room, begging them to look at my amazing free archive of pornography. Thousands of porn-hungry people a day would receive messages from from my script, leading them to my site. Then many of those people would click on every single link on my page, each click resulting in at least one phone call to my victim. Not to mention one unhappy pervert who never received the free porn images that he was promised.

This, of course, resulted in some guy's phone ringing almost nonstop for about six months straight while I was free to go about my life as usual, doing more important and productive things than pressing a button all day to harass someone.

The test subjects who received these nonstop phone calls were a couple of college guys who were my next door neighbors at the time. Their phone line just happened to run through my basement, so I could listen to their line any time I wanted, to see just how effective my harassment was. I estimated that they were receiving approximately one phone call every two minutes and it was slowly driving them insane.

They eventually gave up on yelling at whoever was calling them and just turned their phone's ringer off, which caused their answering machine to be completely filled up with fax tones and test messages. If they wanted to listen to any legitimate messages on their machine, they would have to sift through hundreds of garbage messages until they found it, making the simple act of checking their messages a very time-consuming endeavor.

Many times when they picked up the phone to make a phone call, it was already ringing so they couldn't dial out until the automated service hung up on them. I heard lots of phones slamming down and yelling through the walls when this happened.

They called the phone company many times, begging them to do something about the problem, but the phone company said there was nothing they could do. Tracing the calls would do little good since the calls were coming from companies. My neighbors tried contacting the internet companies and had moderate success in getting a few of them to prevent their number from being called. But there were so many companies to choose from, all I had to do was update the fake porn page with new forms. The police showed up one day to take a report, but weren't able to do anything helpful.

It took them nearly two months to finally break down and change their number so that the calls would stop. I gave them a few days of peace so they could give out their new phone number to all of their friends and family before updating my fake porn site with their new phone number, which wasn't hard to get since I could tap into their line and dial an ANI number that would read their new number to me.

I listened to them speculate many times about who might be responsible for the calls, but surprisingly they never suspected the weird guy next door who had a Phone Losers of America license plate frame on his car.

The calls continued nonstop for a total of about six months, when they finally graduated college and moved to Florida. They learned to live with the phone calls and finally just accepted the fact that they would never be able to use their answering machine again and that making outgoing calls was a crapshoot.

About a month after they moved to Florida, I called the phone company and talked them into giving me the guy's forwarding address. Then I called the phone company in Florida and got them to give me the unlisted number at their new home. I would have loved to hear their reaction when their mysterious phone problems followed them 1,000 miles to Florida.

A few years later, cellular phones and text messaging became very popular with the general public, and every wireless carrier had a form on their web site that would allow a person to send a text message to a cell phone number of their choice. This meant I could set up a new set of modified forms that would text random cell phone users and ask them to give my victim a call.

And then, with the help of my friend Heywood, we were able to add some javascript that would automatically push the buttons on the fake porn sites for us. Each time the button was pushed, it would send a text message to another random cell phone user, asking them to call my victim. Usually the message would imply urgency so that they'd be likely to keep trying my victim's number until he picked up.

Having my home computer repeatedly push the button seemed risky, so I continued to use the fake porn site, but I also set up a special web page with about 10 self-pushing buttons on it that I would visit from display computers in stores. Setting up a password protected screen saver on the same computer would ensure that nobody could shut down the browser until the machine was rebooted. I would sometimes set up that page as the default home page so whenever a customer opened the browser, my page's buttons would be pushed a few times.

My fake sites and scripts went through many changes throughout the years, but they were always effective at driving any phone user nuts with the constant stream of phone calls. There was never a thing they could do about it, other than change their phone number and hope that it ended. Today, the possibilities seem endless since everyone has a cell phone now and there are more telephone websites than ever.

History Lesson

"The college I attended last semester blocked the Phone Losers website because it was classified as tasteless by the content filter, so I dropped out. I'm so happy I can listen to PLA Radio again." -po2okemon

"Well, I'm going to start a really cool hacker group and I'm going to call us the Phone Losers of America!"

That's the sentence that my friend Zak typed onto a computer bulletin board system in 1994, which marked the official beginning of the Phone Losers of America. Zak, also known as el_jefe, was being sarcastic and making fun of some guys who were calling themselves hackers, but I took the name and we ran with it.

It's probably about time that I told you what the PLA is, now that you've been reading the book covering many of the events that have happened during two decades following Zak's proclamation.

Confused yet? Let me explain. In the 1980's and 1990's, computer enthusiasts would write tutorials on hacking into computer systems, circumventing telephone security, making explosives, obtaining things for free, learning things you're not supposed to, and just about any other kind of underground, antisocial topic you could think of. Hundreds of these files were freely available on underground computer bulletin board systems, commonly referred to as a BBS. BBSes were the internet before there was an internet.

I'd even written a few of these tutorials myself, posting them on bulletin boards throughout the country and hoping they would be enjoyed, copied, and distributed even further. But my writings were scattered all over the underground, and were hard to find amongst the thousands of similar files that were already available. What I really wanted was a series of my own text files that would be kept together so that they could be easily found. The only problem was that my text files needed a common name to be associated with them. In late 1994, when Zak threw the Phone Losers of America name out there, I decided that was the perfect name to attach to my writings.

The texts that I'd already written dealt with the usual topics of computers, phones and anarchy, but what set them apart from most of the others available was the humor. My writings dropped the elitist attitude that was common in most text files and replaced it with jokes, pranks, humor, and complete nonsense. While they were entertaining to read, they were still educational, as long as the reader could manage to decipher the facts from the nonsense. At the time, humorous text files on underground topics weren't too common.

Around the end of November 1994, I moved from Oregon to Austin, Texas to find an apartment and a job, but my real reason for moving there was to attend the yearly computer hacker convention called HoHoCon, which would be held at the Ramada Inn in Austin, and which Zak would be attending as well. This would be the perfect place to promote the Phone Losers of America!

After working for a few weeks at a convenience store in Austin, I used some of the money I earned to print up 1,000 business cards with Phone Losers of America written on them, along with a couple of my voicemail numbers and a conference line number. After Zak arrived in Austin, we had lots of fun handing these cards to complete strangers, throwing them around restaurants, licking them and slapping them on storefront windows and handing them out to everyone during HoHoCon.

After HoHoCon was over, I spent a month in Illinois, visiting family and friends. I spent many of my days at my parents' house, editing my old text files, slapping Phone Losers of America headers and footers on them all, and releasing them onto the local computer bulletin boards. At this point there were a total of 13 different PLA text files. The PLA now officially existed.

Before my visit in Illinois was over, the incident with Dino's cordless phone occurred, so the next day I wrote the 14th PLA text file which detailed that story. I finally left Illinois and took an Amtrak back to Austin. Having no place to stay, I planned to sleep in Austin's airport, but since I'd slept in the airport for so many nights during the previous month, the security guard told me that she'd throw me out if I tried to sleep. So to stay awake, I spent the night writing the 15th PLA issue on my laptop, which was about taking over all the phone lines in Celina, Ohio.

The next day, I moved to Corpus Christi, Texas, got an apartment, and used my laptop computer to start my own BBS. I called the BBS Whombat Communications and declared it the world headquarters for the Phone Losers of America. During my eight month stay in Corpus Christi, nineteen more issues of PLA were written and I began distributing them to underground BBSes all over the world. I would ask the owners of these BBS systems to set up special directories just for the PLA files and, in turn, I would list their BBS name and phone number in the PLA issues.

Eventually, issues of PLA began popping up on BBSes that I'd never even heard of, people started contributing material for me to use in PLA, and my BBS was busy most of the day and night with calls coming in from just about everywhere. The owner of a Corpus Christi internet provider, sure that we were up to no good, noticed all of this and announced that he'd hired an investigator to deal with us and it would be his life's mission to bring the PLA down.

The PLA was getting plenty of attention in the Illinois BBS scene too, thanks mostly to Zak. A newspaper reporter became interested and tried to interview us for an article. My girlfriend, Colleen, and I had decided to move out of Corpus Christi to Oregon, with a one week stay in Illinois. The day we arrived in Illinois, a newspaper in Belleville, Illinois ran a front-page article about the Phone Losers of America in their Sunday paper. Not surprisingly, it didn't paint a very good picture of the PLA.

A few days later, on a Wednesday, an editorial about the PLA was published in the same paper, complete with a humorous cartoon depicting a member of the PLA hacking on his computer. And then, the following Sunday, another front-page article was written. We were thrilled to make the front page of the Sunday paper, two weeks in a row. A Madison County Sheriff apparently wasn't as thrilled as we were, though, because he came to arrest me just a few hours after we'd boarded our flight to Oregon. It was a close call.

In Oregon, I immediately set up my BBS again and released the 36th issue of PLA, which included an update on the newspaper publicity we'd received in Illinois. Soon after this, I found my way onto a wonderful new thing called the internet, and I immediately took down the BBS to replace it with a web site. The internet was just beginning to become popular, and having the entire archive of PLA on a website was creating many new readers. During our one year stay in Albany, I released six more issues of PLA, bringing the total number to forty-one.

Our next move was to Ohio, where the last four issues of PLA were released. I had suddenly decided that I wasn't interested in writing them anymore and wanted to move on to other things, so on May 5th, 1997, I released the 46th issue, marking the official end of the PLA texts. But PLA was far from being over.

Soon after announcing the end of the PLA texts, we registered www.phonelosers.org. This not only became the official archive of the Phone Losers of America texts, but it's where I began enlisting people from the internet to create their own regional PLA web sites, which I linked to from the PLA site. Over 100 regional PLA sites sprung up around the world, each detailing information, lists of pay phones and vulnerabilities in the cities that they lived in.

PLA prank call tapes and CDs were released and sold on the website, as well as t-shirts, stickers, and other miscellaneous items with the PLA branded on them. The PLA community remained strong and active, through various email discussion lists, phone conferences, web-based forums and chat rooms.

I quickly learned that I couldn't handle not writing text files and I started up a new 'zine called Peachey Incorporated, which was based around our harassment of an extremely naive girl on IRC. As that event died down, I renamed the 'zine to Pink Fluffy Phreaking Bunnies and began writing about traditional phone topics again, beginning with a huge list of phone numbers that were connected to the OCI telephone company. Then the name was changed once more to Dark Fluffy Phreaking Bunnies so that people would stop making fun of our girly name. This 'zine lasted for over 2 years.

In the late 1990s, after moving to Illinois, my friend EvilCal and I began releasing short video clips, calling them PLA TV. They mostly revolved around various juvenile pranks, and one featured puppets by the name of Elephant and Bird, teaching viewers how simple and profitable phone fraud could be.

In 1998, linear created a spin-off group of the PLA called the United Phone Losers. Though it originally started as a joke, it picked up momentum and became an integral part of the PLA by releasing 30 issues of their own 'zine and setting up their own forums, which became a very active part of the PLA community in the early 2000's. UPL also took over the PLA's quarterly phone directoroy.

In the summer of 2004, Rob T Firefly, murd0c, Big-E, Judas Iscariot, and I-baLL gave a PLA 10th anniversary presentation to a few hundred hackers at the Hackers On Planet Earth convention in New York City. They played a few of the PLA's prank calls, an episode of PLA TV, took questions from the crowd, and gave away free PLA T-shirts and CDs. They organized a similar panel 4 years later, adding Sidepocket to the panel.

In January of 2006, I jumped on the new podcasting bandwagon with PLA, by creating a show called PLA Radio. The show featured original prank calls, skits, songs, and tutorials on various underground-related topics. Just like the old PLA issues, PLA Radio blended plenty of humor to accompany the informative content.

In 2009, PLA was given a 2-hour weekly slot on a New York radio station called Party 934. Spessa, linear and I used it to broadcast The Phone Show, where we took phone calls and talked about various PLA topics for an hour each week. Since then we've moved the show to new stations a few times, but it still exists today.

And now you're reading the PLA in the form of a book. A book that compiles some of the best parts of our foolishness into an easy-to-read collection of stories, based mainly on the history of the Phone Losers of America.

The PLA 'Zine

Much of the content and spirit surrounding the PLA in all of our projects is based on these original 46 issues of the PLA 'zine. This section is dedicated to the 'zine and will describe each issue and hopefully give you a little insight and history behind a few of them.

(illustration by Rob T Firefly)

PLA001.TXT – How To Hack A WWIV BBS. Years earlier, a guy named Chris taught me a trick that allowed access to the hard drive of most people running a WWIV BBS. In our local calling area, there were about thirty WWIV BBSes to choose from, so I caused quite a stir in the community by hacking many of them. Chris and I had a great time, stealing user databases and changing BBS login screens and menus to say all kinds of wacky things. Since most BBSers used the same password on every other BBS, we could log in as just about anyone and pretend to be them, creating nonstop drama on all the boards.

We had a blast, framing other people for the crimes and watching the drama unfold everywhere. After a while, nobody would trust anyone in the community. Eventually people figured out that I was responsible and everyone wanted to kill me, but then some people started begging me to teach them how to hack. Annoyed by the begging and fearful that people might find out that I don't actually have any real hacking skills, I wrote this file that detailed how to hack a WWIV system with an axe, and uploaded it to all the area BBSes that hadn't kicked me off yet.

PLA002.TXT – How To Build A Red Box. I'd been red boxing for about a year when I visited some new hacker friends in Belleville, Illinois. One guy was impressed to see that red boxing still worked and he showed me my first issue of *2600* which explained how to turn a tone dialer into a red box. I was excited at the prospect of using something so tiny to make free calls with, so we drove to a grocery store and used their photocopier to copy the article for me to take home.

I had my doubts that something so easy could work, but after waiting a week for Radio Shack to special order my 6.5536 MHz crystal, I was suddenly red boxing without a bulky tape recorder. I copied some of the text from 2600 along with my own notes and turned it into issue #2. I added to this file frequently as I figured out new tricks and details about red boxing and by the time it was turned into a PLA issue, it was a fairly comprehensive guide.

PLA003.TXT – Revenge Techniques. Chris and I had fun getting revenge on fellow BBSers, so I began compiling a list of things we had done to people and things that we could do to people. The name originally used in this issue was a guy named Darin who Chris and I went to great lengths to torture in our BBSing days, even visiting his house occasionally to screw with him. By the time this file turned into a PLA issue, Chris and I were no longer friends so I rewrote the entire file using Chris' name.

PLA004.TXT – Dumpster Diving & Looting Bell Trucks. I'd been dumpster diving at phone companies for several years and wanted to write a guide on it since I wasn't satisfied with any of the guides I could find on other BBSes. While writing it, I discovered that there wasn't really a whole lot to say about the subject, so I added the part about looting Bell trucks so the issue wouldn't seem so short.

PLA005.TXT – Third-party Billing. I wrote this file while hanging out all night at the 24-hour computer lab on a university campus in Indianapolis. I often spent entire nights there because I was homeless and it was cold outside. I'd discovered the ease of billing my calls to other people while living in Miami and having no other calling options at the time. It was surprisingly easy to do and became a regular method of phone calling for me over the next few years.

PLA006.TXT – Free Money From AT&T. This is another one written in the computer lab at night. I spent so much time at pay phones in the early 1990's that I was often asked by operators if I wanted a refund on my failed calls. Just for fun, I had a few of them mail me checks for twenty-five cents. It was amusing to think about how much time and money they spent, just to mail me a quarter. It wasn't long before I discovered that I could trick operators into sending me checks for $15.00 international phone calls. For a short time, this became an additional stream of income for me.

PLA007.TXT – Numbers to call When You're Bored. I had notebooks full of interesting numbers and I wanted to share them with other people, particularly my giant list of pay phones that I'd been compiling since I was in grade school. This was originally titled FUNNUMBS.TXT and I uploaded it to the famous RipCo BBS in Chicago, then accidentally lost my own copy and completely forgot that I ever wrote it. A year later I was on RipCo and noticed the file, so I downloaded it and was surprised to see that I wrote it.

Not only did I include phone numbers for phone company news lines and funny answering machine messages, but I also created sections for businesses with the name Roy and Cactus, just to make people wonder what I was smoking.

After a few years, I updated the list and copied it to a new file called the PLA Phone Directoroy, which I tried to release a few times a year. The section that caused me the most grief was the Loser List, where I listed phone numbers of people that were fun to mess with. Eventually I started accepting submissions for this section and began receiving legal threats from the victims once they searched the internet and found that I was the source of all their prank calls.

PLA008.TXT – Ruining The Life of a 7-Eleven Employee. Most of this file was written on my laptop computer while working at a 7-Eleven in Portland, Oregon. Having nothing better to do at night, I began compiling a list of things customers did to piss me off. Then I started adding things that they *could* do to piss me off. Then I just started making things up.

This text file caused some problems for me when I uploaded it to a 7-Eleven themed BBS in a town called Albany, Oregon that I'd just moved to. I thought that as a 7-Eleven employee, the sysop would appreciate the humor. Instead, he took the file as a personal threat and called the police on me for uploading it to him, then he began making harassing calls to me. That turned into a really fun battle for me that I'm sure he wished he'd never started.

Some of the examples in this issue were turned into a PLA TV video in 2009, which YouTube promptly took down for violation of their terms of service.

PLA009.TXT – Jim Bayless' Triumph. Colleen Card wrote this play in 1994 for a school project. It was acted out in front of a class by her and some friends and it was awarded an A.

We expected someone to turn the Jim Bayless screenplay into a major motion picture, but sadly that never happened.

(illustration by Shane Lawson)

Jim Bayless was a real security guy for Ameritech who really had a vendetta against me because I occasionally called his work and his home to make fun of him for not being able to catch me. He even showed up at my old job once to request documents on me. I was thrilled to have a phone company security guy take an interest in me.

PLA010.TXT – Scanner Frequencies. I'd always been into radios and after I purchased my first programmable scanner, I created a list of frequencies that had potential for fun. I wrote the file in hopes that other radio enthusiasts would send me more frequencies and ideas for things to do, but I didn't get as much feedback as I hoped for.

PLA011.TXT – Phone Call Transcripts. This issue contains 6 phone call transcripts, transcribed either from recorded calls or from memory. Some of the stories surrounding the calls are made up, which is obvious. My favorite part is definitely the McDonald's call, which was a real phone call that I didn't record.

MCDS: Thank you for calling McDonald's, May I help you?
RBCP: McYes. I'd like to have a 69 piece McNuggets, a McCoke and two orders of McFrench fries delivered right McNow.
MCDS: We don't deliver, sir.
RBCP: McExcuse me? I'm looking at your McAd in the McPaper and it *says* right here in black and McWhite that you McDeliver.
MCDS: Well, that's some sort of printing mistake or something.
RBCP: This is McRidiculous! Let me speak to your McManager!
MCDS: Okay, please hold.
RBCP: McHurry, you McLoser.

The operator death call and the pay phone call were written by me while on a greyhound bus in Texas. The first deaf relay call was to the mother of a girl Colleen Card was always harassing, and the second deaf relay call was based on an actual phone call that I made a year or two earlier to a 411 operator in Iowa.

PLA012.TXT – Converting Your Modem. Back in the dark ages of computer BBSing, I was stuck with a slow 1200 baud modem while all my friends seemed to be bragging about their speedy 2400 baud connections. I wanted to upgrade my internal modem to a 2400 baud, but couldn't afford the $100 it cost at Wal-Mart. So I ended up buying a 2400 baud modem from them and then returned the 1200 baud modem in the box for a refund since they couldn't tell the difference between them.

This issue was renamed several times as baud rates continually increased and I wanted the issue to seem relevant. Also because I kept upgrading my modem each year to the newest speed. After an upgrade in 1995, Zak and I called the store to tell them what we'd done and they weren't amused one bit.

PLA013.TXT – Fone Tricks and Petty Scams. Here's another one that began its life in the 24 hour computer lab at the University. I was trying to compile the ultimate guide for phreakers since all the current ultimate guides were several years out of date, but I quit before I was finished. To make the issue bigger a year or two later, I added the petty scams to it, which, in retrospect, makes very little sense at all.

PLA014.TXT – Dino's Cordless Phone. This event happened while I was spending a few weeks at my parents house for a visit. In the days prior to this issue, I'd been converting all of my old text files into issues of the Phone Losers of America 'zine. The morning after these events occurred, I turned them into the first file written exclusively for the PLA 'zine and immediately uploaded it to every BBS in my local calling area.

PLA015.TXT – Beige Boxing in Celina. After the visit to my parents house, I took a train back to Austin, Texas and attempted to spend the night in Austin's airport. But since I'd been sleeping in Austin's airport so much during the previous month due to homelessness, the nighttime security guard there told me that if I fell asleep that night, she would throw me out of the airport. So I stayed up all night, writing on my laptop, which is where this story came from.

Nothing in the story is true, other than the fact that I lived in Celina, Ohio for a short time the year before. I used the Celina name on the story as an ode to a small town that I kind of missed. A year later, 2600 magazine printed this story in their Spring 1996 issue.

PLA016.TXT – Deaf Fones, Phone Books and Phone Bills. I kept bugging the hell out of Zak to write something for the PLA 'zine. After weeks of pestering him, he finally emailed this issue to me and told me to leave him the hell alone. The phone book ordering trick was something I frequently used to order phone books for myself while charging them to other people, which allowed me to find fun and interesting phone numbers to call in other areas before the internet made things like that so easy. We also sent dozens of phone books to our enemies, billing it to their own phone bills.

PLA017.TXT – Letters From The Phone Company. I was going through my notebooks and noticed that I had many letters from phone companies addressed to me, mostly demanding money for services that I'd stolen or politely accusing me of scamming money from them. All of them are real, except for the one where the CEO of AT&T offers to pay me a monthly salary just so I'll quit stealing from them.

PLA018.TXT – Kevin Mitnick Articles. I'd always been fascinated with the Kevin Mitnick story that I'd first read about in the Cyberpunk book, so while staying on the campus at Illinois State University, I began collecting newspaper articles about him. I was surprised to see him pop up on the front page of the newspaper in 1995, so I immediately created this issue from some of the old Mitnick articles that I'd saved years earlier.

PLA019.TXT – Fun With Call Forwarding. Playing with call forwarding was really fun in the early 90's since you could easily order the service for anyone's line and then access it remotely. This issue detailed some of our pranks using call forwarding and different methods of forwarding phone lines.

PLA020.TXT – Alternatives to CNA. This issue showed readers how to obtain a customer's name and address using just their phone number, mostly based on methods that I used regularly.

PLA021.TXT – PLA Job Application. After the PLA started getting well-known on BBSes, I began receiving emails and voicemails, asking me how they could join with the PLA. Tired of explaining to everyone that PLA was just an e-zine and not a club, I wrote this issue as a sarcastic reply to everyone, just so I could refer people to it when they asked me how to join.

PLA022.TXT – BBS Back Doors & Flaws. A guy named Pestilence was the first person to talk me into letting him put out his own issue of the PLA 'zine. He apparently mixed real BBS hacking tips with complete fantasy, so nobody was sure exactly what worked in this issue.

PLA023.TXT – Long Distance Access Codes. After spending a few days scanning all of the long distance "10" codes, I turned the list into the new PLA issue. Not long after this, the phone company switched to "1010" codes, making this PLA issue completely useless.

PLA024.TXT – Dabbling in Credit Card Fraud. I happened to be wrapping up this file on credit card fraud just as I was busted for credit card fraud in Texas while trying to card a flight to Oregon. After I was released and awaiting my trial, I decided it was probably a bad idea to have a file like this lying around, so I deleted it. After all of the charges against me were dropped, I rewrote it all and turned it into the new issue.

PLA025.TXT – Taking Over Fred Meyer's Intercom. After continuously taking over every Fred Meyer store intercom in Portland, Oregon for most of a year, I wrote this file to explain how it had been done. I didn't release it until after we moved out of the city, though.

The thing I really loved about this issue was that it multiplied the problem for Fred Meyer because suddenly hundreds of people all over the world knew how to remotely connect to the paging system of any Fred Meyer store. I received lots of email from people who tried it out, telling me of their own adventures with the stores. It took Fred Meyer more than 2 years to fix the problem so that it couldn't happen anymore.

PLA026.TXT – Details on Phone Offices. This one was accidentally released on my own BBS in 1995 and a lot of people downloaded it, so I just made it available to everyone. It shows some partial details on just two phone offices, then has a phone call transcript for one of them that seemed funny at the time.

PLA027.TXT – Nursery Rhymes for Baby Phreaks. Colleen Card wrote these poems on an old IBM typewriter while living in Oregon, and then mailed them to me in Texas. It was the only material ever submitted to the PLA that was written on a typewriter and sent by U.S. Mail.

PLA028.TXT – Telephone Calling Cards. This issue shows readers a few different ways to order telephone calling cards for other people and gives tips on using them safely and making them last as long as possible.

At the end of this issue is a small article about a guy named Pheerless who wrote an article on how to disable the transmission of your caller ID. This was common knowledge at the time, so I printed it only to make fun of him.

PLA029.TXT – Stealing Pay Channels From TCI. Another user-submitted issue of PLA, sent in by a guy named Dr. Dre. This issue helped readers disable the pay channel filters on their cable TV lines.

PLA030.TXT - This is the first issue of PLA that turned into more of a 'zine format with multiple articles. It included another submission by Dr. Dre on scamming stores, a newspaper article about a small town in Utah that just had phones installed for the first time a year earlier, some fake news and a list of the adult GIF files found on Zak's BBS.

A huge part of this issue is the introduction, though. I began writing a small introduction, explaining why I took so long in releasing it, and that turned into a lengthy, made-up story involving social engineering, stealing a hospital employee's car, framing some teenagers for the Oklahoma City bombing and driving across the country to avenge my humiliation. It was the best excuse ever.

PLA031.TXT – AcidFlux's Story Time Hour. This really long story by AcidFlux detail's how he owned a system administrator and all the fallout he had to deal with as a result of it.

PLA032.TXT – Another multi-article issue, including a political rant on computer piracy by Lokust, an introduction to CNA departments, a poem by Colleen Card and another poem by Martini about Deter, and a couple of telephone news articles.

PLA033.TXT – Issue 33 included an article on doing horrible things to your neighbors, a fake classifieds section, a very comprehensive section on beige boxing, a news story on the evilness of "free" chat lines, and some more fake news.

Also in this issue was The Official Phreakerz Manual, which was filled with fake information about the history of phone phreaking, nonexistent phone company acronyms and other tricks of the trade. Included was a long series of numbers that I claimed could be typed into a pay phone to make all the money inside come pouring out.

Despite this secret code being surrounded by obviously fake information, people still believed it and kept trying to type it in for years afterwards. I would get regular emails on the subject, asking if the code had changed because they tried it and it wouldn't work. More than a decade later, I turned this fake code into a YouTube video, tricking a new generation of would-be thieves.

One other thing in this issue was a complete phone directory for the city of Roy, New Mexico. The name Roy had always been an inside joke between Zak and I, so I thought it would be funny to list every phone number in that city. We spent years calling everyone in Roy, trying to create widespread panic by telling everyone about UFO sightings and by hacking their answering machines.

PLA034.TXT – BBSing Lameness in the 618 Area Code. It had been 5 years since Chris and I started the hacking scare in the Illinois BBS scene, but people still talked about us and the PLA and all the scary things they thought we could do. So, just for fun, I began dialing all the BBSes in Illinois from my home in Texas. Once again, quite a stir was created in the BBSing community.

One part of it was the Chatterbox BBS, where the sysop gave out my home phone number to another guy and we harassed them about it until they gave a public apology to me. Then there was The Hit Man, who we also persuaded to publicly apologize to people that he'd been antagonizing. And then there was Mr. Hack's BBS where we kept ordering call waiting on his data line to kick his users off.

PLA035.TXT – Update on 618. After causing loads of problems in the BBSing community again, a newspaper in Belleville, Illinois decided to do a front page story about the PLA. This issue reprinted that story and gave some updates about the BBS community there, such as the Chatterbox sysop and The Hit Man quitting BBSing because they couldn't handle our shenanigans. There was also an article about how to deal with phone harassment and an interview with AmigaDOS, who began our obsession with the word cactus.

"We were playing a game called Hero's Quest, but we were playing a really screwed up version that they invented one night when they were tripin' and there were cactuses sprouting up out of the ground because they were making up really stupid creatures. I prank called this girl right as my character was enveloped by a cactus so I said to her, 'cactus?' and she said, 'who?' and I said, 'oh, cactus.' and that's how it started. After that we kept calling her back and saying cactus because it seemed to really get on her nerves. All night we picked random numbers out of the phone book and cactused people. We did it for days and the next thing you know it just became a way of life."

PLA036.TXT – Pages From A Stolen Diary. This is a fictional story, written in stolen diary format, about a religious guy named James Heggie who endured nonstop harassment and wrote about it in his diary. Then there are some phone call transcripts of us bothering operators and an editorial about the PLA, published in another edition of the Illinois newspaper that did a story on us.

PLA037.TXT – Send-A-Song. "T'was the night before Christmas and all around the house, not a creature was stirring except for Redboxchilipepper who was rummaging through this innocent family's network interface box, clipping their lines and running a long extension cord down the block into his own house so he could call a bunch of 900 numbers."

This Christmas issue of PLA starts out with a phone call transcript and some Christmas carols, then explains how a new music-by-telephone service works. There's also some information on the phone company's FACS office and a transcript from a TV show where a guy scams credit cards from prison.

PLA038.TXT – BustCon '96. This issue begins with a fictitious account of a hacker convention in Green Lake, Wisconsin in which much of the town is destroyed. Then there are some documents procured from trashing at the OCI building and another front page newspaper article about the PLA from that same Illinois newspaper.

If the OCI stuff confuses you, let me explain. Back in the late 90's, we loved to bother the operators at a phone company called OCI. Even though they were a phone company, they never knew where you were calling from and they dealt with our harassing calls for years. Whenever we held conference calls, people always called OCI throughout the night. If you insulted an OCI operator, he or she would often retort with, "Yo mama." During the late 90s, the OCI operators became very familiar with our calls and some would tell us that they knew we were "Defcon hackers." It was the most hilarious phone company anyone had ever come across and we theorized that they probably received more prank calls from us than legitimate calls from customers.

PLA039.TXT – After trying to fool readers into thinking we were taken over by Phrack, this issue contains lyrics to a song called Bell Odyssey (Which Rob T Firefly covered in 2009), a very insincere apology to Send-A-Song who called me to complain about the article I wrote, how to steal merchandise with a shrinkwrap machine, how we deal with wrong numbers calling our house, some pay phone calls we interfered with, and some information on a few possible red boxing busts.

PLA040.TXT – Colleen Card's Unauthorized Issue. Colleen Card takes over this issue with kitchen improvised peanut butter & jelly, horoscopes for phreaks and a really bizarre police log.

PLA041.TXT – Digital Dreamer's quest to become a member of the PLA, free groceries, some prank call transcripts and emails from readers.

PLA042.TXT – This issue begins with a fake transcript of a talk show on hackers, then gives an update on where Dino is, 7-Eleven employee terrorism and things to do while on the bus. It also contains a huge advertisement for CuervoCon which was sort of an unofficial PLA convention in Brownsville, Texas.

PLA043.TXT - Learn how to master the art of false identification, and read about our latest adventures in cordless phone eavesdropping. Our new neighbors in Ohio didn't continue using their cordless phones for very long once we moved into the neighborhood and started interfering with their phone calls. There's also a Send-A-Song update in this issue and a lot of reader email.

PLA044.TXT - We manage to stop a cordless phone user from violating copyrights, then teach readers how to profit from owning their own 900 number. We try to rock the boat in the 2600 usenet group by encouraging people to cancel their subscriptions to 2600 Magazine because we're putting the magazines online for free. This was, of course, a lie and we just wanted to see what everyone's reaction would be. pneyz teaches us how to use Pacific Bell's automated system and there are some IRC logs.

PLA045.TXT - After chasing off all the cordless phone users around my new neighborhood in record time, I tried to think of new ways to bring new cordless phone users into the area. Ideas included breaking into their house and replacing their regular phones with cordless phones and following them around the Wal-Mart and tossing a cordless phone into their cart while they weren't looking.

Logic Box publishes an article called Ramsey Forum Fun, which begins our campaign of terror against an online community until it's shut down, and kcochran explains to us that PLA isn't a group. You'll learn some new ways to scam telephone calling cards and free videos, and you'll learn some phone tricks.

PLA046.TXT - The final issue of the PLA 'zine. We say a quick goodbye and assure readers that great things are on the horizon. This issue is full of things, like the history of the PLA and all the issues, the meaning of ibaibaiba, a DefCon review, quitting someone's job for them, more debate about the existence of the PLA, RBCP visits a 7-Eleven, an IRC script, news, letters and tons more.

But what I really love about this issue is the true story of Sommy. Sommy was a mysterious presence in the house of a Canadian family that would jump into their phone conversations, switch the channels on their TV and blink the lights in their house. He would also call and torment the police and anyone else who had contact with the family. The phone company, police and other investigators were completely baffled by Sommy. It got so bad that the family put their house on the market, hoping to sell it quickly and get away from him.

PLA099.TXT - dhate's unauthorized PLA. While the PLA 'zine ended with issue 46, this issue was released during the previous year by a guy named dhate. I always listed it with the rest of the issues because there was so much funny stuff in it, once you waded through the really sick parts. Zak and dhate made great phone calls to Disneyland, a Waffle House and captured the greatness of prank calling OCI.

Phone Mobbing

In the early 2000's, members of Cal's Forums began organizing "phone mobs" on talk radio shows. The idea was that everyone would call into a radio show at the same time, flooding the lines with our silliness in hopes of keeping normal callers off the air. Our first attempt, organized by Judas Iscariot, was to get on the popular call-in show called Love Line. Only one of us, Sarah601, made it through and managed to talk to the hosts about red boxing during sexual play.

Our next attempt was much more successful when we phone mobbed a small AM radio station in Illinois as they were asking people to call in and bid on items that they had for sale. For a full hour, the station was slammed with calls by the PLA, asking for cactus related items. Many of the regular callers who got through just wanted to talk about us and ask why we kept saying "cactus" on the air.

Phone Mobbing briefly turned towards public phone conferences talking about higher powers in pyramids or how to order Russian brides. Since they had no way to remove us from these free conference lines, the hosts and the callers were forced to listen to our bizarre comments until they finally gave up and quit the conference.

With the help of NWBell, we organized several more AM radio station mobs where we confused the locals with the word cactus. And RogueClown organized another mob against the original AM radio station in Illinois.

In 2006, Altalp discovered an online show called Our Prisoner where a guy locked himself into a house with a live 24/7 video feed for 6 months and encouraged viewers to make all of his decisions for him. Each evening they took live calls from the viewers, which turned into our next phone mobbing project. The location of the house was a secret, but it didn't take long for us to figure out where they were located and then blurt out their address on the air. Until the show ended, they dealt with regular calls from the PLA saying bizarre things to them on the air.

Today the PLA runs the online radio station called Cacti Radio and regularly organizes Phone Mobs that are played live on the stream. Regular phone mobs on internet talk radio stations are sometimes carried out after our weekly show and the results are posted to the podcast feed.

April Fools Pranks

Every few years the PLA pulls a terrible April Fools Day prank on its readers. The first major prank was in 2002, when I posted an article on phonelosers.org about some really amazing software that could be downloaded for your Palm organizer. Software like the Pay Phone Commander which allowed a person to change the billing rates on pay phones or empty the coin box with one stroke of their stylus, or the Palm Red Box, which allowed free calls from pay phones. There was also a cell phone tool kit that allowed users to clone cell phones.

Of course, the four programs I went into great detail about didn't exist. I encouraged readers to download the programs from our downloads section, which also didn't exist, then I ignored the emails, guestbook posts and usenet articles, begging everyone to send them these amazing programs.

> "Ive looked all over your site, and i can not find the palm files you talked. ive prolly over looked the link but i was wondering if you could help me out. Thx." -Michael

> "Bright Idea: Next time you advertise some Palm Pilot programs in your download section, SET UP A DOWNLOAD SECTION!!!! As it is, the interest kind of dies off when it becomes apparent that THERE'S NO DOWNLOAD SECTION! Just a thought......" -Eeviac

In 2008, I created a YouTube video that showed users an amazing new way to hijack the speakers at a fast food drive-thru so that they could screw with the customers trying to order their food. It involved modifying a CB radio with a special crystal that could be found inside a toaster. The video even contained footage of us messing with customers, so viewers were sure that it was real. But, of course, it was all a huge lie.

This video was linked on major web sites such as Fark, Consumerist, Digg, Makezine and Gizmodo, who all seemed to believe that it was real. This caused over 100,000 people to suddenly want to tear apart their toasters, looking for a crystal that wasn't there. In the 2 years since that prank, I still receive angry emails from people who have broken their toasters or spent $80 on a new CB radio to modify, only to find out that it wasn't possible.

> "I've canabalized hair blow driers, hair straighteners, and toasters. I have yet to find this crystal.. Back to looking. I also have 2 of the same model CB radio as the video. The crystal is in a different place, and it is marked 10.240 (32PF) But maybe that isnt the frequency?"

> "I bought a brand new hand held CB radio from radio shack and brand new toaster from wal-mart and NEITHER of them had and crystal at all. do i need a more expensive toaster, the one i got was $20, and should i use a not hand held CB radio? please help out guys i really want to do this."

The PLA's most recent prank was a video based on issue #33 of the old PLA 'zine, which gave viewers a secret code to type into pay phones that would make all the money come pouring out of the phone. The video demonstration of it working and the in-depth details on why it worked left little doubt to many people that it was real. Just like in the previous prank, PLA regulars helped out by posting comments about how well it worked and how much money they were able to steal. I still receive regular emails from people telling me that they can't get it to work.

> "I tried this at my local airport. I did the hack in 3 verizon payphones, and 2 at&t phones, and i got nothing from them. either this doesnt work anymore, or the phones had no money inside." -j02305

> "This crap does not work idk wheere u got this info, i did it to like 10 phones." -ElanderSkull8

> "FUC INFORMATIONAL PURPOSES IMA GETTIN MAH SELF RICH" -moonwalklikeMJ

PLA Communities

Ever since the PLA started existing around 1994, there have been various ways that we all come together to talk with each other and plot out our evil plans. It all started with a BBS in Illinois called Roy's Place.

1995 – Roy's Place BBS: This BBS was run by Zak (aka El Jefe) and was the first official distribution site for the PLA 'zine. Zak had run a BBS before PLA was around, but in 1995, after the PLA really started taking off, he changed the BBS name to Roy's Place and set up at least one message section to discuss PLA topics.

Roy's Place was located in Granite City, Illinois, and it ran WWIV BBS software. It attracted mostly BBSers from the 618 area code at first. Roy's was the home of RoyNET, which networked the message areas from several other area BBSes. Soon Roy's Place began receiving calls from all over the United States and even overseas. Roy's Place came to an end when Zak decided that the internet, which everyone was just learning about, was much more exciting than BBSing.

1995 – Whombat Communications BBS: This BBS was run by me while living in Corpus Christi, Texas and became the official BBS for the Phone Losers of America. It ran customized Renegade BBS software. The PLA text files were becoming well-known on BBSes around the world, thanks to my nonstop campaign of begging webmasters of hacker boards to set up special file sections just for the PLA texts, which all had the phone numbers for Roy's Place and Whombat Communications on the bottom of them. This caused many long distance and international callers. Whombat also received lots of traffic from local Corpus Christi users, which is how I was introduced to EvilCal, who later helped create content and his own PLA communities.

Whombat Communications received a sudden surge in traffic from Illinois when I forwarded the phone line of a gas station's credit card machine in Illinois to Whombat Communications and then advertised a new 618 area BBS on most of the Illinois BBSes. Many Illinois users were confused to be reaching a Texas BBS by dialing an Illinois phone number.

Whombat Communications moved to the 541 area code when Colleen Card and I moved to Oregon at the end of 1995. It only lasted a few months there until I discovered the internet and created a website for the PLA called Whombat Communications.

1997 IRC's #rock: With the internet came IRC, and with IRC came the fun of taking over chat room channels. One of El Jefe's channel takeovers occurred in efnet's #rock, which was a place for discussing rock music. After a few months, #rock became the permanent 24-hour home for many people associated with the PLA. Soon after, a #rock channel was created on Dalnet, which was also for PLA people to hang out on.

These channels were used heavily for years and we met two important people on efnet through this takeover. One was Jammie, the co-founder of #rock where she hoped to talk about music. She eventually just gave up getting the channel back and became friends with the PLA and is still around today. The other person is Spessa, who enjoyed going into channels and harassing the people in them. She figured #rock would be an easy target, so she came in and started spouting off nonsense, but was surprised to find the nonsense spouted back at her to be even more hilarious than her own. Her match was met, so she became friends with PLA and has been with us ever since.

IRC's #phonelosers: There's been a #phonelosers on many IRC networks throughout the PLA history. There was even an irc.phonelosers.net IRC server beginning in 1999 for a while. These days #phonelosers is most active on efnet.

1998 – FruitWare BBS Forums: I tried using a few discussion forum scripts in the late 90's, but wasn't happy with any of them, so I created my own and called it FruitWare BBS. It was referred to as a BBS because it was designed to have the feel of an old WWIV or Renegade system. It was full of security holes and it's amazing that nobody ever hacked it. The PLA's FruitWare forums closed in February 1999 because I was tired of having to delete all the phone numbers and credit card numbers that were constantly posted.

1998 – Yahoo PLA/UPL Email List: The email list started out on a service called Topica, which then turned into a company called ONElist, then eGroups, and then was purchased by Yahoo Groups. All of the messages were read and responded to by email. The list was extremely active until February 2001, when Brice Carlson had the list shut down by complaining to Yahoo after I posted his home phone numbers to the list.

1997 – alt.phonelosers: The PLA newsgroup was created in 1997, but was never very active, mostly because of the rampant spam there.

1999 – PLA Voice Bridge: The PLA voice bridge has been around since at least 1999. Back in 1995 through 1997, many of us would hang out on the Defcon voice bridge before it went down. Two years later I discovered a similar conferencing line in the same exchange as the Defcon bridge, run by Beehive Telephone. The bridge has changed numbers many times since then, but it's existed in some form for over ten years now.

1999 – UPL Forums: The UPL Forums started on free board hosting sites like CGI For Me and boardhost.com before switching to the FruitWare BBS software around September 1999. In May 2001, the UPL Forums switched to ikonboard and then to OpenBB in 2002. Then came phpBB in January 2003 until the summer.

2002 – Email list on wearehope.com: Spuds, the webmaster of wearehope.com, set up this email list for the PLA in June 2002 and it lasted until April 2003. It was never quite as active as the old Yahoo email list, but it still received a lot of posts each day.

2002 – Roy BBS: EvilCal set up a Wildcat! BBS and called it Roy's. Users could connect to it through telnet instead of phone lines. It had message areas, games and the other usual BBS stuff.

2002 – Cal's Forums: Soon after becoming the new web host for phonelosers.org, Cal not only set up forums for the PLA community, but he also set up a place for PLA people to submit articles, write blogs, share links and vote on OMG HAX pictures. This was the sole community for the PLA for years, and ended sometime around the end of 2006 when he shut it down to create a new place called Cal's Content Kingdom.

2006 – PLA Forums: The latest PLA Forums started in March 2006 and still exist today. They were originally intended to be used as a commenting system for the pages on phonelosers.org, but evolved into official PLA forums when Cal's Content Kingdom stopped functioning.

2006 – UPL Forums: Soon after the PLA Forums were created, linear got phonelosers.net back from a domain squatter and immediately set up the United Phone Losers forums, which still exists today.

Who knows where the PLA will go from here, but if you search hard enough, you can find us on Facebook, Myspace, Flickr, YouTube, Twitter and just about every other social network in existence these days.

Listening to Cordless Phones

"You take illegal eavesdropping to the extreme. You people really are a bunch of losers." -Kevin in North Carolina.

"So, you got your pictures back yet?" the man's voice coming from my police scanner asked, just as I'd turned it on.

"Well, we got the proofs from Sears when we had them taken, but I don't have the money to buy them yet," a woman replied. I recognized her voice as Julie Campbell, who lived about a block away from me. I'd been listening her to cordless phone conversations for months at that point.

"Bummer," Julie's friend replied.

"Yeah. I was thinking of just taking the proofs to the copy shop and having color copies made. Maybe enlarging them so they can go in frames."

"You can't do that. There's a copyright on the proofs so the copy store won't let you."

"Their color machine is self-service, so they won't even know," Julie said.

"Ah. I see."

"I'm not sure how good they'll come out on the copier if I enlarge them that way, though. Oh, hold on; another call is beeping in," she said and clicked over. "Hello?"

"Hi, Mrs. Campbell?" I said.

"Yes? Who's this?"

"This is Steve from the Copy Super Center in downtown."

"Oh, hello," she replied.

"I'll be blunt with you, Mrs. Campbell. We know all about your dishonest ploy involving the copyright infringement of your photographs from Sears. This is just a friendly warning to stay the hell out of our store and take your illegal activities elsewhere."

"Who is this?" Mrs. Campbell asked.

"I already told you that I'm Steve from the Copy Super Center here in town. We'll have the police here in two minutes if we see you in here so don't even think about trying to make illegal copies of your kids photographs at our store."

With that, I hung up on Mrs. Campbell. I listened as she clicked back over to her friend and told him in a panicked voice that he wasn't going to believe who just called her. They stayed on the phone for the next twenty minutes, theorizing about how the copy shop could have known what they were talking about. In the end, they decided that Steve must live nearby and that he had been listening in on her cordless phone. They never once thought that it could be a prankster listening in on her calls, just pretending to be an employee. She was certain that it really was Steve from the Copy Super Center and she vowed to never use her cordless phone again. This was the last conversation I was ever able to hear from her on my Uniden Bearcat police scanner.

The year was 1996 and I'd just moved into the neighborhood six months earlier. When I first moved in, there were about seven neighbors nearby that regularly talked on their cordless phones, but my regular prank calls to them had slowly caused each of them to switch to corded phones. I listened to their calls often and I kept a list of their names and phone numbers and other related information about each of them. Sometimes it would take months just to find out what their number was. I'd usually have to wait for them to call a business that would ask for their phone number or an automated menu that would ask them to key in their phone number. When this happened, I would turn on a tape recorder so that I could record the touch tones they pressed and then play them back later to figure out what numbers they were. In the days of analog tape recordings, it could take over an hour to decode their tones.

With Mrs. Campbell gone, the only person left on my cordless phone list was an elderly woman named Mildred, who lived three houses down from me. All she ever talked about was her bladder problems or soap operas that her and a friend watched on TV. They were boring people and neither of them had call waiting, so I couldn't even call them while they were on the phone. It seemed that unless I wanted to drive into another neighborhood and listen from my car, my days of listening in on cordless phone conversations were over.

Just a month ago I'd chased off an old man named Harold after he called a clothing company to order an expensive jacket for himself. He was another old person who didn't have call waiting, so I was unable to interrupt his conversation with a phone call. Instead I sat and listened as he read off all of his personal information, which included his Discover card and his daughter's information for shipping. He was having it shipped to his daughter's house because he was going to be vacationing in Hawaii when it would arrive. I wrote everything down so I could add it to my notes on him. After he hung up, I called him and pretended to be with the company that he'd just ordered from.

"Hi, Harold. This is Jim from the shipping department and we're having a little trouble with the jacket that you just ordered," I said.

"Oh?" he replied. "What kind of trouble?"

"Well, you wanted the dark navy teal color, but we seem to be out of that color so we're going to have to substitute it with turquoise instead."

"What color is that?" Harold asked.

"It's this kind of day-glo bright blue color. It's very pantsy-looking."

"Oh, I don't think I'd want that color…"

"Well, you don't have a choice because I've already put it in the box and that's what I'm sending you," I said, quickly pressing my mute button so Harold wouldn't hear me snickering.

"Let's see what else you have here," Harold muttered as he flipped through the clothing catalog.

"*No*, Harold. I said we're sending you the pantsy color and that's what you're getting. Also, we don't have the 35 inch sleeves, so you're going to have to settle for 10 inch sleeves. And there are going to be yellow polka dots all over it too."

"What?" he asked in disbelief.

"This is going to cost an additional $25 on your Discover card too. Thanks for ordering with us and we'll have your order delivered before March 21st," I said and slammed down the phone so that I could burst into laughter.

Once he realized that I'd hung up on him, he called the company back and calmly explained to them what had just happened. The representative on the phone was confused and made a few calls to find out if there had been any changes made to his order. While this was happening, I called the man's daughter and told her that I was from the shipping department and gave her the same spiel about the turquoise color and the polka dots. She insisted that her father wouldn't be interested in that kind of a jacket and I responded with, "Ma'am, I think you need to stop trying to run your father's life by imposing your lame fashion sense on him. This is just a courtesy call to let you know that we changed the order. Goodbye."

I listened for days as Harold and his daughter and other family members repeatedly called each other to rehash details of the bizarre events. They also called the clothing company back a few times to confirm that their order was still okay and they tried to get connected to the shipping department, hoping that they'd recognize the voice of the person who called them. They didn't become suspicious of Harold's cordless phone until a few days later when I called Harold again to talk to him about his upcoming Hawaiian vacation.

"Hello?" Harold answered.

"Hello, is this Harold Zimmerman?" I asked.

"Yes, I am."

"Hello, Mr. Zimmerman. This is Kahuna Jim from the Hawaii Chamber of Commerce. I understand that you're planning on vacationing down here in a few weeks."

"Yes, sir, that's right," Harold replied.

"Well, I'm just calling to inform you that we don't want you here and not to come to Hawaii. Maybe you could vacation in Kansas instead."

"No, I've already bought plane tickets to Hawaii."

"Well, you're gonna have to get a refund on those. You're not welcome here," I said.

"Why not?"

"Because, uh...you might interfere with the hula girls dancing or something."

Harold began laughing and said, "Well, Ima comin' anyway!"

"Well, I'll just have my supervisor meet you at the airport and tell you to go home!" I yelled and hung up. I was impressed with Harold's ability to stay completely calm when presented with deranged prank calls. For the rest of the day I listened to another round of phone calls between Harold and his family. His daughter told him to call the phone company so that they could trace the phone call. She seemed to think an employee from the clothing company was responsible for this call too.

The representative at the phone company listened to Harold's stories and immediately suggested that somebody was probably listening in on his cordless phone. She even knew that he was on a cordless phone by noticing the occasional bursts of static when he moved around, which I found very impressive. She signed him up for a caller ID package and convinced him that he should buy a new, secure cordless phone from the GTE phone store. While it felt great to help stimulate the economy, I was sad that I would lose Harold forever.

With my favorite past time destroyed, I began searching the newspaper for an apartment in a new neighborhood. With each prospective new home or apartment, I would drive to the neighborhoods with my scanner for an evening to see what cordless phone activity in that area was like. While I did find some neighborhoods that seemed like they'd be fun for eavesdropping, the reality of the cost of moving began to hit me. First and last month's rent, a security deposit, boxes, and a moving truck. My one-year lease wasn't up either, so my current land lord would probably use that as an excuse to keep my deposit. It would be months before I could save up enough money to move. This is when I realized that I could spend all that money, a little at a time, growing my own community of cordless phone users, right here in my own neighborhood.

I ripped the map of my neighborhood out of my phone book and started drawing dots on the addresses of each cordless phone user that I'd picked up from my home in the past six months. The furthest person away was two and a half blocks from me, so I marked off a three block radius on my map. With a clipboard in hand, I began walking around the neighborhood, writing down all the house numbers and the names written on their mailboxes. My goal would be to somehow turn every one of these people into cordless phone users.

By the time the evening was over, I'd written down addresses for more than 300 homes that were within my listening range, along with a few of their names. It was hard to believe that none of these 300 people used cordless phones. Cordless phones had been commonplace for more than a decade at that point and you could buy them at Wal-Mart for less than $50. Why weren't more people taking advantage of this modern convenience?

The public library carried a reverse directory of the entire city. Using this, I was able to find the names associated with most of the houses in my three block radius. Then I looked up those names in the phone book to get their phone numbers. Now I just needed to figure out a way to convince these people to use cordless phones. My first plan worked out fairly well when I called Alice, the first phone number on my list.

"Hello?" she answered.

"Hi, this is Carl from 105.6 The Hits, the best hit radio station in the valley! Are you ready to play the Tuesday Telephone Payout game with us for your chance to win $105.6 dollars?"

"Sure, I guess so," she replied.

"Okay then!" I yelled. "Today we're doing a history question! In which year did the United States first celebrate its July 4th birthday by signing the Declaration of Independence? You've got ten seconds..."

"Uhhhhh... Was it in the eighteen hundreds?"

"You tell us, Alice! Five seconds..."

"I'm going to say 1850."

"Ohhh, I'm so sorry Alice, but that's incorrect. You were really close, though! The date was July 4th, 1776."

"Oh, I knew that!" Alice laughed.

"Of course you did, Alice. Well, you lost out on the $105.6 dollars, but since you were within 100 years, we are going to send you a consolation prize which is a brand new Panasonic cordless phone!"

"Well, that's nice!"

"Tell me, Alice, do you use a cordless phone in your home right now?"

"We don't," she said.

"Well, I want to be the first to welcome you to the nineties. Stay on the line and our producer will take down your information to send you a brand new cordless phone!" By the end of that day, I'd promised to give away four cordless phones to people that lived on my street.

After browsing the phone aisle at Wal-Mart, I discovered that my generosity was going to cost me a total of $189.80 plus tax. Sure, it was cheaper than moving to a new neighborhood, but it sure seemed expensive to drop that much money on gifts for my neighbors. Their cheapest cordless phones were $47.45, with the nicer models costing more than $100.

The more expensive models promised "secure communications" which usually only meant that they ran on the 900 megahertz band instead of the 46 and 47 megahertz band like the older models did. Modern police scanners blocked out these new cordless phone frequencies by law, but the scanner I owned could pick them all up. If I was going to buy a lot of cordless phones, though, I had to find a cheaper way. So I put the cordless phones back on the shelf and bought a $7.99 cordless phone replacement battery and a glue stick instead. This would save me hundreds of dollars on cordless phones.

I drove to downtown and stopped at the Copy Super Center to make a few dozen photocopies of the barcode from battery replacement package. Then I drove back to Wal-Mart and glued the bar codes onto the bottom of each of the cordless phone boxes, covering up the original barcodes. My four new cordless phones would now only cost me $31.96! At this price, I would be able to give all 300 houses cordless phones for a total cost of $2,397.00. Without my barcode scam, I would have had to spend $14,235. That night I wrapped each of my four cordless phones with brown paper, addressed them to the winners of my contest, and walked by their houses after dark, slipping the packages into their mail boxes and hoping they wouldn't notice that they weren't postmarked. I didn't want to pay for shipping costs too.

I continued with my fake radio DJ ruse for most of the people on my list, but since I was running out of money, I began shipping cordless phones to people from a mail order catalog, using stolen credit card numbers to pay for them. This way the phones would be shipped to them through the mail, which might make the winners less suspicious of the packages I was leaving in their mailboxes. I just had to hope that they would ignore the invoice that came with it and that they wouldn't mind the flood of junk mail that usually happens after you order something through the mail. A few houses refused to play along with my radio station game, so I sent them all cordless phones from the catalog anyway. Then I called them and pretended to be from the mail order catalog company, letting them know that we'd be sending them a complimentary gift in hopes of them ordering from us in the future.

After fraudulently ordering more than thirty cordless phones, I began to worry that the catalog company would catch on, so I started buying cordless phones at Wal-Mart for $7.99 again. A new family moved into a house across the street from me, which had been up for rent for a couple of months. Since they were new, I couldn't look up their name in the library's reverse directory, so I began taking note of when their cars were gone to get an idea of when I could break into their home and just install some cordless phones. Since it was a new place and they were still moving things in, they probably wouldn't even notice.

They both left for work or school at 7 o'clock in the morning, so I walked around the block just as they left and entered their back yard through the alley. Several of their windows in back were open, so I just had to pop off the screen and climb in.

Their house was clean and organized, but there were still lots of boxes piled in their bedroom and on the kitchen counter. I was able to find three phones in the house, one of them being on the kitchen wall. I'd anticipated this, so I purchased a more expensive cordless wall phone with a built in answering machine, even though it still only cost me $7.99. As expected, there wasn't an electrical outlet on the wall by the phone, so I had to improvise by using the extra pair of wires in the phone jack to run the 9 volts of power that the phone needed. In the basement, I cut into the spare wires and hooked the 9 volt power supply to them, plugging it into an outlet on the ceiling.

I checked the outgoing message on their answering machine, which had the wife saying, "You've reached the Lawrence residence. Todd and Becky aren't here, but if you'll leave a message we'll get back to you as soon as we can." I set up the outgoing message on their new machine by playing the message from the old machine into it. The remaining two phones were easy to replace. One phone was on the computer desk in their bedroom and the other one was in their living room next to the couch. I replaced each of them with cordless phones and kept their old phones and their answering machine so that their only choice would be to use the cordless phones. I wrote down their phone number and their names for my list of cordless phone users, then quickly left their house.

My actions were definitely having a positive effect on the cordless phone scene in my neighborhood. I'd given away more than fifty telephones at that point, but had only logged nine new users in my notebook so far, but this was still more activity than when I'd first moved here. I guessed that people were just lazy about installing their cordless phones once they had them. I was learning a lot about my neighbors and I was doing my best to keep notes on them all.

That evening, as I was listening to cordless phone channels, I heard Becky Lawrence make a call from her new cordless phone, but it wasn't the kind of call I was hoping to hear.

"Police department, how can I help you?"

"Yes, I need an officer sent to my house. Someone broke in today and they stole all of our telephones," Becky said.

"Stole your telephones?" the officer asked.

"Yes, but they replaced them with new phones. I don't understand it, but we really need someone to come here so we can file a report."

I was really bummed that the $25 of phones that I'd installed in their house would probably go to waste. I anxiously watched out the window for the police to arrive as I listened to Becky make a call to her landlord to tell him about the break in. He wasn't home, so she talked to his wife instead. After their conversation, I called Becky and pretended to be the landlord.

"Hi, Becky! Wife tells me you got the present I gave you and Todd! I came in and installed those phones today for you and I hope you like 'em!"

"*You* put these phones in here?" she asked. "I just called the police because I thought someone had broken in and stolen our phones!"

"Why would someone come in and replace your old phones with new phones, Becky?" I asked.

"Well, why would you come into our house and replace our phones without asking us first?" she yelled.

"Because it was a surprise! It wouldn't be much of a surprise if I asked you first, would it?" Becky said nothing in response, so I continued, "Well, okay then! You better call the police and tell them it was a dumb mistake you made and that it's just a gift from me and the wife!"

"Well, wait," Becky said. "I want my old phones back."

"Those things? They were junk so I threw them in the trash."

"You threw away our answering machine? There were messages on there that I needed!"

"Well, you're sure not very appreciative of my kind gesture!"

The police didn't last long at Becky's house because she told them that her landlord had replaced the phones. I got to listen to the drama unfold on my scanner as Becky called her mom and her husband at work and several friends to tell them all what was happening and how insane the landlord must be. She called the police again the next day, though, once they figured out that the landlord didn't really install the phones. At least I got to listen to them for a couple of days, until the police took the phones for evidence. The best part was when they replaced their stolen phones with a cordless phone.

Diana Simms was one of the women who'd won a cordless phone through my fake radio station contest, but I hadn't heard her use it yet, so I gave her a call to check up on her.

"Hello?"

"Hi, Diana. This is Dale Philly from the Federal Telephone Upgrade Committee and it's come to our attention by an anonymous source that the equipment inside your house may not be up to code."

"What's not up to code?" she asked.

"Your telephones, ma'am. I'm running a test on your line right now and I'm able to detect that you're talking to me on a corded phone. Those are illegal and you'll need to upgrade the phones in your house to cordless phones immediately!"

"I've never heard of such a thing," Diana replied.

"Well, ignorance is no excuse to break the law. By continuing to use your old phones you're clogging up the phone lines and using up resources that could cost lives if there were an emergency. Do you have a cordless phone that you could use instead of this corded phone?"

"I got one a few weeks ago in a contest, but I haven't hooked it up yet because I don't know how."

"Well, I suggest that you learn how before you end up getting fined and arrested for misuse of the telephone system or before you cause a fire with that old equipment. Just open the box and plug your cordless phone in. The instructions in the box are very straightforward. Make sure you don't use your corded phone again unless you want a visit from the police. In fact, you should use scissors to cut the cord to the handset because you're not allowed to even own a working corded phone."

"Okay, I will. I'm sorry about this!" Diana said and then hung up. About thirty minutes later, I heard her repeatedly picking up and hanging up her new cordless phone as she fumbled with it, trying to understand how to make it work. I felt good about helping an older woman learn a new technology. If it wasn't for me, Diana would be sitting around the house watching television all evening, but instead she learned how to plug in a phone. I hoped that the experience would give her the confidence to do other things that she felt were too complicated, like setting the clock on her VCR or changing the filter on her air conditioner. I listened happily as Diana called her friends and family to tell them about the telephone laws they didn't know about.

While most of the people didn't believe that I was really with a federal telephone upgrade committee, I did convince a few of the older contest winners to start using their cordless phones.

One man told me that he didn't use his cordless phone because it wasn't in a convenient location like his corded phone was, so I snuck into his house while he was mowing the lawn and rearranged the locations of his phones.

While I was at Wal-Mart restocking my supply of cordless phones, I recognized a lady in the store as a neighbor of mine. I couldn't recall if she was one that had received a cordless phone from me or not, but just in case she wasn't, I tossed one of my $7.99 cordless phones into her shopping cart while she wasn't looking. I hoped that she wouldn't notice it until she got home and would see that it was so cheap that it'd be crazy not to keep it.

At the houses that I didn't have a name or phone number for, I left cordless phones on their porches in a gift bag along with pamphlets from a nearby church. I included a letter that explained the cordless phone was a gift and that Christians only use cordless phones because that's what the Bible says we should do. And I invited them to come to our Sunday services that week.

I wrote an editorial for the local paper about the wonders of cordless phones and how everyone should be using them. I dispelled the myths that they weren't secure, explaining that all modern cordless phones were impossible to listen to. Obviously this was a lie, but the paper seemed to think it was good enough to print in the paper. I knew it was a long shot that the editorial would get me any new users, but it couldn't hurt.

Since my editorial claimed that cordless phones were as cheap as regular phones now, I printed out sheets of bar codes and stuck them on all the cordless phone boxes at Wal-Mart, making their prices range from $7.99 to $24.99. The $24.99 model usually sold for $109.99. I even changed the price stickers on their shelves to reflect the new prices.

Three months after I began, I had a huge community of cordless phone users in my neighborhood with 78 new users logged in my notebook. During any given evening, I could turn on my scanner and choose from a dozen different conversations to listen to. In fact, it was sometimes frustrating having to choose which conversation I would listen to each night since there were so many of them. I flipped through my channels and finally settled on a lady named Marcia Seals who was in the process of ordering pizzas for dinner. After her phone call was over, I called her home.

"Mrs. Seals, this is Terry from Dominos Pizza. It seems we have a small problem with your order. You see, we share customer database information with the Southbrook Health Club where you're a member. And your current weight on file with them is way past the threshold of what they find acceptable for a healthy lifestyle. So until you lose some weight, we're not going to be able to have any pizzas sent to your house."

Homelessness

"I love coming back and reading this story. I wanna walk out on my job right now get in my car and drive to Galveston!" -spizak

When I left my parents' house at age 17, I knew it was likely that I would end up being homeless, but I didn't have a problem with this and I was sure that homelessness would be an interesting, and maybe even fun experience. I was optimistic, but mentally prepared for the worst. So I packed everything I could into my 1979 Dodge Colt and left in the middle of the night. My plan was to drive as far away from my small town in Illinois as possible, which took me to an island in Texas called Galveston.

I only had about $200 in cash and I knew that it would be foolish to blow it all on a place to stay as soon as I arrived, since I would need food until I found a job. I wasn't even sure if I'd be able to find a place to live since I wasn't a legal adult yet. So I mostly slept in my car in the Kroger parking lot, but sometimes I would lay out on the beach, which was right across the street from Kroger, and sleep there. It was great to wake up in the middle of the night and walk across the sand to pee in the ocean. It's not often in life that your nightly pee precedes a short walk along the beach.

Soon after arriving, I started paying a nearby campsite $3.00 each time that I wanted to use their showers, so at the very most being homeless in Galveston would cost me $93 per month. Eventually I found a graveyard shift job at Circle K, right across the street from the beach. Many mornings after work, if there wasn't too much sun in the forecast, I would walk across the street and sleep on the beach during the day for 8 hours.

Being homeless gave me complete freedom from pretty much all financial responsibility. No rent, no utility bills, no place to be, and nobody to answer to. Since I always kept a job and never had any of the normal expenses of life, I had plenty of spending money. I spent my days exploring the island, reading at the library, playing video games and watching TV at the campground, and using the computers at the community college. Eventually I found roommates and got a house, but those first few months of homelessness were quite an experience.

My next experience with homelessness was about 8 months later, in Myrtle Beach, South Carolina. I moved there with barely any money at all so my first month was spent sleeping in my car in various parking lots from North Myrtle Beach to Surfside Beach. Nobody seemed to care that I slept in my car until one night a cop started banging on my car window, I think with his flashlight. I was in a deep sleep and ended up screaming when I opened my eyes and saw him there. This was the first time I'd ever been hassled about sleeping in my car.

He made me get out of my car and attempted to search through all my belongings, I assume for drugs, as I stood by his car half asleep. I told him I was just passing through town on my way to North Carolina. He let me go, but said if he ever caught me sleeping in my car again, he'd arrest me. I slept in my car for another week or so in the next town over, but finally found a place to live with some roommates after I'd received my first paycheck from my new job.

I didn't have to pay for showers in Myrtle Beach while I was homeless. There were many campgrounds along the beaches, and I would ask the guards if I could take a look around their campground to see if I wanted to stay there. I would drive to their shower house, take care of everything, and then leave. Eventually a guard remembered me and told me to get lost and don't come back. After that, I just started entering the campgrounds by getting on the public beaches and walking along the beach until I found the back entrance to a campground.

My girlfriend Sylvia and I were homeless together once or twice. Once we spent the night behind a gas station somewhere in Illinois, the night before we hitchhiked to Normal. Our plan was to be homeless in Normal, but instead she persuaded our friend Chris to let us stay in his dorm room for a couple months. Then we lived in Los Angeles for a while and I really wanted to be homeless there, just for the experience, but instead we stayed with her mom for a while and then a friend of mine. Not that I'm complaining, but being homeless in Hollywood would have been a lot more memorable.

At least I came away from there with two experiences that I associate with homeless people. One was sitting at a freeway onramp all day, holding up a cardboard sign that read, "SPARE ANY CHANGE?" I sat there for more than five hours and ended up with less than ten dollars. You sometimes hear about homeless people making a lot of money doing this kind of thing, but I must have picked the worst onramp ever.

The other experience was selling beads all over Hollywood. We shoplifted enough materials from a Michaels craft store to make hundreds of necklaces and bracelets. Then we sold them to people on Hollywood Boulevard and in Venice Beach. We didn't make a whole lot of money with this, but it was enough to occasionally buy some food.

We met some homeless kids in Hollywood during our stay there and got to visit a few of their squats and hung out with them regularly on Hollywood Boulevard. One group of them lived in an abandoned building that had mostly burned down during the Rodney King riots the previous year.

Several months later, back in Galveston, I stayed in a homeless shelter for the first time. I don't remember why, but it's probably because it was cold out. I'd never stayed in a homeless shelter before and after staying in this one, I was glad I hadn't. They aren't fun. The staff treated us like scum, the residents all seemed mentally impaired and smelled bad, and we had to wake up and be out by 6:00 a.m. I think they provided breakfast, but I skipped that. I spent two nights in a row there, and then never again.

Later that same week I was sleeping under an outdoor stairwell at a Holiday Inn and I noticed that a door was cracked open. I hadn't seen anyone go in or out of it for hours, so I decided to see if anyone was inside. I knocked and there was no answer. I stepped inside and the room was clean with no signs of anyone staying there. So I slept there for the night and had a nice shower and shave in the morning, which felt amazing after having to sleep in the homeless shelter a few days earlier. I blocked the door with a big chair, just in case somebody attempted to come in during the night, planning to make my escape through the window if I needed to. Then I toilet papered the room before I left in the morning. I bet they were surprised.

In 1993 I spent about a month being homeless in Miami. I used various showers by hotel pools and I lived underneath a part of the boardwalk that spans a large part of the beach there. I kept my bags stashed under the boardwalk while I went out looking for a job each day. Each morning around 5 or 6 a.m., joggers pounded by overhead, waking me up for the day.

When I first arrived in Indianapolis, I spent a lot of time in the airport, sometimes sleeping there overnight. It was in this airport that I discovered the luggage carts were worth 25 cents when I returned them to their stations. I routinely patrolled the airport's parking garage, looking for carts to return for cash. I kept this up until I found a job at the airport's gift shop. Being an employee at the airport severely limited my ability to get away with sleeping there since I ended up knowing so many people, so I had to find new places in Indianapolis to stay.

I often switched between being homeless and living in weekly hotels. Several of the nights that I slept outdoors, next to buildings, I woke up covered in snow. It was damn cold that year. Another spot I slept at, next to a parking garage, had bats flying overhead all night. I slept on some giant heating grates a few nights, which were warm, but windy and noisy. Occasionally the owners of buildings would come out and tell me to leave. This mostly seemed to happen around government buildings that had night guards.

I'd sleep in the Greyhound station sometimes, but the manager would often decide to throw me and the other homeless people out of there. His favorite catch phrase to us was, "This isn't the Hilton!" He even yelled at me personally once, telling me that he saw me in there every night. Occasionally I would take Greyhounds to other cities in Indiana, just for fun on my days off, and I would try to make a point to let that manager see that I'd bought a ticket. I wanted him to think that I traveled by bus a lot so I could get away with sleeping there more often.

Eventually I found a perfect indoor home in Indianapolis - the IUPUI campus. The entire campus seemed to be completely unlocked and unguarded all night. Even some of the basement rooms with giant radioactive warning signs on them were unlocked. Some nights I slept in a student lounge or in a random classroom. I'd toss some of my books and notebooks around me, hoping to make anyone walking by think I'd just fallen asleep studying.

The campus was a great place to stay. I used their indoor pool's shower rooms to shave, shower and brush my teeth. I ended up with my own locker there and I spent a lot of my days jumping from the diving boards in their Olympic sized pool. The girl working at the desk in that building even gave me a sticker for my ID card that would identify me as a student to the pool and the computer lab attendants.

My regular sleeping spot ended up being under some stairs on the bottom level of a building. Apparently I wasn't the first one to live there, since there were stickers pasted on the slanted ceiling and burn marks all over the place from a lighter. I guess I must have been snoring when I was eventually caught sleeping there by one of the IUPUI staff. It was early in the morning and when I woke, I saw a lady peeking under the stairs at me, saying, "Hey, you're not supposed to be under there!" I told her I'd leave and I never slept there again. A few days later, I happened to be passing through that building and noticed that they'd stacked hundreds of chairs in front of my old sleeping place.

I worked evenings at the Lafayette Square movie theater and usually wouldn't get off work until 11:00 p.m. or so. Sometimes the city buses wouldn't be running anymore, so I'd walk to a nearby highway overpass and sleep under it. I'd tell my manager that there was still one more bus I could catch and he believed me. I don't think I ever told anyone I worked with, anywhere, that I was homeless.

One night the theater manager insisted on taking me home so I had him drive me to a house that I'd stayed in before and I walked around to the back until he left. After he was gone, I walked to downtown and found a place to sleep next to a building, annoyed that I had to walk around looking for a place to sleep when I could be sleeping under my usual overpass. I always thought about sleeping behind the screens at the theater, maybe on top of the giant speakers, but I'd hate to end up getting caught by the janitor or the manager.

The house that he dropped me off at was one that I occasionally stayed in for a week or two at a time. The living conditions there were enough to make anyone want to remain homeless. Roaches and mice were everywhere, the thin walls had holes in them, most of the furniture was broken, the rooms were dirty, and the beds had some scary-looking stains on them. But the rent sure was cheap!

The house was a three-story Victorian which had seen better days. The man who managed the house was fat, unclean, and smoked cigars. As I filled out a card to stay for a week the first time, he asked me, "You're not a faggot, are you?"

I looked up from my card, and said, "Um. No?"

"Faggots are not welcome here and if I find out anything is going on in your room, you'll be thrown out."

"Oh. Well, you won't have anything to worry about from me," I tried to assure him.

"Well, I *do* have to worry about it," he said, and then continued to rant about faggots and all the problems he'd had with them in the past as I finished filling out the card, handed him my $75, and went upstairs.

Months later, I was staying there again when I had another run-in with the manager. My alarm woke me up for work at 5 a.m. and I got up to use the shower. Each floor of the house had a bathroom for all the visitors to share. About ten minutes into my shower, someone started banging on the door, screaming, "WHO'S IN THERE!?"

I quickly got dressed and opened the door. The manager stood at the door, demanding to know what I was doing.

"I'm getting ready for work."

"Oh!" He seemed surprised by this as he looked into the bathroom. "I thought there were faggots up here. They like to get up early and leave so I won't know they were here. We've caught them in the showers before."

I looked past him and saw a black man standing at the top of the spiral stairs, holding a large metal flashlight. Since the hall was well-lit, I can only assume that it was going to be used to beat the living shit out of some homosexuals. After my week was up, I returned to being homeless on the streets of downtown Indianapolis, which seemed like a much safer option.

In Portland, Oregon I used stolen credit card numbers to fund a week or two of hotel stays, but after that stopped working, it was back to being homeless. I stayed in a weekly run-down hotel called the Jack London for a little while, then I found a college campus and began sleeping in their auditorium occasionally.

Since I worked nights, my girlfriend would sometimes let me stay at her house and sleep since her dad worked all day. But many times I would sleep on a park bench, at a bus stop, or behind some bushes on the ground. Once or twice I even slept in a tree, but that just seemed like a disaster waiting to happen.

The airport in Portland became my home for a few months. I kept my bags in a few of their lockers and spent many of my days and nights there. They had several rooms for businessmen, which included my very own cubicle with a telephone and a data port for my laptop computer. I collected luggage carts for money and since I still had a few pay stubs from my old gift shop job in Indianapolis, my meals in the airport came at a 10% discount since these gift shops were owned by the same company.

Cincinnati was the usual stuff; staying at the college campus and taking advantage of as many of their facilities as I could. I managed to get my own locker there to keep my stuff in. I slept in a few random places around downtown and a few times I slept in grass fields and under bridges.

I'm not going to say I actually miss being homeless today, but it sure was an interesting experience in life and it made things a lot easier financially when I was traveling. Finding a good place to spend the night where I wouldn't get hassled by anyone was sometimes a challenge, but at least I never had to worry about paying any rent or bills. I almost always had money since I would always have a job and not much to spend it on, especially after ditching my car. Basically all I ever had to do was eat, and I rarely ever had to beg for money. When other homeless people would ask me for change, I had the best excuse that you could give a homeless person – that I was homeless too.

Wacky Morning DJ

"After a particularly hot and sweaty fuck-session, RBCP rolled over and told me he had to update the phonelosers.org site. Perplexed, I checked it out, and I was hooked." -murd0c

Around 1998 or so, after moving to Illinois from Ohio, I discovered a quaint little morning show hosted by a guy named Howard Stern. I lasted as a dedicated Stern fan for a little over a year, before suddenly growing bored with his same old routine of boobs and penis discussion, day after day. I needed something new to listen to in the mornings, so I started trying new radio stations each morning until I happened across the Skippy and Dippy Morning Show.

Skippy and Dippy broadcasted from Ohio, but their show was syndicated to the Saint Louis market, which was just across the Mississippi from me. I immediately took a liking to Skippy since he seemed to love making prank calls to people. Not only did he make prank calls to the subjects in the stories they talked about, but he also made prank calls to celebrities.

The best part about Skippy's celebrity prank calls was that he dialed the phone numbers on the air. First the listeners would hear a dial tone, then Skippy pressing touch tones, and then the celebrity would pick up. By recording the touch tones that Skippy typed into his phone, I could later play back my recording and decode the tones so I could find out what numbers he had dialed. This meant my tiny list of celebrity phone numbers started quickly growing with names like Scott Baio, Dan Rather and Judge Wapner.

Skippy was relentless in his prank calls, calling some of his victims all morning, throughout the show, just to continue torturing them. Since his show started at 6:00 a.m. in the Eastern time zone and even earlier everywhere else, his prank calls almost always woke the victims up. I tried to create some drama from within the show by dialing Skippy's victims back and telling them who was responsible.

"Hello," answered the subject of a news story sleepily.

"Hi there." I said. "My name is Don Yarborough and I'm the producer for the Skippy and Dippy Show in Ohio. Our wacky morning DJ just made a prank call to you and I would like to fax you a release form to sign so that Skippy can use your voice in his upcoming prank call CD."

"Are you kidding me?" the man asked in disbelief. "That guy woke us up at five in the morning and said some really rude things to my wife, just because we were in the newspaper yesterday. You may *not* use my voice on your morning show!"

"Oh, we already played the call on the air. We don't need your permission for that. We just need your permission to put it on a CD to sell to Skippy's fans so we can make money from your misfortune."

"What he did wasn't even funny!" He was really getting angry now.

"Well, of course it's not funny to *you*, sir. You were the butt of the joke. But our listeners loved hearing Skippy make a fool of you. If you could just sign this release form then you'll never hear from us again."

"Oh, you're going to hear from me alright! What's the name of your show and how can I get in touch with your supervisor?" the man demanded.

"Let me give you the phone number for our station manager..."

Each time Skippy provoked a prank call victim enough for them to yell at him on the air, I would follow up with this same phone call, giving the victim the number to Skippy's station manager and any other information they requested, the whole time insisting that they should just get a sense of humor and stop being so uptight. I even did this with a few celebrities and hinted that if they didn't comply with the release form, Skippy would probably give out their phone number on the air to all of his listeners.

I realized that I was putting the daily prank calls I loved in jeopardy by making people complain to the station manager all the time, but I was just hoping to hear Skippy mention something about the callbacks on the air. But instead, I guess Skippy and his team figured out that I was getting everyone's phone numbers by decoding his touch tones, because he started muting most of the tones as he dialed the number.

Most of the news stories that Skippy used were taken from Fark's website, and Skippy would sometimes even steal Fark's funny headline. Occasionally the other hosts would chime in with funny comments that I recognized as comments that Fark users had posted the previous day. Using the story links on Fark, I was still able to call the prank call victims by reading the names in the stories and looking up their listed phone numbers.

As I continued to listen to a couple hours of Skippy each morning, I began to notice how uptight Skippy was and what a temper he had. He was always yelling at his interns on the air for doing stupid things or he was complaining about the incompetence of his cohosts. He liked things done a certain way and if he didn't get what he wanted, he would blow up at everyone, live on the air. He went into long rants about terrible service he received at restaurants and other places of business, complaining about the most trivial things. If Skippy didn't make such awesome prank calls to people all the time, I would think he didn't have a sense of humor at all.

One morning, as I listened to Skippy tear into a prank call victim immediately after screaming at one of the other hosts, I realized that Skippy would probably get really upset if he were the victim of a similar prank call. So I decided to test this theory by tracking down Skippy's home phone number and making a few prank calls to him.

I'd tracked down plenty of phone numbers before, so I figured it would be a piece of cake to find Skippy's number, but I was completely wrong about this. Skippy was very protective of his identity and his real name didn't seem to be known by anyone. Every newspaper article I found online mentioned only his DJ name. I called the station and asked a few employees to tell me what his real name was, using various ruses. Some would say that they couldn't tell me that, but most would admit to me that they didn't even know his real name.

Using the few radio station phone numbers I already had, I called their local phone company and convinced them that I was a technician at the station and I needed a list of all the phone lines working there. I tried to get them to fax me the list of numbers, but the phone company representative who was helping me didn't know how to fax documents from her computer, so I listened as she spent nearly thirty minutes reading me the entire list of numbers as I wrote them down by hand.

There were over a hundred numbers and I called every single one of them. I had the private office numbers for Skippy, Dippy and the rest of the staff. I ended up with another number for the station manager and the station's secret hotline number, which was used when a staff member was out pulling a stunt for the show and needed to call into the station without being put on hold. They rarely screened the calls on this line, so I was able to call in and get on the air a few times by calling that number. I also sometimes called it at other times of the day, just to chat with whatever DJ was currently on the air.

I'd hoped that Skippy would mention his real name or his cell number on his office voicemail, but he didn't. It was a dead end for me. But as I called every number at the station, I noticed that some employees would give out their cellular phone number on their office's voice mail box. By calling the wireless provider, I was able to find out that all of these cell phone numbers were owned by the station. So Skippy must have a cell phone provided by the station too!

After a few calls to the wireless provider, I finally found an employee willing to fax me a three page list of all the wireless phones on the station's account. This consumed several more of my days as I called every number on the list, hoping to hear Skippy's voice. I asked every person who answered for Skippy's wireless number, claiming that he'd given me the wrong phone number. None of them fell for it and Skippy didn't appear to use any of the wireless phones on the list. Another dead end.

Since I couldn't find Skippy, I began to concentrate on Dippy. His name was also a secret, but he used one of the cell phones on the list. It didn't take long for me to talk an employee from the wireless company into faxing me the last three months of Dippy's cell phone usage. Skippy and Dippy appeared to be friends in real life, so I reasoned that they must make occasional phone calls to each other. I called every number on Dippy's phone bill that had a duration of more than one minute, and finally recognized Skippy's voice answer one of the numbers. I quickly hung up and began checking into the number I found.

It turned out to be Skippy's home phone number! A call to his phone company gave me Skippy's real name, his home address and the other two lines on their home account. They also gave me the alternate contact number from the account, which turned out to be Skippy's cell phone number. A call to his wireless provider gave me his wife's cell number too. I suddenly had more information on the elusive Skippy than I knew what to do with.

When I called Skippy at home the next day, he already knew someone was trying to track him down since everyone at the station had been telling him that they were getting weird calls from me, asking for him. I had even called Dippy's wife and asked her for his cell phone number.

Skippy was not happy to finally hear from me and our first few phone calls didn't last long. In the first call, he only sighed heavily before slamming down the phone. In the second call, I asked to speak with his wife, but he just told me that my call would be traced and then hung up on me. Later that day he changed both of his home phone numbers. I waited until a week later to call Verizon and ask them for the new phone numbers.

"Hello," Skippy answered.

"Hi, Skippy! Why'd you change your phone number?"

"Do you know what star 57 is?" Skippy asked.

"No, what is it?" I asked.

"You're going to find out very soon, my friend. They know who you are and you will be tracked down."

"If they know who I am, then why do they need to track me down?" I asked.

"Why don't you tell me your phone number?"

"It's unlisted, Skippy. You know how that is. I think this is a classic case of you being able to dish it out but not being able to take it. Correct?"

"It doesn't matter!" he yelled. "I will see you in court!"

"No you won't."

"Yes I will."

"What's star 57 anyway?"

"Star 57 is the automatic tracing service that is accessible only to the police," Skippy explained.

"Why are you so mad, Skippy?"

"Because you obviously got my unlisted numbers last week and now you've gotten them once again after Verizon has changed them. And there's only one way you're getting them. You have access to the Verizon unlisted database. And believe me, Verizon security is extremely interested in this."

"I don't have access to any databases," I replied. "I don't even know what a database is."

"Dude. I will see you in court. The police have your number now."

"Oh, the police can't get my number because it's unlisted."

Of course, I knew exactly what star 57 was already. People had been threatening to trace my calls for most of my life, but it was always just a scare tactic. I was dialing Skippy through a calling card that caused my number to come in from "out of area" so I knew that Skippy's attempts to star 57 my calls were useless.

And I thought it was great that Skippy assumed I had access to some top secret unlisted database of phone numbers. All it took to get an unlisted phone number was a quick call to Verizon. Most of the customer service reps there would easily give up an unlisted number if you knew how to ask them for it. This kind of trickery wasn't even illegal. If anything, the reps should be arrested for handing out people's private information.

It may have taken several weeks of hard research to prove my theory, but I was right. Skippy could dish it out, but he couldn't take it. Just like so many of the victims in Skippy's prank calls, Skippy immediately became angry and threatened to do something about the prank calls. He yelled and gave exasperated sighs and slammed down the phone several times on me. My weeks of obsessive research had finally paid off!

At the time, Napster was a controversial music sharing application on the internet. It was the first easy way for average internet users to obtain pirated music files. While most people only used Napster to share their music collections, other people used it to share their collection of prank call mp3 files. There were even a few dozen prank calls by Skippy on Napster, which I had downloaded and enjoyed immediately after discovering his morning show.

I wanted to share my prank calls to Skippy with other people who were familiar with his morning show, so I began putting my calls up on Napster and labeling them as more of Skippy's hilarious prank calls. I even created a small introduction to some of the calls, telling listeners that Skippy loved making prank calls but he hated to receive them.

Each time I made another call to Skippy or any of his staff, I would add it to my Napster list. I left Napster running all day and night so that his fans could download my prank calls to him, keeping close tabs on the number of downloads. I noticed that other Napster users also began sharing my prank calls on their own accounts. This only encouraged me to continue making as many prank calls to the Skippy and Dippy staff as I could.

It was really crazy how much time I poured into all this research. Even after my initial calls to Skippy's home, I continued to obsess over collecting more information on him and the show. I called the phone company and had several months of his home and cell phone bills faxed to me. I spent hours, sitting at Subway during lunch, looking over his phone bills, crossing off numbers I already had and trying to eliminate duplicates so I could find even more people related to the show.

After the thrill of pestering Skippy on his personal phones wore off and they changed the station's hotline number so I couldn't get on the air instantly anymore, I needed a new way to irritate the staff. They changed the hotline number the day after they put me on the air and I yelled Skippy's real name before they could hang up on me. I had way too much information on the station to just quit harassing them, though. This is when I realized that I had Walt's number.

Walt was the show's inside Hollywood man. Each morning at 9:00, Walt would call into the show with the latest celebrity gossip and news. He claimed to have multiple sources and paparazzi working for him. Several times on the show he expressed paranoia about celebrities figuring out who he was since he and the people working for him used sketchy methods when obtaining their information.

One morning I turned on the radio just as Skippy was assuring Walt that nobody could ever figure out who he was. A challenge! It turned out that I already had Walt's two home phone numbers in my giant stack of Skippy's phone bills. I called every phone number on them that was located in California until I heard Walt's voice answer one of the numbers.

The next morning I called Walt's home fifteen minutes before he was scheduled to go on the air with Skippy. I told him that I was a friend of Skippy's and that Skippy gave me his phone number and said I could call him up for secret information on Tom Cruise. My hope was to make him upset with Skippy for handing out his private number, but he didn't believe that part of my story. Instead, he assumed that I was with the Church of Scientology and that I was angry about the things he was saying on the air about Tom Cruise. Walt talked to me until Skippy called him on the other line, then he said he had to go. I failed at making him angry with the show, but I sure helped fuel his paranoia.

Ten minutes later, Walt was on the air and giving his report. Although Walt was obviously shaken up a little during his report, I was disappointed that nothing was mentioned about my call, so after a few minutes I began calling the phone Walt was using, making his call waiting beep. Each time it beeped, his voice would cut out during his report. I called nonstop throughout his segment that morning, making his voice cut out repeatedly and making him stammer a lot. Skippy kept having to ask him to repeat himself. Twice during the segment Walt actually put Skippy on hold, live on the air, so he could click over and see if it was me.

"Hi, Walt, it's me! Don't say anything about us Scientologists today!" I yelled at him.

He clicked back over to Skippy and said, "Looks like I'll be getting a new phone number."

Skippy told him to stop answering his phone during his segment, but Walt just couldn't resist clicking over once more to ensure that it was really me calling him. The next morning, I tried interfering with his segment again, but he disabled his call waiting so I couldn't get through. I'd dealt with people blocking call waiting before and I knew exactly what to do.

The morning after that, I drove my car up to a pay phone and waited for Walt's Hollywood segment to begin. When it did, I dialed AT&T and talked to the operator.

"AT&T, how may I help you?"

"My brother's phone is busy and I need to emergency interrupt his line so I can tell him to get off the phone."

"The charge will be $21.00. How will you be paying for this?" she asked me.

"In quarters." I replied. I couldn't believe how much the price had gone up. I used to do this same thing less than ten years ago to kick people off of computer data lines and it only cost around $4.00 then.

"In *quarters*?" she replied as if she couldn't believe it.

"That's right. Hurry up, this is important."

Acting as if I'd ruined her day, she began the process of having me insert quarters into the phone, $3.00 at a time, until I reached the full amount. I wasn't putting in real money, of course, but I was using a red box which mimicked the tones that pay phones used to recognize quarters. Once all my pretend money was in, she cut into Walt's on-air report, telling him that Roy was making an emergency phone call and asked if he would release the line.

"Tell him it's about Scientology!" I yelled into the phone, hoping that she hadn't muted me so my voice would go out over the air too.

The next morning I tried calling his line from home again, but he still had his call waiting blocked. So I dialed a number that I suspected of being Walt's cellular phone, but I hadn't confirmed yet. And in the background, on the air, I heard it ringing as Waldo talked about the latest Hollywood gossip. He paused for a few seconds, but he didn't answer.

Less than a week later, Walt's Hollywood segment no longer involved live phone calls. Instead, Walt sent his notes to Skippy and let them read about everything themselves. Walt changed his phone numbers and I didn't bother getting the new ones since he never went on the air anymore. He probably moved and layed low for a few years, hiding from the Scientologists who were out to get him. I pulled similar stunts with other regulars that called into the show since I had their phone numbers, but none were as funny as Walt was.

I felt as if I had created a new era of interactive radio. It wasn't easy to get past the interns screening Skippy's calls so I could get on the air, but it sure wasn't that difficult to cause crazy things to happen on the show by harassing the regulars who were already on the air.

Throughout my campaign against the Skippy and Dippy show, I tried my best to let the listeners know what Skippy's real name was. The few times that I got on the air, I tried to yell his name on the air before they hung up on me. And I posted his real name a few times on the show's internet forums, but the staff would always delete those posts. Skippy had always been secretive about his real name, so I was surprised one morning when he teased his listeners all morning, promising to reveal his real name on the air.

He turned the entire thing into a shtick and actually gave his real name to the listeners at the end of the day, completely ruining my fun of telling the listeners myself. Well played, Skippy...well played.

When his sidekick Dippy announced that he would be in Chicago for a few days to attend a relative's wedding, the conversation turned into a radio bit where Dippy refused to tell Skippy which hotel he would be staying at because he didn't want to be prank called at six in the morning. Skippy assured Dippy that he would figure out where he was staying and that he would call him on the air.

For me, it was easy to find out where they were staying. I called up Dippy's cell phone provider and asked them to read me all of the phone numbers on the bill that were in Illinois. The only recent calls to Illinois were in a Chicago area code, so I called that number and it was the Days Inn. I gave the man there Dippy's real name and confirmed his reservation for later in the week.

On the morning that Dippy was absent from the show, Skippy happily announced that he had figured out which hotel

Dippy was staying in and that after the commercial break, he was going to surprise him with a live phone call. As soon as the commercial break began, I called the hotel and began making calls to both of the rooms Dippy had reserved.

"Hello?" Dippy answered sleepily.

"Hello. This is Roy from the front desk," I said. "We've had several complaints from our guests about the noise coming from your room and the smell of marijuana smoke coming from under the door. We need you to settle down in there or we're going to have to escort you from the hotel."

"There's nobody making noise in here. We're asleep."

"I doubt that, sir. I've been up there myself and I heard the party coming from the other side of your door. If you don't take care of things immediately, I'll have Skippy the security guard come up there and forcibly remove you."

"Oh, this is the show calling me," Dippy realized. "Wait a minute. Who is this?"

"I'm Skippy's new sidekick, motherfucker, and you're not welcome back at the station!" I yelled at him.

Dippy, confused and tired, finally hung up the phone on me. I called his other room, which he had family staying in, and confused everyone there with my randomness as they passed the phone around. I didn't last long with any of them, until the phone was given to Uncle Harold.

"This is Skippy from the radio station, isn't it?" he asked. "Am I on the air right now?"

"You certainly are!" I said. "I couldn't get Dippy to wake up so I'm forced to bother the rest of his family instead. Who am I talking to?"

"This is Dippy's Uncle Harold," he said after a hearty laugh. "Let me tell you a few things about that boy..."

Uncle Harold, obviously pleased that he was on a syndicated radio show, launched into a tirade of boring stories about Dippy.

"Listen, Uncle Harold." I interrupted. "I need your help. I need you to go next door and wake up Dippy. He refuses to talk to me, so I need you to think of a way to get him on your phone so I can talk to him."

Uncle Harold was thrilled to be a part of such a hilarious radio stunt, and immediately ran next door to start pounding on Dippy's door. By this time, Skippy had already called Dippy's room and was talking to him on the air. I listened to the radio as I heard Uncle Harold in the background talking to Dippy's wife and trying to coax Dippy into the next room.

"Uncle Harold, I'm already talking to Skippy on this phone." Dippy said on the air.

Confusion ran deep and the call between Skippy and Dippy didn't last long. Dippy made a small mention of the previous call he'd received and Skippy quickly changed the subject, probably realizing what was happening. Skippy managed to say, "I told you I could find out where you were staying!" a few times before awkwardly ending his call with Dippy. I guess I ruined whatever they had planned together since the whole on-air exchange was pretty boring and awkward.

Months later, the space station Mir was de-orbited and began burning up during re-entry into the Earth's atmosphere over the Pacific Ocean. Skippy turned this into another wacky morning radio bit by burning up a bunch of metal with a blowtorch and listing it on eBay as authentic space station Mir debris. In the item description, he claimed to be a fisherman who saw it come out of the sky, so he fished it out of the water before it sank. People seemed to believe this and began placing bids.

He spent an entire two days talking about the auction, bragging about how many hits it was getting and about all the coverage it was receiving from the media. The auction had less than a day left until it ended and the listeners would finally find out what the final bid would be. But the next day, thanks to me, Skippy never spoke of the auction or Mir again.

As Skippy began his second day of raving about the cleverness of his auction, I just couldn't take it anymore. The prank wasn't funny at all, but Skippy just wouldn't shut up about it and acted as if it were the best thing he'd ever done. Instead of just turning my radio off like a normal person, I decided I would hack Skippy's eBay account. I began by trying some of the passwords that he used on his phone accounts, but none of those worked. So I called eBay's customer service line.

As much as I pleaded with the customer service representative to change his password, she insisted that the only way she could do it was to send a new, randomly generated password to his email account. Luckily, I was able to get Skippy's email address on the account from her, which was an AOL address.

"AOL Support, this is Jim. How may I help you?" the man on the phone asked.

"Hi Jim," I replied. "This is Roy from the sales department. I need you to pull up an account for me so we can change the password on their account."

"Why can't you do this?" Jim asked.

"Because our Merlin systems just went down here and my supervisor is saying they won't be back up for another twenty minutes. I just upgraded their plan, but the system went down before I could take care of his password issue for him."

After a little more coaxing and verifying some information on the account, Jim finally set Skippy's password to a word that I picked, and before he even hung up the phone I had logged into his AOL account from the web. I quickly called eBay back and asked them to reset my password. Several minutes later, the new eBay password was waiting in Skippy's in box.

Since the auction had less than a day left before it ended, I wasn't able to delete any of the auction's description, but I was able to append some extra text onto the end of it. Since Skippy had already told the listeners his real name, I decided to publish his personal phone numbers to the auction. I made a list of about about thirty phone numbers of people related to the Skippy and Dippy morning show, and added them to the auction description. I listed Skippy's home and cell numbers, Dippy's home and cell numbers, the home numbers of a few of the other regular hosts, all of their personal office lines, the station manager's home and office lines, and Walt's cell phone number.

I also saw that eBay would allow me to add some extra pictures to the auction and I just happened to have the perfect picture. A few weeks earlier, I'd noticed that my friend Legend lived in the same city as Skippy, so one day I told him about all the awful things I had been doing to the show. It turned out that Legend also listened to the show occasionally, and he volunteered to drive by Skippy's house and snap a few pictures for me. So I added a picture of Skippy's house to the auction and saved the changes.

Then I locked Skippy out of his eBay account by changing the password and calling eBay customer service back to change some of his personal information so that he couldn't easily log back in and remove the extra information. By the time I was finished, there wasn't much time left in that day's show.

I kept listening, waiting for Skippy to check the page again and hoping to hear his live reaction of what had been done to his auction page. And while he did appear to check the auction once more near the end of the show to give an update on it, I guess he didn't scroll down far enough to notice my changes. As they wrapped up the show, he encouraged everyone to visit the auction page again and promised to have the final results on the bidding first thing in the morning. I could hardly wait.

I can only assume that they didn't see the auction page until the next morning when they prepared to announce it on the air. The auction page stayed up all night and for most of the next day, but Skippy never said another word about it. Later that afternoon, the auction completely disappeared. They did the rest of their show as usual, but nothing more was ever said about the auction or Mir.

One of the cool things about having access to Skippy's email account was seeing how him and a few of the other staff members put their show together each day. Him and Dippy emailed each other throughout the days and evenings, sending each other show notes and ideas, constantly appending to the list, including notes for jokes and comments that different members of the staff should try to work in. It was interesting to see how scripted their morning show was. It was more than just reading from a list of items to talk about – they actually scripted out the jokes that they stole from Fark.com and other sources and they did a very convincing job at casually working their scripted jokes and commentary into the conversation as if they were really clever enough to think up that material on the fly.

Going back to my roots of wondering how Skippy would react to prank phone calls, I began calling him again, but he stopped answering calls from "out of area" phone numbers. So I began calling all of the neighbors living on Skippy's street instead.

"Hello?" Skippy's neighbor answered.

"Hi, Mark! This is Skippy, a couple houses down from you." I said, but using Skippy's real name.

"Oh, hi Skippy."

"Mark, I'm sorry, but I need to be blunt with you. You need to clean up your yard. Spend a little time trimming your trees and stuff. I'm embarrassed to bring my friends or family over because your shitty yard makes it look like we live in the ghetto."

"Are you serious?" Mark asked.

"Yes, I serious!" I yelled. "You realize I'm a celebrity, don't you? Do you know what it's like to have a lazy neighbor like you who can't even take care of his yard work?"

I never could get any of his neighbors to agree that I was a celebrity. I called the woman who lived next door to him and explained to her that I was a celebrity and because of this she needed to avert her eyes whenever she saw me outside because celebrities don't make eye contact with normal people. I told another man that when he saw my BMW passing by on the street, he needed to pull to the side of the road until I passed to avoid having his car throw any rocks or dust onto my car. As hard as I tried, though, I just couldn't get the neighbors to see eye-to-eye with Skippy.

All of these events occurred over the course of maybe one year. During that year, I made frequent prank calls to all of the staff members of the Skippy and Dippy Show, especially the ones who yelled at me the most creatively. As much fun as I had turning a regular morning show into my own personal interactive game, I quit after about a year. Stalking the entire staff of a morning show was just eating up way too much of my time, so just like that, it was over.

Until one morning, several years later, my clock radio woke me up to the sound of the Skippy being really pissed off about something. This wasn't unusual, but as I lay there, trying to wake up, I slowly realized that Skippy's rant was about *me*. He was ranting about a story that had been in the news a lot over the past week, where some pranksters had used their ham radios to talk to the customers of a Burger King drive-thru. But throughout his rant, which I missed the beginning of, he kept making references to a stalker in Illinois.

When I figured out that he was talking about me, I jumped out of bed and grabbed my digital voice recorder so I could record what he was saying and add it to my collection of Skippy calls on Napster. Apparently he'd been refraining from talking about the Burger King prank story on the air for over a week because it reminded him of me. This is because a year earlier, EvilCal and I had mailed a video to Skippy of us pulling similar pranks on drive-thru customers. We sent it as an entry to a contest the morning show was holding about pulling hilarious pranks on people, hoping to win the $5,000 prize.

What was most horrifying about his rant was that he knew exactly who I was. He called me and my wife by name on the air. He even referenced the name of my long distance provider as he talked about how he worked with the phone company and the police to trace my calls and said that he had eight months worth of my personal phone bills. According to him, he knew who I was from the very beginning of those first prank calls to his house.

I spent an entire year interfering with his show, doing things that were incredibly illegal, and for some reason he never sent the police after me or filed a lawsuit like he promised to in several of my prank calls to him. Had I known that he knew who I was, I never would have taken things as far as I did. I thought I was taking adequate precautions when making calls to everyone and logging into his accounts, but I was suddenly finding out that I was wrong.

I had even called his home and taunted him about his threats of subpoenaing me. I reminded him that he promised to see me in court and asked why it hadn't happened yet. He said to me once that maybe it was because I wasn't bothering him that much. I assumed he was saying this because he didn't really know who I was. This was a man who had filed lawsuits against people before, so provoking him was a horrible idea since he actually had all of my information.

For years I'd used certain brands of calling cards to mask my calls. Instead of just making a call show up as "anonymous" on a caller I.D. display, the calling card would cause the call to come in "out of area" which rendered caller I.D. useless. It also made calling codes like star 57 and star 69 not work at all. When you tried to use these features, a recorded voice would tell you that it didn't work.

I occasionally tested my calling card on my home phone, just to ensure that it still properly blocked all of my calls. And I did this at least once during my Skippy harassment, but I guess just because my own phone company didn't allow the calling information to pass through didn't mean that Skippy's phone company worked the same way. I just don't understand why he didn't take action since he knew who I was the whole time.

Another year after waking up to Skippy's tirade against me, I was still a regular listener of the show. Lindsay Lohan was making a lot of news at the time and Skippy was talking about her often, so I decided to finally contribute something to the show by sending them Lindsay Lohan's home and cell phone numbers, which I just happened to have. I started to send it anonymously, but then decided against it and I kept my real name in the email header. I even signed the email, "Your favorite stalker friend, Alex."

The next morning, Skippy began talking about Lindsay again and I was surprised to hear him mention that they had her cell phone number and they'd received it last night from one of their "phone phreak friends" in Illinois. I didn't expect them to even use the number, let alone acknowledge me. They made a few calls to her and then moved on to other things. Lindsay changed her number later that day, so I called T-Mobile and got her new number for Skippy. It felt nice to help out the show for once, even if it was at the expense of a young Hollywood celebrity.

Close to ten years after this story began, I was living in Oregon and hadn't listened to Skippy's show in more than four years. So I was surprised to get an email from an old friend in Illinois, telling me that Skippy had been talking about me again that morning. As one of the other hosts happened to be driving by my old town on a business trip, Skippy began jeering at him, "While you're there, why don't you stop by Alex's house and say hello to him! Here, let me find the address for you!"

It's nice to know I'm still having an effect on Skippy's show, all these years later.

7-Eleven Looting

> "*The PLA is responsible for my endless hours of brute force attacks on answering machines all over the country.*" -BaconStrips

In early 1993, at age 19, my girlfriend Sylvia and I had just moved to Illinois after spending the past few months in California, Texas, and Florida. I was staying with my parents and Sylvia was staying with a friend of ours while I saved up enough money so we could get an apartment of our own. I ended up with a job at a 7-Eleven convenience store in Wood River, working the graveyard shift from 2:00 a.m. until 10:00 a.m. Sylvia hung out with me many nights at the store, playing nonstop pinball with the free quarters I supplied her from the cash register.

On the morning of April 1st, around 1:00 a.m., a business named Clark Boat & Motor called the store and asked if it'd be a problem to come in and buy $2,000 in money orders with cash. I told them it wouldn't be a problem at all, so they agreed to come into the store in an hour or two, to buy the money orders.

Soon after the call, I began thinking about how neither of us were too crazy about being back in that area, and with $2,000 suddenly coming into our lives, it sure would be easy to just leave town and go wherever we wanted. So I suggested to Sylvia that we take the money and run.

"Yeah right," she said. "Like they wouldn't miss that much money."

"Well...since it's grand theft anyway, what if we just took all the money out of the register and safe too? And maybe a bunch of cigarettes and lottery tickets and whatever else we want to take with us?"

Of course, she was completely against the idea at first, but somehow I managed to convince her that it was the best idea we'd ever had. After all, we'd been flying all over the country on stolen credit cards for the past year, so this wasn't too much worse than that. So we sat at the counter for a while and began making plans. We knew this would turn us into fugitives, but neither of us seemed to care about that at all. We figured it would be fun to change our names and be on the run from the law. After looking at a travel atlas, we decided to move somewhere in Georgia since neither of us had ever been there and it was far away from any friends or family.

The safe behind the counter worked the same as every other safe I'd worked with in a convenience store; it stored rolls of coins and bills, but only allowed me to retrieve one roll every two minutes. This was to deter robbers from getting away with more than $10 or $20 from the safe, but with enough time to spare, you could empty out the entire $300 to $400 available in just under two hours by pressing the button every two minutes. So that's what I began to do as we waited for the guy to show up with our $2,000.

The other part of the safe contained all of the money earned for the day, but that was only accessible with the manager's key, which I didn't have. Employees were supposed to drop the large bills into a slot in the safe, which I'd been doing until we'd hatched our devious plan.

Since the store had four surveillance cameras that were running as we were making our plans and stealing all this money, I thought maybe I should steal the video tape out of the machine so there would be less evidence against us. Besides, a tape like that would make an excellent souvenir.

The security monitors and recording equipment were kept inside a locked metal box, mounted on the wall in the manager's office, which was also locked. The manager's door was easy enough to open, using a can opener handle to slip between the door and frame, and the key to the security equipment was right on top of the manager's desk. As I looked for a blank tape to replace my souvenir tape with, I happened to notice a large, square key that looked exactly like the safe key sitting on the manager's desk. I couldn't be that lucky, could I?

I ran out of the office with the key, extremely excited about the prospect of having access to the entire day's cash. My excitement didn't last too long, though. The key fit into the safe and it turned, but nothing happened when I pressed the "open" button. The safe's door was still securely latched, no matter how many times I tried. I figured it wasn't the master key and only had limited functions. Oh well.

Sylvia and I had a great time, running around the store and taking things off the shelves that we planned to bring with us on our trip. We loaded up on candy, sunglasses, snacks, toys, and cigarettes. As we were filling up our second grocery bag, we suddenly heard a loud grinding noise and then a clang, coming from behind the counter. I ran to the counter and peered over to see that the safe was open! I'd completely forgotten that there was a twelve minute delay to open the safe's door, again to deter robbers from getting away with anything more than was in the register.

It took us another hour just to get all the money out of the safe and organized into bags so we could carry it. We made off with around $4,000 in cash, $200 in food stamps, $50 in lottery tickets, $50 in rolls of quarters, and two bags filled with groceries, cigarettes and other supplies. We would have stolen more lottery tickets, but knew we wouldn't be able to cash them in once we left the state.

Now we were faced with the problem of how to leave since neither of us had a car. We called a few friends and tried to get them to drive us to the airport, but they were all either afraid of getting arrested or weren't allowed to leave the house that late at night. Having no other means of transportation, we called a cab.

First, we had the cab drive us by the friend's house where Sylvia was living to pick up her things, and then to my parents' house to pick up my things. The cab driver didn't seem the least bit suspicious that we were leaving an apparently unmanned 7-Eleven and that we were stopping by separate houses to pick up large duffle bags. Not to mention that I had him park down the block from my parents' house while I ran to get my things and we paid him with money from a brown paper bag, which included a $20 tip.

While at my parents' house, I unplugged their phone lines so that the cops or store manager wouldn't be able to immediately contact them, hopefully giving us a little more time to get away. I also left a note for my parents, which I'd written at 7-Eleven, apologizing for my actions and assuring them that we hadn't been abducted by armed robbers at the store. I stuck the note in a copy of Abbie Hoffman's *Steal This Book*, which I'd checked out from the library earlier in the week.

Worried that the cops would figure out that we'd taken a cab, we had the driver drop us off at a mall in Glen Carbon. From there we used a pay phone to call a different cab company to take us to the St. Louis airport. By the time we arrived there, it was nearly 5:00 a.m. We checked into an airport hotel, so that we could get some breakfast, rest, and call in our flight reservations.

There were two flights departing to Atlanta that morning, one at 8:00 a.m. and the other at 10:00 a.m. I wanted to take the earlier flight, just to quickly get us further away from the scene of the crime, but Sylvia insisted that we take the later flight so she could rest for an extra hour. She finally won the argument, so I called TWA and reserved two seats under the names Susan and Kevin Mitnick for 10:00.

As we ate our continental breakfast and organized our huge piles of money, we began to discuss our future. I'd just made over $5,000 from working at a 7-Eleven for only a month. We theorized that I could continue to take jobs in convenience stores all over the country, maybe even two at a time, and then skip town with all the money and merchandise we could carry.

With a little more planning, we could easily cut down on the amount of time I'd need to work there before looting the place, and if we bought a car, we could fill it with merchandise from the store. All the cigarettes, cash, money orders, and lottery tickets that we could stuff into the trunk and back seat! We could even take expensive hardware with us, like the security camera equipment, computers, and the money order machine. By using different fake IDs each time, they'd never be able to tie all these crimes to the same person. We were sure that this plan was foolproof and that our future was set.

Exhausted from our activities, we slept for a couple of hours. And just before 9:00 a.m., when our alarm clock was about to wake us up to catch our flight to Atlanta, our life of crime abruptly ended as a voice from the hall yelled out, "Wood River police!"

I opened my eyes and sat up in bed, just as a maid and two Wood River detectives burst into our room and arrested us. The first thing they said to me was, "Where's the security tape?"

"In there," I said, pointing to one of my duffle bags.

After retrieving the tape and the money, they searched through our other bags for the rest of the stolen merchandise. The two detectives were in extremely good spirits and seemed strangely amused about the entire thing. They smiled a lot and were friendly to both Sylvia and I. They marveled at my huge collection of fake IDs and laughed at the Missouri ID that claimed I was a 5' 4" black male. I guess they thought the whole incident was a nice break from the usual, boring crimes that they had to deal with in Wood River.

The detectives drove us back to Wood River where we were booked into jail. We spent the morning giving statements, chatting with the police, and going to court. I sat in a room with an officer for about an hour as he slowly inventoried everything we'd stolen and he chuckled, "You sure have caused me a lot of paperwork this morning, Alex."

When the cops and manager arrived at the store that night, they viewed the new security tape that I put into the machine. I was afraid that leaving the machine empty might trigger an alarm, so I put in an old tape just to be safe. I didn't realize that any of the cameras pointed at the front windows, but one did and the police were able to see that we climbed into a cab and drove away.

After finding out that we'd been dropped off at a mall 20 miles away, they must have called the cabs in that area to find out that we were picked up from there and taken to the airport. It would have all gone as planned if we'd just taken the earlier flight that morning. That is, unless they found out where we were going in time and had the Atlanta police waiting for us, which would have been a much more interesting situation.

The next day we were transferred to the county jail in Edwardsville, Illinois. My cell block was overcrowded and they didn't have a bed for me, so I spent the first few days sleeping in a common area on the floor. I placed my mattress directly underneath the pay phone in the room, so I could sit up and play on the phone late into the night, which made me feel right at home.

I ended up spending a week in jail, while Sylvia somehow ended up with two weeks. We wrote each other notes and slipped them to each other as we passed on the way to court. This was noticed once, and a guard took the note and read it, telling us he wanted to make sure that we weren't planning to meet someone out in the parking lot with a machine gun to bust us out.

The courts released us both, making us promise that we would come back for our court hearings. It seemed a little strange that they'd trust us to come back, considering they knew our original plan was to flee the state and change our names.

We didn't run, though. After being let out of jail, we moved to Highland, Illinois, which was about 30 miles away. My tax refund money had just arrived, so we used that, along with my last paycheck from 7-Eleven, to get a small apartment there. We both found jobs and diligently attended our court proceedings in Edwardsville every few weeks.

At some point during booking, Sylvia had told the police that we'd planned to use all that money to visit Disneyland. And during one of our hearings, a man in the court room who had to read the charges against us, read them in a monotonous drone, ending the whole thing with the sentence, "with the intentions of using the money to go to Disneyland." Sylvia and I snickered uncontrollably.

By the time summer was over, Sylvia and I had broken up and had moved out of our new apartment to go our separate ways. In the end, I was ordered to pay restitution for all the money we blew on cabs and the hotel, which came out to just under $300.00. I think there may have been a small fine involved too, but I can't remember how much it was.

Neither of us did anymore jail time. We were both sentenced to two years of supervised probation. Sylvia served all of hers, but I only served a few weeks of mine before fleeing the state, moving to Indianapolis and changing my name to Glen Carbon.

Sylvia and I, in a hotel, holding up our piles of money.

Red Boxing

"I'm eager to get the PLA book so I can pirate it on the internet and sell my own digital copies for $5 apiece. Brad and I are like a team!" -taintedbloop

Once upon a time I worked at a movie theater in East Alton, Illinois. It was a lazy job with lots of down time, and me and the other employees there sometimes passed the time away by prank calling the pay phones in the shopping center across the street from us. We would talk to kids walking by, trying to freak them out by telling them what they were doing or what they were wearing.

Sometimes we'd end up staying on the phone with them for hours, just killing time and chatting with them about nothing in particular. A few times the random strangers would figure out who we were and they'd come over to visit with us. We made a few friends that way.

One afternoon in the theater, I saw a lady pull up to one of the phone-from-car pay phones in the parking lot. As soon as she rolled her window down, I dialed the pay phone to make it ring and she picked it up.

"Hello, ma'am," I said to her. "This is the Illinois Bell operator. I need you to deposit the remaining twenty-five cents for the phone call you just made."

"I didn't make a phone call. I just pulled up."

"I know it was you that made the phone call. I was listening in on the conversation and I recognize your voice, so there's no use in denying it. Just put the quarter in the phone or I'm not going to let you use this phone."

I can only assume that I won this argument, because she finally gave in and deposited a quarter into the phone, just to shut me up. That's when I heard the tone for the first time. As I watched her stick a quarter into the phone, I heard a strange chirping noise come out of my phone. I'd never heard it before, but I knew that it must be the sound that a pay phone makes when you deposit a quarter into it. I was only slightly intrigued at the time, not realizing how valuable those tones were.

The tones were referred to as "red box tones" by phone phreaks, and they were used to signal the phone company's equipment that a quarter had been deposited. There were five chirps for a quarter, two chirps for a dime and one for a nickel. By simply using a tape recorder to record those tones as quarters were deposited, a person could later replay them back into a pay phone to get free calls.

It was just a few months later, on a computer bulletin board system, that I found an article explaining to me what I'd heard. I began asking around about red boxing in the message areas on hacker BBSes. Everyone I encountered about it told me that red boxing was really big in the 70's and early 80's, but the phone company had fixed their system nearly a decade ago to make red boxing impossible. Trying to build a red box would be pointless, they told me. I decided not to listen to anyone and I tried it anyway. I'm in a small town and it might still work here, I reasoned.

"This sounds illegal," my manager, Phillip, replied after I asked if he would pick up the phone and record tones for me while I ran over to a pay phone and deposited some quarters.

"It might be," I said. "But I just want to see if it works."

"I'm going to pass on this one, Alex. You can do this on your own time. I have to draw the line somewhere."

This particular manager was normally so easy going when it came to my shenanigans, so I was really disappointed when he wouldn't help me out with this experiment. That night after work, I stopped by a closed gas station that had a pay phone on each side of its parking lot. I deposited a quarter into one phone and dialed the other one, then ran across the parking lot and picked up the ringing phone. I pulled out my portable Panasonic tape recorder and plugged a suction cup microphone into it, then licked the suction cup and stuck it onto the pay phone's receiver.

It was nearing midnight now and I suddenly remembered that the city's police station was right across the street from me and they might find it suspicious that a guy was running back and forth between two pay phones, but it was too late to stop now. I ran back to the first pay phone and began depositing quarters. I couldn't hear the chirping sound from my pay phone, but I knew that the other phone would. After I used up all four dollars of my pocket change, I hung up the phone and ran back to the other phone to turn off the tape recorder. Not surprisingly, the pay phone kept all the quarters I put in.

I played back the tape and the tones sounded exactly as I remembered them from that day at the movie theater. I rewound the tape and got it ready to try and make a call. I dialed a random phone number in South Carolina, which was the only far away area code I knew, and the automated voice asked me to deposit $2.75. I began playing the tones and the voice told me to hold for a live operator, letting me know that it wasn't working.

I turned the volume down on my tape recorder, thinking that maybe the tones were distorted. This time when I began playing my tones, I was able to play almost two dollars before the automated voice interrupted me to tell me to hold for a live operator. I hung up before the operator came on, excited that it seemed like it might be working.

I turned the volume down another notch and tried again, this time making it all the way to $2.75 with my 11 bursts of chirping noises. A second later I was rewarded with the automated voice thanking me for using AT&T. The phone in South Carolina began to ring and someone's answering machine picked up.

I was beyond excited that it actually worked. I hung up the phone and began to laugh and exclaim things like, "Oh my God!" and "Holy shit!" and "I can't believe this!" as I paced around in front of the pay phone. After a while, I began dialing more numbers in South Carolina until I finally reached a sleepy woman. I can't recall what I said to her, but I decided to leave when a police car slowly passed by.

It felt so surreal that something like this was possible. I thought that it must be the pay phone I was using; it must be really old and outdated so that's why it was working. Over the next few weeks, I began trying different pay phones all over town and every one I tried worked. It sometimes took a few tries, but it always worked in the end.

A week later, I made a better recording of my tones by using one of the indoor pay phones at the mall and calling my answering machine at home. When my machine asked me to leave a message at the beep, I deposited as much as I could and then hung up. Waiting for me at home was a cassette tape with perfect sounding red box tones on it.

My new tape, combined with using perfected volume levels and just the right distance away from the pay phone's mouthpiece, allowed me to make flawless calls every time. Since I didn't know many people who lived in other states, I would just dial random numbers and talk to anybody that would talk back to me. I would explain to them how I was calling by tricking the pay phones. Some of them would lecture me about being honest but almost everybody else I talked to thought it was impressive or at least kind of interesting.

So when I left home and arrived in Galveston, I managed to keep myself occupied on the pay phones by red boxing calls to old friends and random people. I had a notebook full of cool numbers to call like phone company news hotlines and test lines. Then there were all the overseas numbers, just calling them to hear their old recordings and trying to talk to foreigners.

I also sold phone calls to people walking by in a few of the larger cities I lived in. I didn't realize it at the time, but I could have easily gotten myself into serious trouble by selling illegal phone calls. I guess I was lucky, though, because nobody ever reported me. If I saw a person about to make a phone call, I would stop them and ask if I could have the quarter if I'd give them a free call. Showing strangers how the tape recorded tones worked was a great way to meet people. I wasn't even charging very much for the calls, I was mainly doing it just because I was bored and liked to impress people with it.

A year later, I was at a friend's house in Illinois and he showed me a recent article from a hacker magazine called 2600. The article explained a very simple method of converting a small device from Radio Shack called a tone dialer into a red box. It cost less than $30 to build, and a week later I had my very first tone dialer red box.

It was only a quarter the size of the tape recorder that I'd been using for the past year, and it had 3 memory buttons along the top, which I was able to program as a quarter, a dime and a nickel. The tones it produced were slightly slower than authentic tones, but it wasn't enough for AT&T's computer to notice. As far as I was concerned, it was flawless, compared to my tape recordings, and it made red boxing long distance calls easier than ever since I no longer had to deal with a volume knob.

From that moment on, I was never without my tone dialer red box. I would make marathon phone calls, both to friends of mine and complete strangers. I would sit at pay phones for hours at a time, pausing our conversations every few minutes to deposit more "money."

Occasionally a live operator would come on the line to ask for the money. Normally they wouldn't give me any problems, but sometimes they'd be able to recognize them as fraudulent tones and they would lecture or threaten me. Considering the endless hours that I spent on certain pay phones, it's hard to believe they

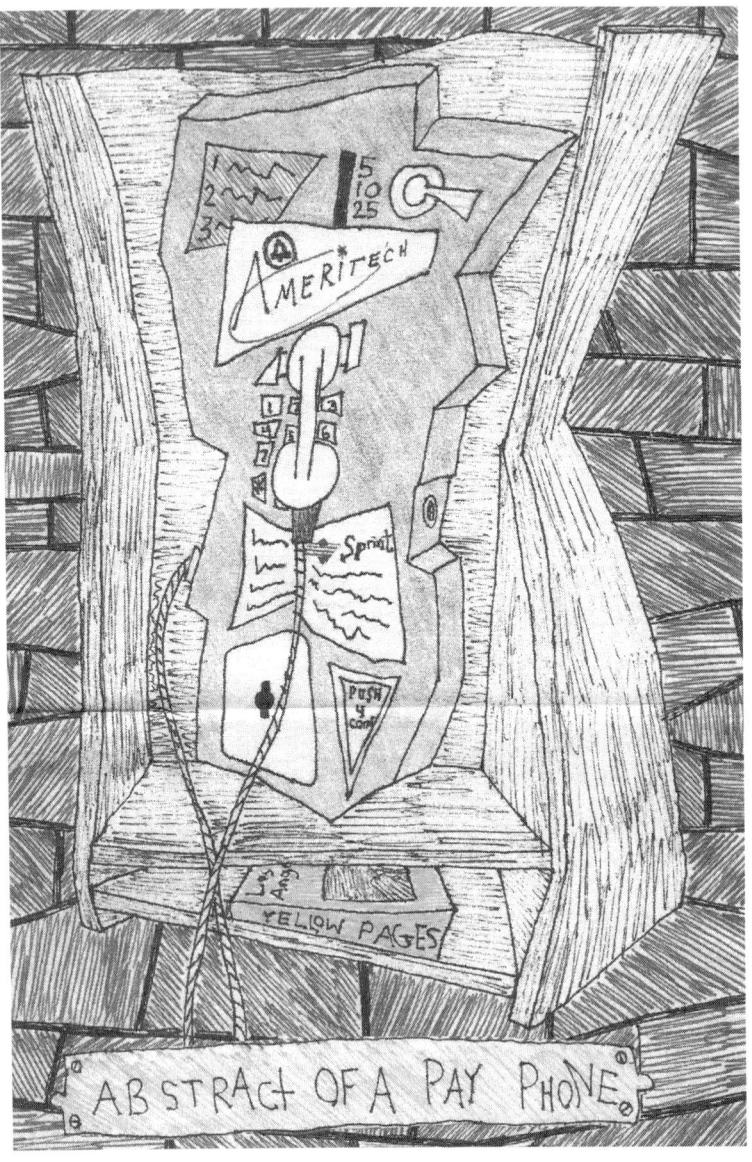

never noticed the money missing from them. Or if they did, they sure never did anything about it.

While red boxing a call outside of a convenience store in Texas, I got quite a scare from a phone company guy who seemed to come out of nowhere. I had just inserted a few dollars of tones for a call I was making. Right as I finished inserting the money and I set my tape recorder down, a man behind me touches me on the shoulder and says, "Excuse me."

I turned around and was horrified to see a Southwestern Bell guy standing there, looking at me. I'm positive my face turned white as my stomach dropped. But then he reached for the pay phone and unlocked the coin box, scooting my tape recorder out of the way in the process. He was just there to empty the phone's coin box. After emptying the money into a bag and locking the phone, he left without saying another word to me.

Another frightening incident happened to me while I was working at a Circle K in League City, Texas when a cop walked in and purchased a coffee from me. We were the only ones in the store, and as he approached the counter and I was ringing up his purchase, he said to me, "We've got a problem with those pay phones outside."

"Oh yeah?" I replied.

"Yeah," he said slowly. "Apparently someone has been using a little grey box to make phone calls out there. This little grey box makes these beeping tones." And he began to do an impression of the tones that a red box makes.

The police officer was eyeing me the whole time he said all this and it was obvious he knew something. I regularly used the pay phones outside of the store to make phone calls, before and after my shift. I had no idea how the officer could know about it or how he could know that I was the one responsible.

His stare was unnerving, and I was at a complete loss for words, but before I could say anything, he smiled at me and said, "Scott told me about your tape recorder."

I replied with, "Oh!"

"It sounds like an interesting little toy. I've never heard of anything like that." He paused and smiled again before walking out the door. "Just don't do it anymore in this town."

"I won't," I stammered.

Scott was the assistant manager and I'd shown him how the tape recorded red box tones worked a few weeks before that. The next time I worked with Scott, he laughed and told me that the cop said I looked like I was about to faint.

That wasn't the only time my various red boxes had encounters with the police. While in Cincinnati, an officer stopped me and a few friends on suspicion of vandalizing a pay phone earlier in the day. (Yes, it was us.) He searched my bag and held up the red box, asking what it was. I explained to him that it was a tone dialer that I used to store phone numbers and he seemed satisfied with that answer. I gave a similar answer to the officer that arrested me for credit card fraud in Corpus Christi. When I was let out of jail there, my red box was returned to me in a ziplock bag along with my wallet, money and keys.

I was often selling my red box to people for a profit, causing me to revert to using a tape recorder until I got around to buying a new tone dialer for myself. I once decided that it would be awhile before I could afford to buy a tone dialer since money was so tight at the time, so I improvised by encasing the innards of a tone dialer inside of an old Walkman tape deck.

Of course, first I needed the innards of a tone dialer, so I purchased a tone dialer from Radio Shack, removed the circuit board and speaker from inside of it, put it back together and then got a refund for it. I was certain that a red box hidden inside of a Walkman tape deck was going to be the coolest thing ever and that it would be sleek and completely inconspicuous, just like something James Bond would carry, but it fell just a little short of all that. Instead it had multicolored buttons sticking out of the top of it for the coin and programming buttons, toggle switches sticking out of the back and punch labels to identify everything. I even used a punch label to write "Ghetto 1200 Plus" along the bottom of the device. It was the most suspicious looking thing I'd ever owned.

As atrocious as it looked, I used it for over and year and it never failed me. It was bigger than a tone dialer, but slightly smaller than my usual tape recorder. When people saw it for the first time, they usually reacted with something along the lines of, "Oh my God! What the fuck is that thing?" Luckily the police never saw it during the year I used it since it looked a lot more scary than a tone dialer.

It didn't take me too long to discover that I could also make international calls with my red box. The process was a bit more complicated and tedious than making a call within the United States, because I had to use a live operator and I could only insert $3.00 at a time. Some of the calls to other countries would end up being close to $15.00 and it would take more than five minutes just to initiate the call. From there, I would have to be interrupted every few minutes to deposit more money.

I enjoyed trying to talk to people with the different accents. I called up a lot of overseas airlines, since they could usually speak at least a little English, and kept them on the phone as long as I possibly could. Then I made calls to random numbers in English speaking countries, just to talk to strangers. The foreigners were usually intrigued enough by an American calling them to stay on the line and talk to me.

I also liked hearing the different error recordings from around the world. I began to compile tapes full of error messages from all the different countries. The operators would sometimes interrupt the error messages when I would try to record them, telling me that the number was disconnected, and I'd have to yell at them to shut up and to put my disconnected number back on the line.

Some operators could tell the difference between real tones and fake tones, mostly because the chirps on a tone dialer were spaced a little further apart. So they would forward my call to their supervisor or threaten to send the police to my phone. I always scoffed at their threats, but I never hung around a phone much longer after they said they were going to send the police, just in case.

Sometimes the operators would offer to send me a refund for the initial $3.00 or $6.00 that I deposited if the number was disconnected. At first, I declined, saying that I was a billionaire and that all these quarters were mere chump change to me. But after a while, I began accepting their offers for free money. Before long, my post office box began filling up with $3.00 and $6.00 checks from AT&T.

After realizing how easy it was to receive refund checks, I stopped caring so much about making international calls and began to concentrate on receiving larger refunds. I made a list of international phone numbers and exactly how much each international call would cost. I kept trying different countries and taking note of the most expensive places to call. Then I would make a call to the AT&T operator, not even bothering with inserting any of the fake money.

"AT&T, how may I help you?" the operator would ask.

"Hi. I was making an international call using my spare pocket change that I stole by breaking open a Pepsi machine on Eighty-Sixth Street and the phone went dead and kept all of my money. Could you redial the call for me?"

"I'm really sorry about that, sir. Our policy won't let me put the call through for you, but I can refund the money to you in the mail."

"Oh, all right," I replied.

"How much money did you lose, sir?"

"Eleven dollars and eighty-five cents."

"How could you lose that much? We only let you deposit $3.00 at a time."

"Well, I dialed the number and the operator came on the line. She told me it was going to be $11.85. So she had me put in $3.00 three different times. Then she had me put in $2.85. She told me thank you and then the phone went dead."

After asking which number I was calling and confirming that the amount for that call was the same amount that I was claiming to lose, the operator would agree to mail a check to me. The key was to know exactly how much money a particular international call would cost. As long as I had that information, they always seemed to believe me.

Once I perfected this routine, I started making about $100 each week from it. For someone who worked a minimum wage job, an extra $100 every week was quite a bit of money. Just as I was considering quitting my regular job to do coin refunds full time, I received a letter from AT&T.

It read, "Dear Alex Carbon. Our records indicate a large number of coin refund requests. In light of this history, we cannot provide a refund until AT&T investigates and verifies this claim. As part of this investigation, please provide us with the written detail of the call and circumstances in which you lost your money."

The letter provided me with an address where I was expected to write to them with the details of my loss. Of course, I never attempted to go that far with it. It looked like my coin refund days were over. That is, until I got the idea to use my fake IDs to start mailing myself checks under different names and addresses.

So that I wouldn't appear to be the same person, I looked up a random person in the phone book and filled out a change of address card using their address and my new fake name. This way, all of the mail being sent to this random address under my fake name would arrive at my post office box. Then I just used my check cashing account at a supermarket to continue to cash my refund checks.

I filled out change of address cards for random addresses all over the country, using different fake names, and I kept the occasional AT&T refund checks coming to me for several more years. I made sure to keep them under $100 per month, hoping that it wouldn't raise their suspicions too much. I still received a few more letters from AT&T, though, sent to some of the other addresses.

My red boxing habit died down a little as I discovered easier ways to make free phone calls with calling cards, credit cards and with call forwarding, but I always kept my red box with me and enjoyed showing it off to people and helping them build their own.

In 2002, AT&T stopped accepting coins for long distance calls. This had nothing to do with red box phone fraud, but was because most people were beginning to use wireless phones and prepaid phone cards. Today it's still possible to red box local and intrastate phone calls. Some people can even manage to make long distance calls with a red box, but apparently it's getting harder every year and it's barely worth the effort just to save 50 cents.

It's amazing to think that for thirty years, AT&T couldn't figure out a way to stop people from using red boxes. And the ability is only just now beginning to diminish because they're completely turning off the equipment used to complete phone calls made with coins, mostly because pay phones aren't used as much as they used to be.

For me, it was a fun decade of free calls, giving me a head start before the rest of the country would begin experiencing super cheap long distance rates around the beginning of the millennium, with flat rate long distance and free nights and weekends. Thanks for making it so easy, AT&T!

Taking Revenge Too Far

"This is great. It gives me wonderful ideas for my neighbors, who have a loud stereo, barking dog, and teenagers. Thanks!" -Nancy from Minnesota

"Hello?"
"Hello, could I speak to Chris McCall please?" I asked.
"This is Chris," said the cautious voice on the phone.
"Hi, Mr. McCall. This is Stephen from Flicks Video in Wood River. You've got a few videos checked out with us that are more than a week overdue now. Any idea when you'll be able to bring those back?"
Chris replied with a short pause, and then a heavy, exasperated breath into the phone.
"Mr. McCall?"
"I haven't rented movies from there in more than a year now," Chris replied.
"Oh. Well, maybe a family member used your card then?"
"I don't think so," he said. "Some people have been messing with my accounts everywhere for the past year. They must have checked out videos under my name."

"Oh really? Well, I remember the guy that checked these movies out. Tall skinny guy, right?"

"Yeah, that's probably him."

"Well, I have a surveillance video of him checking out the videos here."

"You do?" Chris seemed to perk up at this news.

"Yeah," I said. "Maybe you could come down here some time and identify him to us."

"Could I come down right now?" Chris asked, sounding more excited by the moment.

"Sure, that'd be fine. I'll be here until midnight."

"I'm leaving right now. I'll be there in just a few minutes!" he said, and then hung up the phone.

I'd never worked in a video store in my life, though, and I didn't check out any videos under Chris' account either. I was several hundred miles away from Chris at the time, sitting on the floor under a pay phone in the Indianapolis Greyhound bus station. My friend Zak was on the phone and had dialed Chris' house with his 3-way calling.

"I can't believe he actually believed all that," I said to Zak.

"The guy at the video store is going to think Chris is on crack when he comes in there," laughed Zak.

"I got an idea!" I said. "Call the video store!" After a quick call to information, the video store's phone was ringing.

"Thanks for calling Flicks Video. This is Shane."

"You're gonna die, Shane!" I blurted out. "Both of these videos I rented are messed up. This is fucking bullshit, man. I can't believe you rented me this garbage. I'm coming to the video store and I'm going to kick your ass for wasting my time!"

"Okay, first of all you need to stop threatening me," Shane replied, trying his best to be in control of the conversation.

"Do you sell all of your customers faulty video tapes?"

"When did you rent the videos, sir?"

"Earlier today. Don't you remember me? My name is Chris McCall. This is pointless even talking to you about it. I'm going to hang up, drive over there, and *kill* you."

Taking Revenge Too Far - 161

"If you threaten me again I'm going to call the police."

"Go ahead and call the police!" I yelled, making several people in the bus station turn to look at me. "I hope the police are there so I can have you arrested for scamming your customers! I'll be there in a few minutes. When I come in there and tell you that my name is Chris McCall, you better be ready because I'm going to jump over the counter and *pulverize* you!"

Zak disconnected the line and we laughed together over the potential outcome of confrontation that was about to occur. I would have given anything to see what happened, especially if it involved a fight or an arrest. Unfortunately, both Zak and I lived too far away from Chris to be able to witness the mayhem.

At this point we had been harassing Chris for almost a year. It started out as simple revenge, but slowly evolved into our favorite pastime. Both Zak and I had lots of free time to spare, and pulling hilarious revenge-style pranks on Chris eventually became a daily routine for us. Each day I would call Zak and our conversations would usually begin with something along the lines of, "What should we do to Chris today?"

A couple of years earlier, Chris, Zak and I had all been friends. But we later found out that Chris had been stealing things from us. Chris later admitted, to a mutual friend of ours, that he'd stolen cassette tapes from my house and video games from Zak's. During the first few months of harassment, we regularly called Chris and asked him for reimbursement for the stolen items, but he always refused. After a while we stopped asking, but continued with the revenge.

Chris attended a University in Illinois, which is where he experienced most of his grief from us. We called everyone we could think of to try and interfere with his life. Campus security ended up being a regular visitor to Chris' room because of the things we did to him, from calling in anonymous tips about drug use in his room to framing Chris for crimes that students would end up reporting to security. Chris became very well-acquainted with the campus security officers.

"Campus Security, this is Derek" the man on the phone answered.

"Hello, my name is Roy and I'm elderly!" I shouted in my best old man voice.

"Er, okay," Derek replied. "How can I help you?"

"I need you to have Chris McCall arrested immediately! He assaulted me today as I was walking through campus."

"What did Chris do to you?"

"He dropped a cinderblock on my head from his window, just as I was passing beneath the Van Buren building."

"A *cinderblock*?"

"That's right, young man," I responded, pressing the mute button on my phone immediately afterward so he wouldn't hear me giggling.

"How could you possibly know it was Chris? He lives on the fifth floor there."

"Because I looked up after the cinderblock hit me and Chris and his roommate were pointing and laughing at me," I said.

"Listen, you need to stop calling here about Chris. We're getting tired of your calls. If you keep it up we're going to have you arrested."

Eventually security stopped taking our calls seriously and Chris stopped answering his dorm phone at all, so we resorted to calling the rooms of everyone else on his floor. I ended up with a directory of students at his school which included their phone numbers and which rooms they were in. We called just about everyone that was in his building, especially the people who were on the same floor as him, hoping to start some sort of confrontation with them.

"Hey, is this Gary?" we asked one guy who lived just a few doors down from him.

"Yeah, this is Gary," he replied.

"Hey, this is Chris McCall in room 525, and I'm sick of you looking at me like that whenever we pass in the hall. If you don't cut it the fuck out, I'm going to knock your teeth in!"

"Who'd you say this is?"

"Chris McCall. I'm in room 525 and I don't want you looking at me anymore. Got it?"

We pulled this same scenario with about a dozen different students in his building. Some were afraid of the confrontation and others were pissed and wanted to immediately come to his room to either talk it out or fight. We called up girls in his building and confessed that we had crushes on them, insisting that we were destined to be together forever, whether she wanted to be or not. We did the same with guys. We called his teachers and accused them of favoring other students over him or offered to pay them for better grades. We called other students and begged to be invited to parties, saying we'd never been to one before. Things got so bad that Chris' father ended up giving an interview to a local newspaper because of the harassment where he told the paper that we "really ruined Chris' social life."

We called up every business in the area and canceled his membership cards, claiming the card had been stolen. Renting anything from a video store or a library for Chris became a hassle, since he would usually have to reinstate his account each time he went in. Figuring he was probably using his roommate's cards too, we also routinely canceled those. We canceled Chris' credit cards, put holds on his bank account, canceled his calling cards, and even set up new calling cards that we could charge our long distance calls to. Quite a bit of the harassment towards Chris ended up being charged to his own phone bill.

We put ads in the paper about once a month, selling things for Chris. We would set up really good deals on things like apartments and automobiles, then list Chris' dorm number for them in the classified ads, causing his phone to ring all day. It was common for Chris' answering machine to contain a message explaining that the ad in the paper had been a mistake.

Eventually the newspapers stopped allowing us to place ads using Chris' phone number since he never paid for the bills that arrived for these ads. So we started placing the ads for other students at the University, only we would be sure to write in the ad, "Ask for Chris McCall, Room 525." Sometimes we'd call the student who was receiving all the calls and explain things to them.

"Hi, this is Chris McCall. I placed an ad in the classifieds for a boat I'm selling and I put your number in the ad."

"Why would you put my number in there?" the student would ask.

"Because I need my line to be available, in case my mother calls. Anyway, what I need you to do is write down all the messages that people leave so I can call them back. I'll come down each evening to collect the messages. Or you can just bring them up here for me."

"*What?* I'm not taking messages for you! I don't even know you!"

Not one person we did this to was nice enough to write down the messages for Chris. We even tried this with a few of his teacher's numbers and with campus security, but nobody would cooperate.

When Chris went home to his parents for the summer and holiday breaks, we would shift our harassment to Chris' neighbors and the businesses around town that him and his parents used. We started calling up all the neighbors that were within a few blocks of Chris' house, making outlandish claims to them.

"Hi, is this Mrs. Phillips?" we would ask a neighbor of his that lived on the other side of the block.

"Yes it is," Mrs. Phillips replied.

"Hi. I'm Chris McCall and I live at 8714 Bowman Street. This is a little embarrassing to admit, but the other night I was passing through your yard and I thought it would be funny to piss on your doorknob. So I did. I told my mother about it and she insisted that I call you and apologize."

"You *what* on my doorknob?" she asked in disbelief.

"I, uh, peed on it. It seemed funny at the time, knowing that your hand would touch it. I'm surprised you don't see the humor in it. I did it to the house next door to you too. Anyway, I'm sorry for what I've done. And you may want to wash your hands. And your doorknob since its got pee all over it."

"I can't believe this! I should call the police on you!"

These conversations with his neighbors would go on and on like that. We would confess to all sorts of vandalism and other crimes. Even the ones that didn't call the police or visit his house probably looked at him differently after our calls.

We even checked the police logs in the paper a few times for thefts, then called up the people who had been stolen from and confessed that we were the ones responsible. We apologized, but said that we couldn't return the stolen item since we'd already sold it for drugs. We were always happy to give these people Chris' name and address, but would ask them to please just accept our apology and not involve the police.

Chris' parents, tired of the bizarre phones calls they constantly received, tried changing their phone number but we always managed to get the new number by calling the phone company and impersonating Chris' dad. Within a day of the phone number changing, we would have the new one, then we could call up the various classified services that we had ads with and update them with his new phone number so he wouldn't miss any calls for all the things he was selling.

Chris' parents would password protect their phone line, but it wasn't too hard to fool the Ameritech reps into giving us the secret password on the line. Once we had that, we could change the password to something new, meaning that when Chris' dad called the phone company to make another change on his line, he wouldn't be able to since he didn't know the password. We doubted that he was as savvy at tricking Ameritech reps out of his account password as we were. He would be completely locked out.

We ordered all kinds of custom services to his line, such as call blocking and speed dial, which increased the amount of their monthly bill. We canceled his calling cards and ordered new ones that only we had the PIN numbers to. Then we used the calling cards to continue to harass Chris without the long distance charges. We even managed to forward his phone number overseas once, to some random person's line in Germany.

We filled out hundreds of magazine subscriptions for Chris, checking "bill me" on the subscription cards that I took out of magazines at the library. This meant that either Chris had to try and ignore the 2 or 3 magazines arriving at his home each day, or he had to call and cancel each one of them. Not only did we fill out the cards at Chris' address, but we also filled them out with his neighbor's addresses too, but still using variations of Chris McCall's name. So besides having 100 magazines per month arrive at his door, he also had neighbors occasionally dropping by to bring him his misrouted mail. After awhile, the magazines would start sending letters to Chris, demanding payment for his subscriptions. And since magazines love selling their customers' information to other companies, this resulted in more junk mail for Chris and his neighbors.

We filled out dozens of credit card application forms for Chris. Every time I walked through a store and noticed an application on the counter, I would grab one, fill out Chris' information on it, and mail it in. He either got a lot of unwanted credit cards or a lot of letters of denial. Either way, I'm sure applying for that many credit cards didn't do much for his credit rating.

After the summer was over and Chris went back to college, we forwarded all of his parent's mail to his dorm address. After they fixed that problem, we started forwarding all of his dorm mail to his grandparents' house. Then I'd forward all his grandparents' mail to a random person in Alabama. Back then, the post office didn't send confirmation letters to people when their mail was forwarded, so a person wouldn't know that it had been forwarded until they happened to notice that they hadn't gotten any mail in the past couple of days. About once a month I'd fill out a new change-of-address card, forwarding Chris' mail to a new place. Sometimes I would fill out several at once, causing Chris' mail to cross the country several times to random addresses. I'm not sure if Chris and his parents ever tracked down their mail when I did that, since it was forwarded to so many places.

Chris and his college roommate, Ryan, went through several answering machines because of us. Whenever we called and they didn't answer, we would try to guess their answering machine's remote access code. The first machine was easy since it was just a 2-digit code. We had to sit through dozens of messages of people calling about our fake newspaper ads, but if we waited long enough we'd find an occasional gem.

We'd sometimes hear messages from campus security or the police, regarding their investigation of us. And sometimes there would be messages from his friends and family, some who even left their phone numbers. Any personal information people left about themselves would go into my extensive collection of notes on Chris so we could begin harassing those people as well.

When a police officer left a message for Chris about our harassment, we called up the police station to have a word with him.

"This is Officer Bailey."

"Hey, this is Chris McCall. You called me a few days ago about these people harassing me."

"Hi, Chris. How's it going?"

"Great!" I said. "I just wanted to let you know that since you've been too incompetent to capture Alex, I did it myself. I caught him in my building today and I've got him tied up right here."

"You're holding him there?" he asked in disbelief. "Chris, you can't do that."

"Just hurry up and send one of your goons over here to pick him up before I beat him any worse than I already have. You know the address."

And with that I hung up, hoping to keep the conversation short enough so that Officer Bailey wouldn't be able to figure out that I wasn't Chris. Soon after this, a new answering machine ended up on their line. This one had a 4-digit code and it took us weeks to crack it. During one attempt, Chris picked up the phone.

"What do you think you're doing?" he demanded.

"Hacking your machine!" I said happily.

"Alex, listen...if I replace your cassette tapes or give you some money for them, will you quit doing this?"

"NO!" Zak and I both screamed and hung up on him.

(illustration by Sakerobot)

The new machine lasted just a few weeks before they unplugged it from their line once they noticed that we were checking it regularly. For months they didn't have a machine on their line, until one day a new one appeared that didn't allow remote access.

At the same time I was hacking Chris' answering machine, I'd been hacking into voicemail boxes belonging to random people in Indianapolis too. I learned how easy it was to call the owner of a box and trick them out of their voicemail's PIN number by claiming to be an employee of the voicemail company. Once I had the PIN, I could lock them out of their own box and play with the features on their account.

One company had an interesting feature to notify their customers of new voicemails. Once a message was left, the system would automatically call the customer at home and play their messages for them. But just to make sure the correct person answered the phone, the system would require the customer to enter their secret PIN. The system could be configured to call the customer back every five minutes until the correct PIN was entered.

I used this company's system to harass Chris and everyone related to him. I would configure a person's voicemail box to call Chris every five minutes, prompting him for the PIN. Since Chris didn't know the PIN, the system would continue to call him back for days. Twenty-four hours a day, this system would call Chris' dorm, driving him and his roommate mad, and it wouldn't stop until the owner of the voicemail noticed that their account had been hacked and changed their PIN. We also set up other voicemail boxes on the same system to call his parents and other friends of his. None of them had any way of knowing what company was calling them or how to stop it. Whenever a customer locked us out of their account, we had another one ready to take its place.

After just two months of this, the company removed the call-back feature from their system. Our guess is that it was our fault, since we were causing several of their lines to constantly dial out at all hours of the day and night. Also, many of the numbers we were instructing it to call were long distance so the company probably noticed the huge increase in their phone bill, all happening from hacked accounts.

When we found out that Chris had taken a job at his school's library, we began placing ads in the newspaper for items using the library's phone numbers. Most of the ads we placed were for cars for sale and houses for rent, since those generated the most calls, but we also placed a few ads for library items that Chris was selling, such as books for 25 cents each, computers and the card catalog. The library had six different floors, each having their own phone number and each being able to transfer calls to Chris' extension. This greatly extended our ability to place ads, since the newspaper would allow us to place several ads on a phone number before blacklisting the number for nonpayment.

The other librarians, inexperienced with our harassment of Chris, were usually willing to hand us personal information about Chris if we had an appropriate story prepared. We easily got his work schedule from a different employee each week. Then we began harassing students about their overdue books.

"Hello?" the girl answered.

"Hello, is this Ashley?" I asked, looking at the student directory.

"Yes it is."

"Hi, this is Chris McCall at the campus library. You have a few overdue books with us and those need to be returned immediately. Your late fees are up to $78."

"*What?*" she screamed. "I don't even have any books checked out from you guys."

After confirming her information, I said, "Ashley, it's obvious that you're lying to me. Quit being such a deadbeat and take some responsibility for yourself. You need to bring those books back now and you need to pay the seventy-eight dollar fine. If you don't, I will personally see to it that you're kicked out of this school forever."

It never took long for them to start screaming at me or to start making threats. Ashley assured me that her boyfriend was going to kill me for talking to her that way and dozens of other students also made similar threats of bodily harm against me. We were never sure if any of them followed through with the threats, but having a constant stream of angry students coming into the library to yell at him surely kept him on edge.

The library staff began receiving regular complaints about Chris McCall. We confirmed this by calling a few random librarians and pretending to be students that were a victim of Chris' rude collection calls. Most of the librarians told us that they received calls like this about Chris every day and did their best to explain to us that they were prank calls.

The harassment of Chris McCall came to a sudden end when both Zak and I received packages from him containing the missing items that he'd taken from us, along with a letter of apology to each of us. When Zak told me that he'd received his, I called my parents to ask if anything had arrived in the mail for me and they confirmed that I had a package with Chris' return address on it.

It's not that we felt bad for Chris for everything we'd done. It'd just been over a year of steady harassment towards Chris and this seemed like an easy way out of it since we were both starting to get bored with the whole thing. We're not sure if Chris gave us back the original items he took or if he actually went out and bought replacements. At that point I didn't even care about the music that he'd taken from me since I'd moved on to new genres years earlier. And surely Zak didn't care that much about the video games. We only used the stolen items as an excuse to mess with him.

We tried to think of a grand finale of something awful to do before leaving him alone forever. Or perhaps calling up everyone that we'd harassed and driving them nuts by personally apologizing to them nonstop for years straight. But in the end, we simply called up Chris at work and thanked him for the packages, being careful not to apologize for anything we'd done since we felt it would take away from the hilarity if Chris felt that he'd made us feel guilty. Chris would never learn his lesson then.

We never really found out how our actions impacted Chris' university life in the end. Did the other students continue to glare at him for the remaining years or did they maybe see the humor in it after a while and become friends with him because of us? We sure put him in touch with a lot of students during our yearlong campaign, so surely he made a few acquaintances and friends as a result. At least some of them must have thought the personal harassment made him kind of interesting.

Maybe he even met his soulmate because of us. That's how I'm going to pretend this story ended. Chris met a beautiful girl one day when she came into the library to yell at him for being so rude to her about her overdue books. After successfully convincing her that the whole thing was a prank, she saw the humor in it and he asked her on a date.

They immediately hit it off and dated regularly for their remaining years at the university. Upon graduating, her father offered Chris a job at his corporation. Chris and the girl married several years later, having three children and living happily ever after. You're welcome, Chris.

Big Larry

"Thanks for the endless hours of entertainment and enlightenment, PLA." -El Gato

Big Larry was the type of person that I expected Dino to become someday. He was about 6' tall, had white hair that he rarely combed, and a big handlebar mustache. He smelled really bad and constantly made these disgusting hacking and snorting sounds. A few years before our adventure with Larry, he had hurt himself on the job and he claimed to be disabled so that he could receive a disability check each month, which he appeared to spend only on beer and cigarettes.
 Colleen and I met Larry in Albany, Oregon when he moved into our house, which was a large house where many rooms were rented out. We immediately took a disliking to him when he began eating our food from the pantry and fridge. He couldn't afford his own food, of course, because that would cut into his beer and cigarette funds. At the beginning of each month, Larry got his disability check which kept him drunk until about the middle of the month when his money ran out. Then he slept in his room for a few days to sober up.
 The remainder of his month was spent playing with the power tools in the shed and building things in his room. For a

discount on his rent, he remodeled the entire basement of the house and it looked really great. Kind of made me wonder why he was getting a disability check each month when he was obviously a very able carpenter.

I began trying my best to irritate Larry, first by imitating his coughing and hacking sounds whenever he walked by, then by stealing the few items of food he had in the pantry. Since it was nothing I would eat, I would take an item or two each day as I left for work, stuff them in my backpack, and then toss them in the garbage can as I arrived to work.

I also began unplugging his extension cords whenever he used the power saw in the shed, and then I ran back inside. I always hoped that it would throw him off balance when I did this and he'd cut off his arm, but I was never that lucky. Instead he just cursed a lot as he walked across the yard to plug it back in. A few times I even leaned out the upstairs bathroom window with a fishing line and hook so I could wiggle the cord loose while he worked. It was plugged into a loose outlet, so I never knew if he suspected me or if he just thought it was falling out on its own.

Colleen and I would constantly flush toilets or run hot water when we heard him in the shower and I even turned off the water supply valve running to his room a couple of times. I know this wasn't too subtle, but he apparently never complained about me to the owner of the house.

In the middle of this particular summer, Colleen and I moved into a bigger room when another tenant moved out, which put us directly over Larry's room. This had several advantages in my pursuit to annoy the living hell out of him. For one, since he stayed out at the bar all night and slept most of the day, we could be really loud all day by playing music and stomping around and he couldn't really say much since it was the middle of the day.

Another really great thing was that his favorite past time, aside from drinkin' beer, burnin' steak and runnin' power tools, was watching massive amounts of television. Day and night, his TV was on, and right outside our window was the connection for his cable TV. Each time I unscrewed the coax that ran into his room, Colleen and I giggled uncontrollably as Larry cursed up a storm, ranting about his TV mysteriously going out. What I really wanted to do was plug his cable line into a power outlet in an attempt to blow up his TV, but Colleen, always the voice of reason, seemed to think that was too much and talked me out of it.

When Big Larry's TV went out, he listened to the oldies station on the radio. I tried using several FM transmitters to take over his radio broadcasts, but I just didn't have enough power. I could sometimes tune his station out or create some annoying static in his music, but I never managed to fully take over the station so that I could imitate his gross coughing noises into his radio.

The fun *really* started when I realized that Larry's heating vent was directly below ours. I had nailed a board over ours to keep his cigarette smoke from stinking up our room when we first moved in. Larry would sometimes get pissed and yell at us through the floor if our music was too loud, so I found an old 35 watt speaker and dangled it down the heating duct by the wire, approximately a foot above where I estimated his heating vent to be. I attached a 1/4" jack to the end of the wire and nailed the board back over our vent. Whenever I wanted to hear Larry scream really loud at us, I'd plug the jack into our stereo and crank the volume up to 10. The music would blast into his room while we could barely even hear it from upstairs.

Usually I would put in a CD and make it repeat the same song over and over for the entire time I left the house, a few times even during my eight hour shift at work. I assumed that Larry's favorite songs to hear all day were "I Remember Larry" by Weird Al Yankovic and "Living in the Fast Lane" by Urban Dance Squad. Anytime Larry got too loud for us, I'd crank up one of those songs and let them repeat for a few times. When I turned it back off, he'd usually be a little quieter. It saved us the effort of going downstairs and nicely asking him to be quiet.

Of course, this only worked when he was sober, which was about half of the month. When he was drunk and I did this, he'd start pounding on the walls, screaming things like, "You fucking little punk-ass mother fucker! I'll fucking kill you!" I always expected him to go out and start smashing up my car with his tools but he never did. Strangely enough, as much as Larry screamed threats at me through the floor, he never once confronted me in person.

One night he had a party in his room that lasted from about 2 a.m. until 6 a.m., which kept us awake until we quietly got up and moved into a vacant room in a different part of the house. His party consisted mostly of him and two other buddies, drinkin' beer and swappin' fishin' stories and talkin' about what a cock suckin' mother fucker I was. The next morning I awoke at 8:30 a.m. and crept into our room. I stood quietly in the middle of the room for a few minutes until I heard Larry snoring loudly. Cool, I thought, he's passed out. I plugged in Larry's speaker and cranked up some "Rest in Peace" by Extreme.

After falling out of his bed, Larry was banging on the wall and screaming at me, it sounded as if in pain, to shut it the hell off. I screamed back, "*No!*" This didn't go over well with him, so after a little more screaming, he suddenly figured out an ingenious way to shut my stereo off - he opened up the circuit breaker panel that was outside his door and shut off every switch. Not just the main switch or just our room, but every switch. Now us and four other tenants were without electricity. Oh well, I wasn't phased in the least.

I suddenly noticed that the step coming into our room could use a little work, so I whipped out my trusty hammer and began hammering the hell out of it just to make sure it was secure. About three seconds into my hammering, I noticed that Big Lar wasn't taking kindly to this. He began banging on his walls, screaming, and then running back and forth across his room, slamming both of his doors over and over. I suddenly had the urge to sing country songs at the top of my lungs while I hammered. So I did.

I was finally sure that the step was secure, so I looked around for other things in our room that might need a good hammering. It suddenly became quiet downstairs, so I slowly tip-toed down the stairs, carefully looking around corners and hoping to be prepared when Larry jumped out to stab me with a screwdriver. I walked down the steps, onto the landing, and turned all the circuit breakers back on, expecting Larry to pop out of his door and start strangling me. He didn't, so I quickly bolted back into the kitchen. As I passed the window, I saw that Big Lar was out in the driveway, stumbling away and probably headed to Fred Meyer for more alcohol. I considered following him there, then once inside, getting on the store's paging system and singing country songs, but I chickened out.

The phone line in Larry's room just happened to come into our room as well. A few weeks after we moved above Larry's room, I couldn't bear to not hear his conversations anymore, because he kept calling up someone and yelling at them. So I hooked up an in-line recorder onto his line and left the stereo on at a low level while I was in the room so I would hear when he picked up. Usually he would call his girlfriend and yell at her. We never heard any reason for his yelling; he was just mad at her and she seemed willing to put up with the abuse.

Larry had a big yellow car that he kept parked in front of the house, but it didn't run too well and his license had been revoked, so he relied on taxicabs to pick him up and take him to the bar, which was a staggering one mile away. Clearly too far to walk to. But Larry would constantly reach wrong numbers when he tried to call a taxi or his girlfriend because halfway through his slow, drunken dialing I would pick up an extension phone and hit an extra touch tone for him. He would either hang up on whoever he reached, or he would curse at them and *then* hang up.

Sometimes when he reached a cab, I would bridge his phone wires together, making his line go dead. But sometimes I would allow him to speak to the cab company and order his cab, so that I could immediately call the company back from my own phone line when Larry finished his conversation. Using my best drunken Larry voice, I would say, "Yeah, this is Lar. I don't need no fuckin' cab after all. I'm gonna drink my beer right here by myself so stay the fuck away from my house."

A half hour later, Larry would call the cab company once again, wanting to know why they weren't there yet, but not before reaching a half-dozen wrong numbers first, thanks to my interference. The taxi guy, assuming he was dealing with a drunk, would once again arrange to send a cab come and pick him up. Then afterwards I would call them back again and say something like, "You known what? Fuck this shit. I'm tired of dealing with you. I'll just call a different cab company that knows how to get to my goddamn house." Larry would eventually call a different cab company and the whole process would be repeated. Getting a ride to the bar was tough for Larry.

Larry eventually moved out of the house and the fun with him ended forever. Colleen and I, saddened by the loss of Larry, moved out soon after that and we never saw him again. But Larry's spirit still lives on today, in his story and from the sound clips of his recorded phone calls that have been on the internet for more than a decade.

eBay Feedback

"Your good work shall continue. I shall now try to live up to the standards you have set for smartassdom in this land of eBay. I am now buying shit I don't even need just to have the excuse to feedback."
  -Chill Winston

If you're unfamiliar with eBay, it's fairly simple concept to understand: you can buy things from people on the internet and you can sell things to people on the internet. How do you know you're not dealing with a thief? Because eBay uses a very effective user rating and comment system. You're able to rate users that you do business with as "good" or "bad" on their eBay profile so that everyone knows whether or not they're an upstanding eBay citizen. You're also able to leave a short comment next to your rating.

I signed up with eBay at some point in 2000, and I've been using it frequently ever since then. It's a great way to get rid of old stuff that you don't need and an even better way to *buy* lots of old stuff that you don't need. Several years after signing up, a user that I bought something from left me some unusual feedback, so I returned the favor and left that user some unusual feedback of my own. This was the very moment that my eBay feedback issues spiraled completely out of control.

From that point on, I began to leave strange and sarcastic feedback to everyone that I encountered on eBay. Then, after awhile, that just wasn't enough so I started replying to all of the nice feedback people left about me with mean and sarcastic remarks. Every day, from 9 to 5, while I was supposed to be working, I would pass the boring hours away by reading and responding to my feedback. I even began to respond to feedback that was left for me years earlier. All of the feedback I left became a permanent part of my eBay account, and it all still exists today.

Keep in mind, even though I was leaving bizarre feedback, I was still giving them a "good" rating, so I wasn't exactly causing problems for all of these eBay users. Many of them probably never even noticed the feedback. Some of the users that did notice got a laugh out of it and returned the odd feedback to me. Others became confused or angry about it.

The next thing I knew, my weird feedback started becoming quite a hit on the internet. It began, as all great things do, with the Fark website linking to it. Once Fark showed my feedback to the world, countless morning radio DJ's across the country began reading it on the air, in between their yuk-yuking. Links to my feedback were showcased on several humorous auction sites, in blogs and talked about in various eBay seller forums. A book about eBay even dedicated a page to my feedback. I received a constant flow of "fan mail" via eBay during all of this.

My fun abruptly ended in February of 2005 when eBay canceled my account for abuse of their feedback system. They had sent me several warnings over the previous years, asking me to not use certain language or suggestions in the feedback. I always complied and tried to tone it down a bit, but I never actually stopped leaving bizarre feedback for everyone. Even though I complied with eBay's policies the best that I could, I still managed to occasionally break a rule or go just a tad too far with my silliness. After more than a year of friendly warnings from them, they finally canceled my account.

The comments they appeared to have a problem with were the ones referring to homosexuals and the Taliban. My letter of suspension ended with, "Due to the suspension of this account, please be advised you are prohibited from using eBay in any way including registering a new account."

Several days later I managed to convince eBay to reinstate my account by pleading with them and promising never to abuse their feedback system again. Reluctantly, they gave my account back, with all the zany feedback still intact. Since then I've more or less stopped tormenting eBay users with the feedback system and I make it a point to keep my comments as generic and boring as possible. Below is a list of some of the feedback comments that I've left for eBay users throughout the years.

Feedback I've responded to:

Their feedback: lightning speed; well-packaged.
My reply: Do you know how fast lightning travels? Buyer obviously not a scientist.

Their feedback: Very fast shipment. Thanks!!! Item exactly as described.
My reply: I didn't describe all the little scratches and dents but buyer didn't mind.

Their feedback: QuickResponseToWiningBid..Highly reccommended
My reply: Seller should look into an ebay auction for a new space bar and a dictionary.

Their feedback: fast payment, nice transaction A+++++++
My reply: You gave me considerably less +'s than you give other buyers. I'm offended.

Their feedback: Great Ebayer! Prompt Payment! A++++
My reply: You should tell Ebay I'm great so they'll stop threatening to kill my account.

Their feedback: Thanks for a fine transaction. A+++ Hope to see you again soon.
My reply: You've never seen me. We arranged all this by email. Quit being delusional.

Their feedback: Item as promised.
My reply: I did indeed promise buyer that this would be an item. And it was.

Their feedback: All was perfect. Thanks. De primera
My reply: It wasn't so perfect - I tripped over the threshold going into the post office.

Their feedback: excellent product, better than described, fast shipping thanks alot!!
My reply: I don't see how they could be any better. You must be on crack.

Their feedback: Good seller. Item arrived well-packaged and in good time. Thanks!
My reply: Used wadded pages of porn mags to pack things, they always love that.

Their feedback: Quick shipping, good communication, definitely recommended
My reply: Roses are red, violets are blue, 2XL was a robot, I sometimes sniff glue.

Items: Assorted x-10 home automation components
Their feedback: Received the items, and they work, thank you.
My reply: Just don't get it close to magnets or it'll explode like a bomb.

Their feedback: Very quick payment........ HIGHLY recomended ebayer....... thanks so much again
My reply: I bought this video only to hear that hot Beach Boys song on the end.

Their feedback: super fast shipping ! Very satisfied!!
My reply: You're not the first person to tell me that I really know how to satisfy a woman

Their feedback: Simply Awesome! Instant Payment and Great Communications A++ Seller
My reply: We communicated by email. Really, what alternative did we have?

Their feedback: Smooth transaction. Good product.
My reply: Not a GREAT product?? No A++++++?? What a jerk.

Their feedback: shipping fast and simple, check sent in mail a little slow getting to the seller
My reply: It's okay, the Betty Boop checks were so cute that I immediately forgave you.

Their feedback: Exactly as described. Super fast.
My reply: I did not describe the item as being super fast. Buyer is confused.

Their feedback: Thanks very much for shopping with us; you are a great ebayer; come back soon!
My reply: If I'm so great then why does Ebay always send me threatening emails?

Their feedback: Immediate payment. Great communication. Outstanding transaction!
My reply: Seller really knows his adverbs!

Their feedback: Quick shipping, recieved as described
My reply: Dude - I before E except after C! I'm a dropout and even I know that!

Their feedback: Great buyer! Would love to do business with them again!
My reply: "Buyer" is singular and "them" is plural. Seller makes no sense! B+ for effort.

Their feedback: Fast shipper & good deal. Thank you
My reply: My new Ford Focus allowed me to get to the post office quickly.

This following is a negative feedback comment left on my account. It was for my old car stereo, which the buyer claimed was broken, even though it worked just fine for me when I took it out of my car a week earlier. He asked for a refund and I refused. Even though he claims he got his money back from me, he never did.

Their feedback: ITEM RECEIVED BROKEN. Don't worry, got my money back. loser.
My reply: Buyer does crack, lives with his mom, wets the bed.

Their feedback: Prompt payment!!! Nice comunication, a pleasure to deal with. A+
My reply: I'm from Illinois. Your misspellings and exclamation marks do not scare me.

Their feedback: Payment received. An asset to ebay. A PLEASURE!
My reply: *lights a cigarette* It was good for me too baby...

Their feedback: Quick shipment, great commincation
My reply: TOO BAD I DIDN'T SELL YOU A DICTIONARY! HAHAHA! I KILL ME!

Their feedback: GREAT !!!!!! I wish all sellers are like you !!!!!!!!!!!!!!!!!!!!!!!!!!!!! A+++++
My reply: What a racist thing to say!

Their feedback: Great to deal with
My reply: It's been a year now and I'm starting to miss this CD. I want it back, kc.

Their feedback: Received the CD very promptly!!
My reply: Hope you enjoy the 1 good song on this CD.

Their feedback: Thanks a million!
My reply: Buyer is being misleading, only thanked me 2 times.

Their feedback: CD was in great condition Fast shipping
My reply: Great condition because I only listened to it once before learning it sucked.

Their feedback: Great seller! Would buy from again anytime!
My reply: I have listed other items since this transaction, he never bought any of them.

Their feedback: Thanks, just what the doctor ordered.
My reply: I'm glad I could help, I hope the itching goes away.

Their feedback: EXCELLENT TRANSACTION...MY CD ROCKS! and it was cheap :-)
My reply: BUHAHAHAHAHA, buyer thinks that Billy Joel rocks! LMAO!!!!

Their feedback: easy transaction. speedy delivery. a pleasure to do business!
My reply: Thank you, Mr. McFeely.

Their feedback: Thanks, rec'd as promised, Great product
My reply: Item was not really rec'd, I packed it very carefully.

Their feedback: Very fast shipment, my kid is happy IM HAPPY Thank you.A+++++
My reply: Um, sir, that WASN'T a kid's toy. Did you miss the XXX packaging???

Their feedback: Good buyer but he is a Joker.
My reply: I am a Christian, I do NOT joke.

Their feedback: nice product - as described. recommend this ebayer; would deal with again.
My reply: Product was not very nice, buyer obviously can't tell the difference.

Their feedback: WARNING do not do business with this guy! VERY RUDE! Did not reply me for weeks
My reply: Yeah, well you're ugly mister!

Their feedback: Payment recieved very quickly. Great Transaction!!! A+++++
My reply: I paid with counterfeit money. Seller didn't notice.

Those were just the replies to the feedback that other people left for me. The following is the feedback that I initially left for other people. Some of them responded to me, as you'll see in the first one, but most of them didn't. Many of the things I've written here are complete nonsense and have nothing to do with the items I bought.

My feedback: Buyer is insisting that I leave him positive feedback. Won't leave me alone.
Their reply: It took a few weeks for him the leave feedback, I just had asked that he do so.

My feedback: Never paid for item, ignored my emails, supports the taliban, is a big homo.

My feedback: Thanks for being my virtual girlfriend! Hope it makes people think I'm not gay.

My feedback: My friend went to a federal pound-me-in-ass prison for hacking a Gibson once.

My feedback: My friends say that I'm a big homo for listening to Dean Friedman. AA++++!!!!

My feedback: I am leaving nice and unsarcastic feedback, as required by Ebay. A+++!!

My feedback: What a terrible movie. But thanks!

My feedback: OMG GREAT TRANSACTION!
Their reply: Can't really reply in a witty & earthly straight-forward manner...so gee thanks!

Item: My old Sony cell phone
My feedback: If you had any idea how I used the vibrating feature on this phone... Tee Hee!

My feedback: Thanks for buying the only button I have that's not a cheap replica knockoff.

Item: TRS-80 Color Computer
My feedback: A REAL man would be into C64's and Apple IIe's, not TRS-80's. You wimp.

My feedback: This machine didn't really fly around my house or do the dishes. Oh well...

My feedback: Didn't pay me but said I better leave good FB or she would declare jihad on me.
Their reply: I didn't say "jihad," I said 'I'LL DECLARE YEE-HAW" which is totally acceptable!

My feedback: Told me exactly what she was going to do with the item. Disgusting!

My feedback: I haven't finished this book yet, but I'll give you the benefit of the doubt...

My feedback: No words to describe buyer. They should've sent a poet. So beautiful.

Item: 35mm movie theater trailer film for Sgt. Bilko
My feedback: Hope you don't mind the bits of porn I spliced in, Tyler Durden style.

My feedback: You bought a Socket Rocket from me. Doesn't that sound pornographic?

My feedback: I'm leaving you positive feedback so you better leave some for me too or else.

My feedback: This guy didn't pay me yet but what the heck, it's been a crazy day!

My feedback: Seller paid me so fast that I question his sanity. A+++@$(*!#(&@

Item: TRS-80 Color Computer
My feedback: Roses are red, violets are blue, Tandy makes sucky computers, I sell them to you

My feedback: This guy has way too much CoCo computer stuff but he bought mine anyway.

My feedback: 64k of RAM. Because you'll never need more than 64k.

My feedback: I had to attend an extra 2 hours of therapy after selling this item to you.

My feedback: Swiped this cell phone off a dead hooker, hope all the blood came out!

My feedback: Filled up this mp3 player with mp3s of me brushing my teeth. Hope you liked it.

Item: Problem Child on DVD
My feedback: Seller promised me that this DVD had deleted nude scenes with John Ritter in it.

My feedback: I hope you will derive decades of good, clean learning with this 2XL cartridge!

My feedback: So here's the thing with this buyer. This is a really long story but I assure y

(I deliberately cut the sentence off in that one, just to make the buyer wonder what I was trying to say about her. It worked because she emailed me and asked me to finish.)

My feedback: Jimi Jimi 99, he's so fine, I'm gonna make him mine. Oh Jimi Jimni 99! BAM!

My feedback: Great magnetic antenna, using it for a fridge magnet to hold up drawings.

My feedback: Paid quickly and didn't curse at me. Good buyer! B++++++++++++++

⊕ **My feedback:** I bought this satanic PS2 game just so I could burn it with my church group.

⊕ **My feedback:** Using this battery to power my meth-lab. Working great so far!

⊕ **My feedback:** This panoramic map will aid in my hostile takeover of Alton, Illinois.

⊕ **My feedback:** Once left, I cannot edit or retract this feedback. So thank you for paying me.

⊕ **My feedback:** Heath Ledger is my hero, as me buying this rare VHS undoubtedly proves.

⊕ **My feedback:** Fast payment, all the money went to the church. Praise the Lord and thank you!

⊕ **My feedback:** Item is haunted and I'm only selling it so the ghosts will get out of my house!

⊕ **My feedback:** Paid quick! Please don't use this mp3 player to steal from the RIAA!

⊕ **My feedback:** Payment for wang extender received very promptly. Enjoy & good luck!

⊕ **My feedback:** Wireless card received quickly, using it to balance the leg of a wobbly table.

⊕ **My feedback:** Remote works great, I'm using it to control all of my sex and bondage equipment.

⊕ **My feedback:** fast shipment, I will use this new camera lens to set ants on fire!

⊕ **Item:** Dual display VGA card
 My feedback: item arrived quickly and works great! now I can watch 2 porn sites at once!

⊕ **Item:** Weird Al Yankovic's UHF videotape.
 My feedback: Good seller, she gets to drink from the FIRE HOSE!!!!!!!!!!!!!

My feedback: Buyer paid me all $12.50 with pennies but he was quick! Good transaction!

My feedback: I hope the buyer enjoys the one good song on this CD!

My feedback: I will use the money from this transaction to buy lots and lots of drugs.

My feedback: This guy's fast payment saved my marriage.

My feedback: Buyer paid extremely fast, I used the money to buy lots and lots of crack.

My feedback: Payment received within 3 hours via delivery monkey. Monkey wanted a tip though

My feedback: Seller drove 100 miles to my house so I wouldn't have to wait for shipping!

My feedback: Buyer kept pestering me to personally autograph the CD but she sure paid quick!

My feedback: I've used these Chinese learning tapes to fool my friends and family.

My feedback: This tshirt made a perfect dustrag to clean my house with!

My feedback: Seller keeps pestering me to hurry up and leave feedback. Go away seller.
Their reply: Didn't pester, emailed ONCE saying I've left feedback and that he do the same

My feedback: Seller didn't get mad at me when I didn't pay for my winning bid. Nice guy!

My feedback: I ran out of toilet paper and used this shirt to wipe my bottom. Worked great!

➕ **My feedback:** fast payment, netsexed me in exchange for shipping costs, was good netsex.

➕ **My feedback:** Item arrived so fast that my head spun. I am in the hospital now. Thanks Jenny

Besides leaving crazy feedback for everyone, I also began selling collectible postcards on eBay that had been sitting around my house for years. The postcards were unused and didn't have writing on the backs of them, but in the auction I claimed that they did have writing on them. I only showed the picture side of the postcard in the auction so that they couldn't see any writing on the opposite side.

Once a buyer won a postcard auction and paid me, I wouldn't carefully insert their postcard in a protective plastic wrap and mail it to them in a padded envelope. Instead, I would just write their name and address on the back of the postcard, along with a weird message to them, stick a stamp on it and mail it like a regular postcard. Like this one...

And this one...

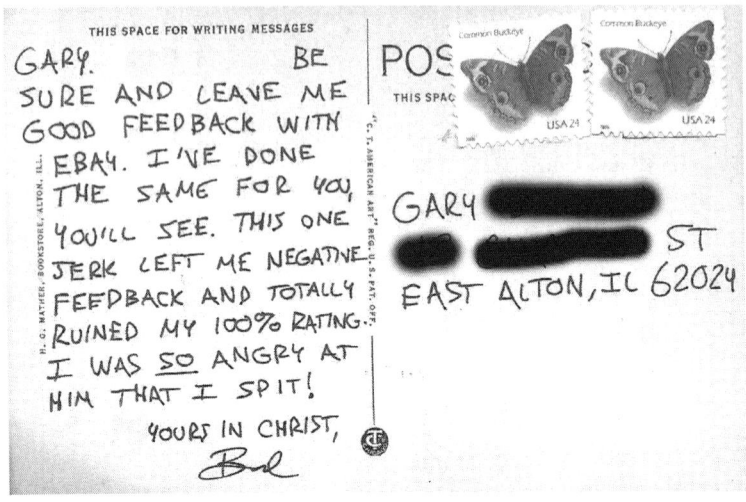

I did this for the sole purpose of enraging the buyers so that they would send me hilariously angry messages that I could display on my website. My intent wasn't to rip them off, and I didn't feel that my auction descriptions were misleading at all. Selling an old postcard with writing on the other side is very common in postcard auctions, and I even told them that the postcards were used, but even still, Gary wrote me the following angry email:

```
hello Alex
I received the post cards and I am VERY unhappy
with them.I cannot believe that you put messages
on them and then mailed them regular postage.
Basicly destroying the cards. I bought them as
vintage collectables and thought you would mail
them in an envelope.I understand that I did not
pay much for them, but that was your starting
price.As for feed back I should leave negative. I
may not leave any.In the future if you sell post
cards PLEASE send them as they are listed.

VERY UPSET - Gary
```

I replied to Gary with this email:

```
I can't believe that you're threatening me with
bad feedback when you got exactly what I
described in the auction. The description said
that the postcards were used, had writing on them
and were postmarked. How the hell did I ruin
anything? I even took a loss on these by
combining your shipping, just to be nice!
```

After exchanging a few more emails with Gary, I did make things right with him and I think he was more or less happy with the transaction, even if I did screw with him for a bit. I sent dozens of postcards to eBay buyers like this and received many angry and confused replies, but I always refunded their money if they insisted they'd been ripped off. Now I just need to start doing the same thing with rare stamps.

Several months after having my eBay account reinstated, I began selling collectable buttons that I made myself. They were replicas, obviously, and I mentioned this in the auctions so that nobody would feel cheated. I sold vintage logos, cartoon characters, band names, holiday themes and anything else that looked like it was making a profit on eBay.

It wasn't until the famous author Hunter S. Thompson committed suicide that I quickly learned that selling buttons of recently deceased people is extremely profitable. Through the months following Hunter's death, I made quite a killing (ahem) by selling lots of Hunter S. Thompson buttons.

I kept experimenting with different pictures and words on the buttons, and eventually scanned some drawings of Hunter S. Thompson from a friend's book and turned those into buttons. The drawings were done by an artist named Ralph Steadman, who has illustrated much of Hunter S. Thompson's writings. Those buttons also did extremely well, but just a week after offering them for sale on eBay, I got an angry, and slightly unintelligible, email from Ralph Steadman himself!

> Do you do not have authority to offer my work for sale.? please remove this item from ebay.....

After checking the eBay account that this message was written from and doing a little internet research on Ralph, I decided that this actually was from the real Ralph Steadman. What an honor, to be chewed out by the famous Ralph Steadman! So I wrote back to him.

> Before Hunter died, he said (and I quote), "Alex, you're welcome to sell that pigfucker's art in the form of buttons any time you want." So you see, Hunter would have wanted it this way. You really don't want to go against a dying man's wishes, do you?
>
> Thoughtfully,
> Alex

My response didn't set well with Ralph. He replied...

> He wasn't dying, you thieving bastard- he shot himself!!

I noticed that he sent a carbon copy of that email to his publisher in America. Since I was in contact with the one and only Ralph Steadman, I decided to try and use this to my advantage to maximize my eBay profits. I wrote back to Ralph, asking for his help.

> Hey Ralph, do you think if I sent you a whole
> bunch of these Ralph Steadman art buttons, could
> you autograph them for me and send them back so I
> can make more money on them? Please let me know!
> Or if not, perhaps you could send me an
> autographed cease & desist letter? I could
> probably get mad bids on that too!
>
> Thanks! And I'm sorry to hear about your friend
> shooting himself.
> Alex

After a whole day of not hearing from back from Ralph, I started to feel bad for stealing his work, trying to exploit him for more money and then making fun of his dead friend. Call me a softie. So before bed that night, I wrote Ralph the following email.

> Ralph, I was just kidding in my previous emails.
> The auction ends tomorrow and after it ends I
> promise not to sell those buttons anymore. I'm
> actually a big fan of your work - I own all of
> your books and even a print of The Alchemist.
>
> Your favorite thieving bastard,
> Alex

The next morning I awoke to find a new email from Ralph. He seemed to be in much better spirits this time.

```
Oh, shit! Alex I've just sent the Hell's Angels
over to your place to have a little word or two
about deep morality issues. Shall I call them off
then??

Bless your heart. You made me laugh just in the
nick of time.....

RALPH
```

So it appears that me and Ralph are the best of friends now, even if he wouldn't help me out by autographing any of my buttons. He even attached a giant picture of his artwork to the email.

If you'd like to learn a little more about Ralph Steadman and view (or even buy) his art, visit www.ralphsteadman.com. If you'd like to purchase a set of the Ralph Steadman Hunter S. Thompson buttons that I was selling on eBay, send me $19.95 plus $2.50 for shipping and handling to P.O. Box... just kidding, Ralph!

McDonald's Sign Prank

"That was very immature. I mean funny, of course. I laughed hard, but seriously, how old are you? I am a manager of McDonald's and that's very stupid. Grow Up!" -Brian, Michigan

One cold, winter morning in 2003 I was sitting at the McDonald's drive-thru window, waiting for my McGriddle, when I noticed a sign ahead of me that didn't make much sense. It was across the parking lot, directly in front of anyone waiting for their food at the drive-thru window. It said, "OUR TEAM IS EMPOWERED TO GUARANTEE YOUR SATISFACTION. THANK YOU FOR CHOOSING McDONALDS." What a strangely-worded sign, I thought.

I noticed how the sign frame was built – it was a couple of 4x4 wooden posts, joined together by two more 4x4 wooden posts. The sign itself was a sheet of aluminum mounted in the middle of the posts. The whole thing looked horribly unprofessional, from the wording of the sign, to the rotting wooden posts, the off-centered McDonald's logo and the extra writing on the bottom of the sign which had, for some reason, been blocked out with white paint.

As I sat there waiting for them to hand me my food, I thought to myself, I could do such a better job of making a sign than they did. Then I began to think, well then why shouldn't I? I certainly have the time to spare and the tools at home to do the job. If their service that morning had been just a little faster, I probably never would have come up with the idea. But by the time I pulled out of their parking lot, McGriddle in hand, I had decided to make them a brand new, yet slightly more offensive, sign.

At lunch that day, I was eating at Subway with my friend Amy. I explained my discovery to her and told her what I wanted to do. Amy thought the idea was hysterical and we tried to come up with new ideas for what we could write on their sign. After lunch, we stopped by the McDonald's so that I could show it to her. I stopped the car and she took a few pictures of the sign while I got out with a tape measure and measured the aluminum part of the sign. It measured 35¼" wide and 22" tall.

"Jesus, Alex, I thought we were just taking pictures! I didn't know you were going to get out and measure the thing!" She looked nervously at the long line of drive-thru customers waiting for their lunch.

My idea was to cut a piece of plywood to that exact size and use drywall screws to attach it on top of the existing sign. The aluminum sign was kind of set back about two inches from the 4x4 posts, so if I cut it to the right size, it would slip right on top of the existing sign and it would look like it belonged there.

The one thing my plan was lacking was a catchy new phrase to put on the sign. So I turned to the users of Cal's internet forums to help. Explaining my idea and posting a picture of the sign, I asked them to come up with some suggestions. Below are a few of their ideas.

> "I would keep it very similar to what's up there. Maybe something like 'Our Team is Empowered with the Dark Side of the force. Thank you for choosing McVader's.' If nothing else, all the Star Wars freaks and fan sites would be hosting it and talking about it."
> **–judasiscariot**

> "Well, an obvious edit would be to include the word sex so it's 'Our team is empowered to guarantee your sexual satisfaction' but that's not very original."
> **–jedibebop**

> "Happy Meals now with 50% less happiness due to bad economy." **-Murdoc**

> "I think what would be funny is 'Our team is empowered to guarantee your gratifaction. Thank you for choosing McDonalds' It's just changed enough that it would stay up for a long time and people would be wondering....gratifaction? Is that even a word?"
> **-Moose-Alini**

> "Least polluted fast food place, 1999-2001 2001-2002"
> **-Big-E**

"Our team would like to thank our lawyer for winning our food poisoning court battle" **–jedibebop**

"Our team wants to let you know, Don't eat the chicken nuggets!" **–judasiscariot**

"How about 'Our team is guaranteed to enhance your stratification.' And then put 'Please ask for an application.' Even without that last sentence, it would still be kinda funny. Especially with the whole 'McJob' dictionary definition making the news." **-sarah601**

"DID YOU REALLY NEED ANOTHER CHEESEBURGER, FATTY?" **-tacojon**

"You didn't really think that was hamburger did you?" **-LethalDosage**

"IF YOU DON'T TURN LEFT RIGHT NOW, YOU WILL RUN OVER THIS SIGN. -THE MANAGEMENT" **-rbcp**

"We now use real chicken in our McNuggets!" **-mr_doc**

"We are not responsible for your obesity. Please eat responsibly" **-mr_doc**

"Fresh food made from people just like you!" **-Somebody**

"We've gone 4 months without a class action lawsuit!" **-mr_doc**

"All your money are belong to us" **-hellview**

"Gerbil deliveries: please use rear door" **-mr_doc**

"Breakfast now served until 12:00 pm" **-mr_doc**

"Put a heading across the top that says 'MCDONALD'S EMPLOYEE MEMORIAL WALL'. Underneath that, attach a photo of a person in a McDonald's uniform. Label it with a name, his birth and death dates (i.e. 1979-2003), and the caption 'LOST IN TRAGIC FRYER

ACCIDENT.' Beneath that, add the words 'CHECK YOUR SANDWICH FOR OUR FALLEN COMRADES' in bold red letters." **-tacojon**

"How about 'Our team is endowed to guarantee your satisfaction'. Subtle sexual double-meanings make me giggle." **-Mithrandir_too**

"You have water, come to my house. Thank you for choosing McDonalds" **-Liife**

"Due to constant complaints, we are now asking all patrons to please check your cheeseburgers for rat feces. We apologize for the inconvenience."
–Mrpeanut

"Our team is imploding, please get help! Thank you for saving lives." **–Mrpeanut**

"You could put something up there that says 'Warning!' and put everything below it in Polish, Czech, or even Gaelic."
–hellview

"You could do a good deed and tell people to be careful not to spill coffee on their pee pee." **–Nelsonmandela**

"CAUTION: SIGN" **–RTFirefly**

"Our staff is empowered to gun you down in the event of shoplifting a happy meal" **–PuRewiReZ**

"If we team up with Walmart we will own all of you!" **-14D**

"Thanks for Choosing McDonald's -- We Lubricate Your Arteries! Brought to you by Dr. Wilhem Maosos, Cardiologist, St. Emmanuel Hospital" **–Spessa**

"We apologize, but cows and chickens have become extinct due to our harvesting techniques." **–tk**

I didn't want to use any of the ideas that defamed the quality of McDonald's food or falsely advertised their products. My intent was mostly to amuse people, not piss them off. I wanted something offensive, yet amusing to most people. I finally decided to pick Mithrandir_too's suggestion of "Our team is endowed to guarantee your satisfaction" but I changed his wording slightly to read, "Our team is well-endowed to guarantee your pleasure!" Even if this was false advertising, I didn't think the employees were going to say, "Hey, that's not true! Our wieners aren't that big!"

The next day I began construction of the sign. I started out by Googling for the McDonald's logo and placing it in Microsoft Word along with our new slogan and printed it all out on transparency paper.

I had plenty of plywood in my basement to work with so I used a sheet of quarter-inch plywood and cut it to the correct dimensions. Then I painted it white with a can of ceiling paint.

McDonald's Sign Prank - 203

Later that evening, after the paint had dried, I nailed the plywood on the wall and shined the transparent sheets at it with my overhead projector. Then I used a pencil to trace the logo and wording onto the plywood.

Then it was time to paint! I had the colors I needed already, except for red, so I went out and bought a quart of red paint and a package of Crayola watercolor brushes. My paints ended up being a combination of water-based and oil-based paints. I wasn't sure if any of it was meant for outdoor use but I didn't expect the sign to last too long so I figured that wouldn't be a problem. My friend Spessa suggested coating the entire thing with polyurethane to help protect it against the weather, but I decided against that, fearing it might smear all of my hard work.

Once it was all finished, I stepped back to admire my work and was very impressed with the results My sign was completely flawless, with a perfect McDonald's logo on top. I wrote the "well-endowed" line in red paint and then on the bottom I wrote, "Thank you for choosing McDonald's" in black paint. Everything was perfectly centered and looked awesome! I snapped a few pictures of it to show off to the forum users, before retiring for the night.

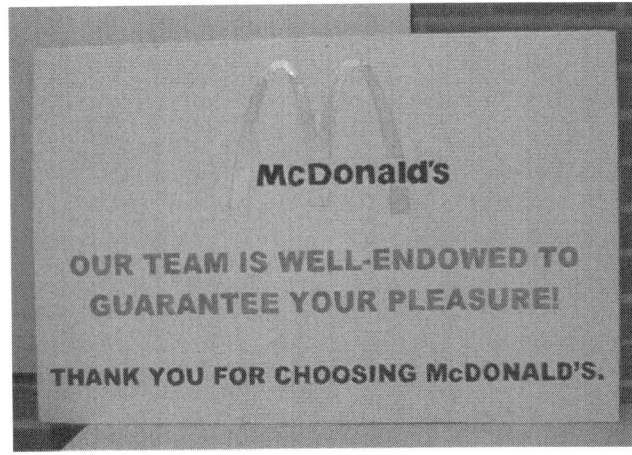

Just a couple of days later, I drove to McDonald's by myself to install the sign. It was on a Saturday at around 1:00 p.m. and the snow was coming down quite hard. I felt that the snow was perfect and would provide extra cover for me as I installed the sign. The drive-thru was packed with the lunch crowd so I felt safe, knowing that the employees inside would be too swamped to notice me, even if they could see through the giant flakes of snow.

I grabbed the sign, my cordless power drill and a bunch of screws. I pulled up to the sign, making sure my car was partially blocking the view from the drive-thru customers and the drive-thru window so they would have a harder time noticing what I was up to if they happened to look my way. I calmly exited my car, took the sign out of the passenger side and attempted to fit it into the sign's opening. This is when I discovered that my carefully measured sign was too big to fit! The height of my sign ended up being not even 1/8" too much. I tried to squeeze it into the opening but it wouldn't budge. I suppose my measuring and arithmetic skills could stand a little improvement. Disappointed, I put everything back into my car and drove home.

Using a circular saw, I chopped 1/8th of an inch off the bottom of the sign. Thankfully, it wasn't enough to mess up my perfectly centered letters. Several days later I went out to try again. This time it was about 9:00 p.m., McDonalds was completely dead and two employees sat at the window and stared at me as I drove through the parking lot. I decided that it would be a bad night to install the sign. I threw the sign in my trunk and it remained there for a couple of weeks.

I needed to have a friend drive me there during a busy lunch period so they could pull up and I could just lean out the window and quickly install it while they kept a lookout. My lucky break came when my friend Tami and her boyfriend showed up at my house one day and it just happened to be noon. I told them about the sign and asked if they could give me a ride to McDonald's, and they were happy to help out.

I wasn't able to lean out of the window like I'd hoped so I just had Tami stop the car and I got out to install it. My sign fit into the opening perfectly, although not quite as tightly as I'd hoped. I drove a single drywall screw through the middle of the sign to hold it in place and hoped that gravity would take care of the rest. I should have used more screws but I didn't want to ruin my white paint job with black drywall screws. The whole event took maybe twenty seconds. We exited quickly, but came back a few minutes later so that we could snap a picture of the new sign.

An interesting coincidence was that there were several huge trucks parked right next to the sign and they were for some kind of sign company! We assumed that they were just inside having some lunch. But when we came back ten minutes later to take a picture, they were actually doing some work on the big McDonalds sign by the highway. It's a good thing they weren't working on the big sign when we came there the first time or I'm sure I would have chickened out.

The sign lasted for just three days. On December 13th, I went there for breakfast and was disappointed to see that it was gone. The strange part was that nobody at McDonalds seemed to know anything about it. I called their store later that day, pretending to be a regional manager responding to a complaint about the sign and they had no idea what I was referring to. In fact, the person I talked to didn't even know they had a sign in the parking lot.

So what happened to it then? Did a customer decide to steal it because they thought it was funny? Did an employee steal it and not tell anyone? Should I have called the police about the theft? Maybe the manager from the day before took it down and just didn't get around to telling anyone about it. Maybe the actual owner of that McDonalds took it and just hadn't told the store about it yet. We may never know. I'm sure it didn't just fall down on its own, but I definitely should have secured it up there a little better to keep people from walking off with it.

I never intended to make another sign and give it another try, but I was just so disappointed that my previous sign disappeared that quickly. I seriously thought that my "well-endowed" sign would go unnoticed for at least the entire winter. So one evening, I made a two new signs. The first sign warned drivers to turn left or they would run into the sign. The second sign used tacojon's idea of, "Did you really need another cheeseburger, fatty??" but I also added an idea that EvilCal gave me on the phone earlier that day - "Try our new atkins-approved menu!"

Why two signs this time? That was the ingenious part! The "Turn left" sign was made with plywood, just like the original sign. But the "Fatty" sign was done on a sheet of poster board. Then I used thumbtacks to tack the posterboard "fatty" sign onto the top of the wooden "Turn left" sign. My hope was that the employee or manager would see the sign tacked there and think, "Oh, I'll just take these tacks off and throw this sign away!" and they wouldn't even notice the *other* fake sign underneath.

Would my "sign on a sign" trick work? I seriously doubted it, but never underestimate a McDonald's employee! To help divert attention away from the fake sign underneath I wrote a sloppy note on the back of the poster board sign with a blue Sharpie, reading, "Hey! Don't be mad about this sign. It was just a joke." I purposely wrote this message sloppy and in smaller letters near the end. I even messed up the word "joke" and wrote over it and I wrote on top of the part where the lettering from the other side bled through the poster board. My hope was that the McDonald's employee would be so occupied with trying to read my message on the back that they wouldn't have time to notice the "Please Turn Left." sign that they'd uncovered.

After leaving the signs sitting in my kitchen for months, we finally got around to putting them up. This time I decided that I needed someone with a van to drive me there, to help better cover my activities. So I asked Tom, my only neighbor with a minivan, to drive me, EvilCal and his girlfriend.

We arrived in the minivan at 9:00 p.m. As we pulled up to the sign, I threw open the sliding side door and jumped out with a sign in one hand and a power drill in the other. Blaring from the van's stereo was the theme to The A-Team. Well, okay, not really. Anyway, I drilled the new signs into place in just a few seconds, jumped back into the van and we sped off, right past the employee sweeping the parking lot. It's okay, he didn't see us. This time I used some brackets, screwed into the wooden frame of the sign, to secure my new sign into place. Unfortunately these were quite visible, but at least the sign was more securely in place than the last one and nobody could just walk off with it.

We swung around the parking lot one more time to snap a picture of the sign, and then went home. Early the next morning, I went back for some breakfast and to make sure the sign was still there. It was, so I snapped another picture and then went home.

Throughout the morning, I received hourly reports from various people that the sign was still up. A friend on his way to work stopped by and checked on it and reported to me. EvilCal and his girlfriend stopped by there for breakfast and reported that both signs were still intact. I got reports up until 11:00 a.m. And that's when it disappeared. Not just the posterboard part of it, but the sign underneath too. My evil plan to trick McDonald's had failed! But it was okay, because the sign lasted about fourteen hours and the entire breakfast crowd got to see it. I knew a sign that called the customers fat wouldn't last long and I was surprised it stayed there all morning. It's too bad nobody got to see the sign underneath, though.

Sometime during the evening, things turned a little bizarre. Tom, returning from work, stopped by to check on the sign for me. He called me up to tell me the sign was gone and I told him I already knew. He said, "No, the *whole sign* is gone! It's just two posts sticking out of the ground now!" So I raced to McDonald's to get a picture of it, passing Tom on the way there. Sure enough, the top board and the sign itself were completely missing.

I thought they either took the sign down because it was just more trouble than it was worth for them, or they'd shipped the sign off to the crime lab to dust it for fingerprints so they could put me away for life. The half-sign stayed there for two days, then the entire thing was gone. It was looking kind of ratty anyway, and the posts were starting to warp because of the weather, so I guess they decided to just get rid of it. I hoped that after seeing my perfect, professional-looking sign, they realized how much theirs sucked so they took it down in a fit of depression. I walked over to where it once stood, looked down and noticed that they just sawed off the posts at the ground.

So the new plan was this: I felt bad that they had to take down their sign just because of my prank, so I would build a completely new sign for them, constructed out of 4x4 posts and a sheet of plywood. The front would read, "QUIT TAKING DOWN MY FUNNY SIGNS, YOU DAMN EMPLOYEES!" Okay, I'm kidding. That was the end of it. It was fun while it lasted, but it was just time to leave that poor place alone.

To officially close the prank and to satisfy my own curiosity about their thoughts on the event, I made a phone call to them several days after the sign posts were gone. I identified myself as Roy from their corporate office and told them I'd received a few letters of complaint about an offensive sign on their property.

The manager I spoke to told me that they'd taken the sign posts down to prevent anyone from putting more signs up there. She commented on how perfectly the lettering was stenciled on the sign, making my ego very happy, and she told me that they threw my sign away. Near the end of the phone call, I came clean with her, admitting that I was actually the prankster that put up the sign.

"I'm just kidding, I'm not actually in the corporate office in Kansas City," I said to her. "I'm the guy that made the sign. I just wanted to see what you would say about it."

"Oh... Okay," she said, taken a little off guard. "Well, why did you put the signs out there?"

"I thought it was funny," I replied.

"Why did you think it was funny?"

"*You* thought it was funny, come on!"

"No we didn't think it was funny," she said and hung up the phone.

I resisted the urge, several days later, to call back and say that I was with the corporate office, investigating some prank calls that were made to their store where a man claimed to be from the corporate office.

There's no doubt that the positive impact of this event shall be felt for years to come. When trainees ask, "Why are there wooden stumps in the ground here?" the manager will reply, "Oh those. Well, it's a long story. Why don't I tell you over a Big Mac..."

Boulder News Frenzy

"I love how you people have turned the craziest media hype of a child's death into a PLA discussion. It just goes to show that even an exploited child's demise is not safe from the jurisdiction of the PLA. If Jon-Benet were around right now, she'd have her application in to join." -Spessa

Soon after the murder of child beauty queen JonBenet Ramsey, a newspaper web site in Boulder, Colorado decided to open up discussion forums on the internet to talk about the case. Suddenly, dozens of bored housewives decided that they were hardcore detectives and spent their entire days picking apart the JonBenet case, looking for clues and hoping to solve the murder since they all deemed the Boulder police too incompetent to do it themselves.

This was in 1997, when the internet was still new and exciting, and discussion forum software wasn't yet very advanced. This particular forum software didn't even allow people to log into an account, trusting everyone to be honest about who they were when posting messages. We could easily post messages using the names of the regular members there and nobody could tell the difference. And so we did.

It all started when Logic Box and Tannest, regulars in the PLA chat rooms and forums, found the Boulder News Forum and started impersonating other users there and saying crazy things as them, just to watch everyone else's reactions. Reactions included, but were not limited to, regular users getting upset enough to leave the forums forever.

When they brought me into it, it had already been going on for several months. I started bringing up the PLA name as often as I could and we all began posting new theories about the murder that involved toll fraud devices called red boxes, saying that stacks of them had been found in the walls of the Ramsey home. We also dropped names, locations and events related to the PLA 'zine. Some people took our claims seriously and our different theories were occasionally mentioned by the regulars when discussing the case. Soon there were about a dozen of us watching the forums regularly and constantly posting to it.

After another month or two, Logic Box wrote a short article about the Boulder News Forums for the then-thriving PLA e-zine, suggesting that it had been fun, but we were pretty much done pestering them. I don't think he realized at the time that we would continue torturing various JonBenet forums for another two years. It was far from over.

Once Logic Box's article appeared in the PLA e-zine, suddenly a lot of people knew about the Boulder News Forum and decided to join in the fun. I started receiving emails from PLA readers, telling me about things they'd done on the forums, which encouraged all of us to return and continue trolling them.

Between us and the rest of the PLA readers, some really bizarre theories about the JonBenet case began showing up on the forums, from members of the PLA being involved to the whole thing actually being a suicide. Legitimate information about the case was being released at the same time, so our fake information confused many of the regulars and casual visitors of the newspaper's web site. Then there were the regular members who became increasingly angry since they knew we were just screwing with them. They felt as if we were interfering with a police investigation because of the nonsense we posted.

We also attacked theories about the case that seemed legitimate, coming up with insane reasons about why the information couldn't possibly be true. Soon I was spending nearly all of my free time on the Boulder News Forum and it seemed like Spessa, Tannest and Logic Box were too. I wanted to keep the regulars talking about the PLA as much as possible, so I brought up our own names and details about the PLA as often as I could. The regulars began to hate "the PLA" and some came to the conclusion that we must work for JonBenet's parents and that they had hired us to take attention away from them since everyone seemed to suspect they were involved in the murder.

```
Posted by: Faith

The good news is that an arrest is near. Then
Ramsey won't be able to afford to pay the PLA
anymore and they will have to get real jobs. The
PLA will be known forever as losers who worked
for scum. They might as well have helped twist
the rope around JonBenet's neck.
```

These pseudo-investigators seemed to think that the Boulder News Forum actually mattered to the police's investigation and that our campaign of misinformation was going to confuse the police and cause the killer to remain free. The administrators of the Boulder News site knew that we were tormenting the users on their forums, but seemed to have very little time or resources to deal with us. Occasionally they would try something to stop our posts, such as imposing a limit of only one new post per user each hour or displaying our IP addresses.

```
Posted by: BoulderNews

Due to rampant abuse of the software, some
changes have been made to the forum. These
changes will not affect most people (legitimate
users).

To those who feel they need to ruin this space
and harass others, we simply ask you to please
respect this space as one of public discourse and
conversation.

All previous threads that were listed have been
archived or deleted. This is not to censor, but
to "start-over," so to speak, as certain
individuals had flooded the boards with posts.

Thank you.
BoulderNews Administrative Staff
```

When they started displaying everyone's IP address, we were thrilled because the once-anonymous forums were now able to tell us approximately where each of the regular users lived. We used this information to begin building profiles of all the users and some of the PLA began WinNuking the IP addresses of the regulars, causing their computers to crash. Having our IP addresses displayed didn't matter to us, since half of us didn't care and the other half could just go to the site via proxies to hide our locations. Displaying IP addresses only hurt the regular users of the forums, and the administrators removed this feature less than a month after implementing it.

Imposing the one post per hour limit for each user did have a slight effect on our efforts for a while. All of our posts about the PLA had been coming in so fast that they were quickly scrolling away any legitimate discussions about the case. Finding a normal thread that wasn't laced with our silliness was next to impossible for the regulars, so when they limited how many posts we could create, that solved part of their problems, but only for a few days.

At the time, I'd only been creating web pages for about a year and I had just a basic grasp of how the posting forms on web sites worked. One day, while making the 20 minute drive to work, I was trying to think of a way to overcome the posting limit and I came up with the perfect solution which seemed revolutionary at the time. It was the simple act of copying the Boulder News Forum's posting form and changing the fields so that the actual forms became hidden, showing only the "submit" button. The posting forms would be filled with whatever content I chose. Then I'd just have to figure out a way to get a lot of different people to push this button on my website.

Then this revolutionary idea turned into complete brilliance. I would create a page that claimed to have secret information on all of the PLA members that were disrupting the forums. To access each section, you would have to push a button. Only the buttons they pushed would actually be the secret form buttons to create new posts. Each new post would contain the URL to the page with the buttons. This would cause the regulars to spam their own forums! I laughed hysterically at the thought of this as I pulled into work. I couldn't believe my luck when nobody showed up for work that day, meaning that I couldn't get inside and had to turn around and go home. I drove as fast as I could, eager to tell Spessa about my idea and get started on the new forms.

My fake forms worked much better than I expected. I set up the page on a free hosting site called Tripod and turned the buttons into graphics of chili peppers. There were three chili peppers on the page, each one promising different kinds of personal information on the PLA, but each one actually posting a new garbage thread to the Boulder News Forum. I only had to click one of the buttons once, which posted a single thread about the PLA, giving out the URL to get their information from. This caused an endless loop of people visiting that page and clicking on all of the buttons, each time unwittingly creating another post. The Boulder News Forum filled up with these posts almost immediately, completely scrolling away all the real conversations.

```
Posted by:    elf watch

Don't go on the Jameson URL. PLA made it. It is
clever. It makes new threads when you click on
the red peppers. They don't seem active but they
are. The "PLA is on your mind" and spessa threads
are created by this.
```

By the next day, the regulars knew not to click the buttons anymore, so the spamming slowed down considerably. Then another day passed and one of the regulars made a complaint to Tripod and had my page taken down. So I set up a new page on Tripod and didn't tell them where it was located. This page promised free pornography by clicking on the images. Then I sat in a few IRC chat rooms for porn image trading and wrote a script that would automatically message everyone entering the room with the porn URL.

The fake porn site created threads even faster than before. During the evenings, at least one new thread was being created each minute, effectively destroying any chance of normal conversation. The porn site was divided up into six sections, each one posting a different kind of thread. As long as I left my script running in the chat rooms, the nonstop posts continued. I left it running for days and the regulars couldn't understand why it wouldn't stop. They desperately tried to keep their own threads on top of the mess, but nothing they did would last very long because of the nonstop threads burying real conversations. Finally, Tannest asked me to remove the page so we could continue screwing with their conversations, so I did.

We wanted to get right back into the business of making up new murder theories and adding disinformation about the

JonBenet case, but suddenly the regulars didn't seem to care about the case anymore. All they wanted to talk about was the PLA and how they could stop us.

They obsessed over the destruction of the PLA and all associated with it. They seemed even more passionate about this subject than they were about the JonBenet murder. They began posting our personal information and discussing ways that they could bring down the PLA forever. One of them posted my home address and another promised to get some friends together to come to my house and rip my limbs off. They called Tannest's work and Logic Box's school, hoping to get them both in trouble with their superiors. They even claimed to call the mayor, the sheriff and the newspaper in the city I lived in to tell them all about me. All of this attention just caused us to laugh hysterically and try even harder to create problems for them.

Just like we did with the JonBenet case, we "helped" them out in their quest to bring us all down, posting fake information about ourselves and claiming to make phone calls to people associated with us so that we'd stop terrorizing the forums.

While they did eventually go back to talking about the JonBenet case, they still continued to talk about the PLA all the time, even without our help. One user, who called himself 31373, became even more hated than the PLA because of the amount of threads he created to post our personal information and to tell everyone how badly we would all go down.

```
Posted by: Concerned Reader
Subject: STOP 31373 NOW!!!!

I know his/her heart is in the right place, but
it's making things worse. Please do not provoke
the PLA further. I know what they can do!
```

```
Posted by: 31373
Subject: Apologies

I really apologize for all of the garbage posts
to and from the PLA. I've just had about enough
harassment from them and it *will* stop. I was
hacking vax boxes before they were born, and they
need to be taught a lesson. WE CAN FIGHT BACK!!!

I also know what they can do. And I know WHAT WE
CAN DO! Don't take it! Email every admin at every
ISP they are on. Complain, and have them kicked
off. Their ISP's get sick of hearing all of the
complaints from these jerks on dalnet.

I will stop when I see a post from Eric, RBCP,
Logic Box, Tannest, or Colleen, or all of the
above, apologizing for disrupting the BNF, and
promising not to ever come here again.

They can stop it if they want. The ball is in
their court. If they come back with more
harassment, we bring out the big guns.
They have NO idea who they screwed with this
time. And they will regret it, as GOD is my
witness. I'll back off and see what their
response is now. It's their move.
```

The regulars began attacking PLA's website by posting garbage to the site's guestbook and the PLA forums. I had to clean it up several times a day, which was a tedious process back then, but they kept at it until I figured out a hilarious way to fight back. I modified the posting forms on my own forums to contain code for the Boulder News Forum so whenever they attempted to post garbage to my forums, it would go to their forums instead.

Of course, this meant that none of my users could post on my own site either, but the irony was just too great to care about that. And just so visitors of my own site wouldn't have to go without forums, I encouraged them to instead go to the Boulder News Forums. This caused a steady stream of posts from users on my website, asking general questions about telephones, hacking and the PLA.

The regulars quickly realized what was happening and they stopped trying to spam my forums. Whenever they started back up again, I would replace the code to make them spam themselves. This caused extreme paranoia from the regulars that the simple act of visiting any web page associated with the PLA would create phantom posts on their own forums.

```
Posted by: Anonymous
Subject: Had Enough


This forum has turned into a virtual cesspool.
There is no demarcation now between the good guys
and the bad guys. Deep Shadow, I have always
admired your posts and enjoyed your take on
things concerning this case. But your last post
has proven to me that this situation has finally
eroded to the point even the good posters have
turned vile and dangerous. It sounds like it's
time for you to leave the forum. Your intents
here are not the JonBenet case, you have become a
bounty hunter and it's not pretty. None the less,
I will not return to these threads, it makes me
ill.
```

A woman named Jameson, who was one of the regulars, was really into the JonBenet case and, of course, hated the PLA. When Spessa managed to find Jameson's home phone number, she thought it'd be a riot to call her up at 4:00 a.m. and pretend that JonBenet's mother had just been arrested for the murder.

After about a dozen rings, Jameson finally answered, and the conversation went something like this:

Jameson: Hello?

Spessa: Go turn on the news *now!* Theres been an arrest.

Jameson: Oh my God.

Spessa: Patsy's been arrested.

Jameson: Who is it? Patsy has?

Spessa: Yes, turn it on. Goodness, can you believe that?

Jameson: I'm on channel 19 and it's not on. Give me another one.

Spessa: CNN?

Jameson: That's 19. It's not on.

Spessa: It was about four minutes ago...You got it yet?

Jameson: Nope, there's another man talking.

Spessa: Oh geez. Well, it *will* be on. It was on about 5 minutes ago.

Jameson: What did they say?

Spessa: Um, they're not releasing any of the information at the moment, but theres been an arrest, and that got me intrigued, so I watched for a few more minutes and then they said that the arrest was Patsy. I just cannot believe this. I was convinced that it wasn't her. Poor baby. (Pretending as if she's about to cry.) I just think they're setting her up or something.

Jameson: Well, yes, Ella really does believe its her. She really does believe its her. But did he do this without giving any information to Hunter?

Spessa: Right... I don't know if it had anything to do with these handwriting samples or what, I don't know why they would, just out of the blue in the middle of the night..my husband woke me up to tell me. (sigh)

Jameson: I'm still not finding it on TV.

The call ended with Jameson realizing that she had no idea who she was talking to, but offering to call Spessa back if she found out any further information. She said that Spessa had woken her from a sound sleep, but that she was going to call some other people interested in the case to find out if they knew the mother had been arrested. It's unknown how long Jameson spent making phone calls to other JonBenet fanatics in the middle of the night, but her and the other regulars on the forums sure weren't happy to find out that she'd been duped.

```
Posted by: Dave
Location: North Dakota
Subject: Spessa is the one we are going to put away!!

We have a new target, ladies and gentlemen, and
her name is Spessa on IRC! She is the one who
made the call to Jameson and states this clearly
on her web page at members.tripod.com/~wartally .
After we're done with RBCP, she will be the next
in line to fall which LogicBox shortly
thereafter. PLA is going to die, member by
member, and there's nothing anyone can do to stop
me from taking them out.

Spessa lives in Beaverton, Oregon, a suburb of
Portland where RBCP used to live and her real
name is Jennifer. I will keep posting new
information as it arrives. I now have
professionals working on both of them.
```

Spessa was one of the few of us that didn't have her real information posted freely on the net, so Dave's quest to take her down was even more of a failure than with the rest of us since every bit of the information on her was wrong. Most of the things he posted about Spessa were fed to him by the PLA, so his "professionals" didn't seem to be helping out much.

```
Posted by: Patsy
Location: Colorado
Subject: Spessa is the one we are going to put away!!
```

```
I don't see what putting Spessa away is going to
do. She's obviously the most involved here but if
she's arrested then all of the conversation is
going to shift to THAT topic and take away even
more of the JBR attention. I suggest that all you
adults quit acting like CHILDREN and quit
responding to these kids. If you ignore them,
they WILL go away.
```

```
Posted by: Logical Container
Subject: Spessa is the one we are going to put away!!
```

```
Oh yeah.. ignoring them has worked wonders since
they first appeared here five months ago.
```

The Boulder forum regulars began to get desperate for the PLA to leave them alone. Even though they had contact information on several of us, they still couldn't seem to accomplish anything with it. Their calls to my local police and mayor in Celina had done nothing. One of them posted about a lengthy conversation he had with Logic Box's school principal, proud of himself and sure it would end everything, but Logic Box's principal did nothing more than ask him about the strange phone call he'd received. Calls to Tannest's work didn't help since her brother owned the business and was merely amused with the whole thing. Calls to PLA's web host resulted in the owner, Micah, happily sharing their lunacy with everyone on the Boulder forums and laughing with the rest of us.

Then a few of the Boulder regulars came up with their most amazing plan yet. Something that would finally get rid of us once and for all. They began using their mysterious Native American powers to put curses on the PLA and to project maladies for offending their inner being.

```
Posted by: Black Wolf
Subject: TOO FAR!
Location: Universe of the Great Spirit
```

```
To those who would destroy, I come from an old
and respected tribe of Native Americans. We have
known for many, many generations how to project
certain maladies onto those who offend our inner
being. We do not use this ability often or
without just cause.

You have offended me and my people with your
profanity and injustices being sent out into the
universe. My people have come together to place a
terrible curse on you and the one you serve. You
will suffer extreme embarrassment and mental
anguish. We are placing this curse on various
organs in your bodies. Some have to do with a
sexual nature. I know you won't take this
seriously. Many haven't and the results have not
been pleasant. It is my obligation to foretell
you of this.
```

As if Black Wolf's curse wasn't bad enough, Snow Leopard joined in with a curse of her own, putting a spell on the forums itself with the help of the four winds!

```
Posted by: Snow Leopard
Subject: TOO FAR!
Location: Universe of the Great Spirit
```
```
I know exactly what can be done to the humans
behind the keyboards. I don't have to know where
they live, or what their true identity is. If
they have a soul, black or white, it can be
reached.

I know the ways of the Native Americans, and the
distance that can be traveled by the four winds.
The soul of JonBenet has been troubled by this
blatant display of the dark minded, and must be
stopped. Let the ritual begin.

There's to be a spell put on this forum, and my
warning to those of you that want to tempt the
boundaries of this spell...Don't! You may taunt
this warning, but you will pay a big price for
your disbelief. May the dissenters fall like rain
on a parched ground, and may their souls dance
before them in the pain they've inflicted on
others throughout their lives.
```

Whenever activity from the PLA slowed down, everyone would quickly begin assuming that their tactics against us had worked and some would begin declaring total victory in the war against the PLA, thinking that calling up our ISPs and our webhosts and employers had finally put a stop to our nonsense and that we were gone forever.

```
Posted by:   31373
Subject: The PLA is all but gone...
```
```
The little cretins are begging for mercy now.
They are bewildered that a group of 80 year old
women can bring them to their knees. I would like
to thank Lisa, jameson, Kuan-Yin, Wendy and
Windsor for all their efforts in bringing down
the law.
```

```
Posted by:    Bayou
Subject: XOXOX
```
```
Things have been so much better now that the PLA
are completely gone, it's starting to feel like
our same old forum again.  I whole heartedly hope
people will start posting with their original
hats again and once again participating as we did
last Winter. We had some spectacular sessions
here and I know we can again.
```

Their celebrations were often short-lived, though, since the PLA would always come back after a few days and start things up again. This endless circle continued until the day that we all logged in to see the forums gone and replaced with a short message to tell us that the forums were being closed down forever.

```
Welcome to BoulderNews
Our forums are now closed.

Despite several efforts, BoulderNews was unable
to keep obscene and indecent language off the web
site. Not only did the hackers who broke into the
forum go far beyond the measure of good taste,
they also put private information about many
people on the web site. For this reason we had no
choice but to close the forums.

We appreciate your understanding in these
matters.
```

The great part about their reasons for shutting down the forums was that we weren't even the ones posting personal information about forum members. It was always the regulars who were posting personal information and making physical threats towards us. When the forums closed, most of the regulars convened on another web site to hold their vigil for the forums they once loved. The forums came back a few more times, but never stayed up for very long. Eventually, they were closed forever.

```
Posted by: BeaHaven

I am just sick. I am sure that they have spent
some money trying to keep up the forum. I really
didn't think they would stop just when they
almost had it licked.
```

```
Posted by: Rockford
```
I'm so mad I could spit nails! I thought they were this close to putting an end to the trasher nonsense! Well, I hope they're satisfied. What pathetic lives they must lead.

```
Posted by: DavidWill
```
I was just sitting here wondering how long it would take till the PLA started here. I can understand the BNF feeling they had to do something, but oh how I hate giving those **** any satisfaction at the PLA. I'm sure Dan and David have built some protection here, but you know those little vermin will paint a big bullseye here. So sad, silly, and useless.

```
Posted by: GSH
```
Hi, all..Reporting in for the Night Shift, and trying not to cry on my keyboard. We have spent so many nights together that it is with sadness I post here. Something went wrong on the BNF that they couldn't have banned ISP's of those that started all of the trashing in the beginning.

At this point, you may be wondering *why* we targeted a bunch of make-believe investigators and tormented them until their forums were shut down. Were we disgusted over their obsession of this poor, dead child, and hoped to teach them that finding pleasure over something so horrible was repulsing? Did the fact that each piece of evidence released to the public resulted in complete delight for them as they mused over the disturbing details make us want to put a stop to what they were doing to the memory of this girl? Perhaps it was amusement at the fact that these people actually thought they were going to solve the case? Was it simply because we were fascinated with this nutty group of people who couldn't seem to get enough of the sickening details of a little girl's murder?

Nah, we were just bored and had nothing better to do.

* * *

For most of the people involved in screwing with the forums, the fun ended when Boulder News shut down the forums. The regulars all ran off to alternate forums about JonBenet and continued to obsess over the case, just like some of them still do today, still thinking that they're really close to solving the murder. Spessa, Tannest and I occasionally checked in with them to say hello on the other sites until they booted us off, but we left them all alone for the most part. We expected to never hear from them again, but eleven years after the Boulder News Forums were shut down, in 2008, I was surprised to find myself named as a suspect in the kidnapping and murder of JonBenet.

Of course, I wasn't a suspect in any *real* case. It was another case put together by one of these JonBenet-obsessed nuts named Richard. It wasn't a name I was familiar with, but I was fairly certain he had to be someone from the old Boulder News Forums since he appeared to live in the area of Colorado where JonBenet was murdered.

This wasn't just some theory that Richard came up with one night and published the next day for everyone to read. It turned out that he'd put *years* of research into implicating me and a few other people related to the PLA in the kidnapping and murder of JonBenet. He put together hours of video evidence regarding the case, meticulously comparing my own handwriting to that of the ransom note writer. He displayed screen shots from various web sites of mine, using side-by-side comparisons of the JonBenet ransom note to prove that I was involved. Some of the web site captures were from 2002, meaning that it's possible he spent at least six years working on this. From an email that he sent to my ex-wife and Jammie in 2005, we knew that he'd put at least three years into it, using Google as his primary detective tool.

It was hard to believe that that this man in his mid-40's could be serious about all the evidence against us since none of it came even close to checking out. But as time went on, he continued to release videos that analyzed the true meaning behind the ransom note and other aspects of the case, using an overhead projector, a whiteboard and a yardstick to thwack at it with to emphasize his points.

We never figured out if he was trying to frame us for murder or if he was just completely insane, but he did use his real name and he displayed himself in many of the videos. A little research on him led us to find that he was honest about who he was and that he didn't seem like the type to pour years of research into what might be a practical joke. He seemed completely sincere in thinking that he blew the JonBenet case wide open.

When I brought Richard's insanity to the attention of visitors on the PLA website, he grudgingly welcomed all the new visitors and continued on with his investigation. When I emailed him, he insulted me for several paragraphs and then attempted to secure an interview with me to get my side of the story for his videos.

After I made a parody video of his investigative videos, he became angry, made threats to sue me and bragged that he had a made major deal with Penguin Classics to turn his findings on the case into a book. He then complained to YouTube and had my parody video taken down. After seeing how easy it was to have videos removed with complaints, me and Patty (a girl he accused of being deeply involved in the kidnapping and murder with me) began making our own complaints to YouTube and having Richard's videos taken down. I can't imagine he was too happy to have years of his hard work disappear from the internet.

Spessa's husband came up with the hilarious idea of having me mail a letter to Richard that would simply state, "I, Alex, hereby do confess to the murder of JonBenet." and then sign my name to it, just so he would take it to the local police and beg them to arrest me. I really wanted to do this, but our friend RogueClown, the voice of reason, advised against it since I might get into trouble for interfering with a police investigation.

Throughout all of our fun with Richard, he maintained that he was completely serious in his investigation and that he found me through good old-fashioned detective work (meaning Google) and not because I used to pester the members of the Boulder News Forums. He says that his findings in the ransom note led him to me and that it was only later he realized that I was someone who was involved in the forums back in 1997.

As of this writing, no arrests within the PLA have been made in the JonBenet case, we've yet to see Richard's book published, and the Boulder News web site still doesn't have any forums.

Cactus

"To live the cactus is to live like no man." -Amigados

Cactus was cactus about Cactus' cactus, when she cactused Cactus, that cactused away his low cactus and made him cactus again. He started to cactus and had the cactus of cactus upon Cacti at the head of Cactus Lane. His cactus always determined his cactus. Without a cacti's cactus he ran to Cactus and said, "I cactused cactus today, Cactus, and I'm so cactus. I won't ever cactus that cactus again, as long as I cactus!"

The cactus cactused and cactused him cactusly in the cactus.

"I'll cactus you to cactus yourself, Mr. Cactus. I'll never cactus to *cactus*!"

She cactused her cactus and cactused on. Cactus was so cacti that he had not even cactus to say, "Cactus cactus cactus cactus, cactus cactus?" So he said cactus. But he cactus in a fine cactus, nevertheless. He cactused into the cactus wishing she were a cactus, and cactusing how he would cactus her if she cactused. He cactused her and cactused a stinging cactus as he cactused. She cactused one in return, and the cactus was complete. It seemed to Cactus, in her cactus, that she could cactus for cactus to "cactus," she was so cactus to see Cactus cactused for the cactused cactus. If she cactused any lingering cactus of cactusing Cactus Cactus, Cactus' cactus had cactused it entirely cactus.

Poor cactus, she didn't cactus how cactus she was nearing cactus herself. The cactus, Mr. Cactus, had cactused cactus with an unsatisfied cactus. The cactus of his cactus was, to be a cactus, but cactus had cactused that he should be cactuser than a cactus. Every cactus he took a cactus book out of his cactus and cactused himself.

"Cactus, you are cactus as cactus, to cactus up on a cactus and cactus at what they're cactusing," Cactus cactused.

"How could I cactus you were cactusing at cactus?"

"You cactus to be cactused of cactus, Cactus Cactus; you know cactus to cactus on me! I'll be cactused, and I was never cactused in cactus."

Then she cactused her little cactus and cactused, "Be so cactus if you want! I know cactus that's going to cactus. You just cactus and you'll cactus! Cactus, cactus, cactus!" -- and she cactused out of the cactus with a new cactus of cactus.

Cactus stood cactus, rather cactused by this cactus. He said to cactus, "What a cactus kind of cactus a cactus is! Never been cactused in cactus! Cactus! What's a cactus! That's cactus like a cactus -- they're so cactused and cactus. Well, of course I cactused to tell old Cactus on this little cactus, because cactus cactus of getting cactus on her, that cactus so cactus; but cactus of it?"

Cactus took his cactus and went back to his cactus not at all cactused, for he cactused it was cactusy that he had cactused the cactus on the cactus himself, in some cactus cactus -- he had cactused it for cactus and because it was cactus, and had cactused to the cactus from cactus.

A whole cactus cactused by, the cactus sat cactusing in his cactus, the cactus was cactusy with the cactus of cactus. By and by, Mr. Cactus cactused cactus up, cactused, then cactused his cactus, and cactused for his cactus, but seemed cactused whether to cactus it or cactus it. Most of the cacti cactused up cactusly, but there were two among cactus that cactused his cactus with intent cacti. Mr. Cactus cactused his cactus absently for a cactus, then cactused it out and cactused himself in his cactus to cactus!

Cactus shot a cactus at Cactus. He had seen a cactus and cactus cactus look as she cactus, with a cactus cactused at its cactus. Instantly he cactused his cactus with her. Cactus -- something must be cactus! cactus in a cactus, too! But the very cactus of the cactus cactused his cactus. Cactus! -- he had a cactus! He would cactus and cactus the cactus, spring through the cactus and cactus. But his cactus shook for one little cactus, and the cactus was lost -- the cactus opened the cactus. If Cactus only had the wasted cactus! Too cactus. There was no cactus for Cactus now, he cactused. The next cactus the cactus faced the cactus. Every cactus cactused under his cactus. There was cactus in it which cactused even the cactus with cactus. There was cactus while one might cactus -- the cactus was cactusing his cactus. Then he cactused: "Who cactused this cactus?"

There was not a cactus. One could have cactused a cactus. The cactus continued; the cactus cactused cactus after cactus for signs of cactus.

"Cactus, did you cactus this cactus?"

A cactus. Another cactus.

"Cactus Cactus, did you cactus?"

Another cactus. Cactus' cactus grew more cactus under the slow cactus of these cacti. The cactus cactused the ranks of cacti -- considered a cactus, then turned to the cactus:

"Cactus Cactus?"

A shake of the cactus.

"Cactus Cactus?"

The cactus sign.

"Cactus Cactus, did you cactus?"

Another cactus. The next cactus was Cactus. Cactus was cactusing from cactus to cactus with cactus and a sense of the cactusness of the cactus.

"Cactus Cactus" [Cactus glanced at her cactus -- it was cactus with cactus] -- "did you cactus -- no, cactus me in the cactus" [her cacti rose in cactus] -- "did you cactus this cactus?"

A cactus shot like cactus through Cactus' cactus. He cactused to his cactus and cactused -- "I cactused!"

The cactus stared in cactusity at this cacticle cactus. Cactus cactused a cactus, to gather his cactus; and when he cactused cactus to go to his cactus the cactus, the cactus, the cactus that cactused upon cactus out of poor Cactus' cactus seemed cactus enough for a cactus.

Cactused by the cactus of his own cactus, he took the most cactusy cactus that even Mr. Cactus had ever cactused; and also cactused with cactus the added cactus of a cactus to remain cactus after cactus. He cactused who would cactus him outside till his cactus was cactused, and not cactus the cactus as cactus, either.

Cactus went to cactus that cactus cactusing cactus against Cactus; for with cactus and cactus Cactus had cactused him, not cactusing her own cactus; but even the cactusing for cactus had to give cactus to cactus, and he fell cactus at last with Cactus' latest cactus lingering cactusly in his cactus --

"Cactus, how could you be so *cactus*!"

(illustration by aftershocks, 2002)

Beige Boxing Celina

"If you have all this time and talent on your hands, why aren't you using it to help others instead of fucking around?" -Howie in Michigan

I really don't know why I decided to move to Celina, Ohio. I'd been living in big cities all over the United States for several years at that point, and I guess I just wanted a break from that. I'd been spending a lot of time in a book store's travel section, trying to decide on a new place to live, and somehow Celina ended up being the choice. It was a small town in the middle of nowhere, right on the edge of a lake.

After a few hours on a Greyhound bus, and then an expensive 45 minute cab ride from Lima, I was in Celina. Since neither the cab driver nor me knew anything about Celina, she dropped me off at Hardees and I began walking aimlessly around the city. With a population of just 9,000 people, I knew the local police would probably have an issue with me trying to sleep outdoors somewhere. Pulling my Celina map out of my backpack, I found I had to walk a half mile to the nearest hotel, along with my extremely heavy, oversized duffle bags.

Days later, I'd finally settled into a nice efficiency apartment which sat on top of some downtown businesses. It consisted of a small bedroom and a small living room with a TV, couch and a fridge. All the comforts of home. Luckily, the phone company seemed to be overly trusting and didn't expect me to pay any kind of deposit to have a phone line installed, even though I'd just rattled off nine random digits for a social security number since I was living under a false name.

I found a job doing telemarketing for the Fraternal Order of Police which seemed just a little ironic to me. I spent my mornings there calling up local residents and begging them to donate money to help fund the police department, then I spent my evenings breaking laws that might lead to the police department spending money on me. So I reasoned that in the end it all seemed to balance out.

Being in a small town, I didn't do too many illegal things, but I was still a chronic red boxer and I messed with other peoples' phone services when trying out new ideas. And as I became more familiar with the town, I started going on beige boxing expeditions, plugging my phone company test set into the green telco cans in peoples' back yards to make free calls and to set up call forwarding services on their lines.

I began setting up voice conferences through AT&T by ordering call forwarding for a person whose line I had access to. Then I would forward their phone line during one of my beige boxing trips to the number for AT&T's Alliance conferencing services. This meant that anyone calling that person would end up reaching AT&T Alliance instead. The person could still make normal outgoing calls and it'd sometimes be a day or two before they even noticed that they weren't getting any phone calls.

After the forwarding was set up I'd just go to my apartment and dial their local phone number to reach the teleconferencing service. From there I could call up to 15 of my friends at the same time and talk to them as long as I wanted. We held marathon conferences, staying on the line together for 24 hours at a time until the conferences automatically disconnected us. In most cases the person would have their phones unforwarded by the time the conferences ended. But sometimes I would venture out just a few hours before they ended to set up another conference line so we could keep chatting for days at a time.

One night a conference was just a few hours from ending and only me and some girl named Martini were left on the line. I didn't know her personally but she'd ended up on the conference line through a friend of a friend of mine, which is how most people ended up on our conferences. We could hear a few people snoring in the background. Since these conferences went on for days at a time it wasn't unusual for people to fall asleep on the line.

"I'm getting sort of bored with the conferences," I admitted to her. "We need to do something different on here to spice them up. You know, like get more strangers on the line to chat with us instead of just talking to each other."

"Well, don't you do that already? Seems like you do nothing but prank phone calls on these things sometimes," she replied.

"Yeah, but that's not the same. With the prank calls you rarely end up with somebody on the line who'll stay there and talk to you. And when you do, they usually just want to yell at everyone and try to cause problems until we kick them off."

"You ever heard of a party line? People call in from all over the country to talk to each other. They're supposed to be pretty popular."

"I know that these conference bridges used to be really big in the phone phreak community. But supposedly those are long dead," I told her.

"No, I'm talking about normal party lines with normal people. Not phreaking lines."

"I've never heard of such a thing. Why would regular people pay to call a line and talk to people they don't even know?" I asked.

"You may find this shocking, but regular people actually pay for their long distance phone calls. There was a story about people being addicted to these lines on the news earlier this year.

I'm pretty sure if you look in the back of a Rolling Stone magazine you'll find the numbers to some party lines."

After she told me that I started digging through my piles of junk, looking for a copy of Rolling Stone. I found one and flipped to the back pages. Sure enough, there were about a dozen different chat lines to choose from, hidden between ads for psychics and phone sex services. I couldn't believe I'd never noticed them before. Using the third party billing trick, I started calling the lines. The first few I tried appeared to be nothing but guys and girls hitting on each other. But after a little searching I finally found one that was just a lot of people talking to each other, sharing stories, telling jokes and spending hours upon hours on these lines together. I was instantly hooked, and my favorite party line was called Hotel California where there were nine different rooms to choose from on one single line. I hopped from room to room, talking to different people and almost always ending up asking the same question, "How can you afford to be on this line all day?"

One guy replied to me, "Well not everybody here stays on all day. And those that do usually end up getting their phones turned off because they can't handle the bills. And then there's a few that know different ways to make free calls to get here."

"No way," I replied, "So you mean there's actually phone phreaks on this thing?"

"Phone phreaks?" he replied. He seemed confused about the term.

"A phone phreak is a person who's really into the phone system," I explained, "and a phreak usually knows how to get free phone calls.".

"I've never heard someone call me a phone phreak before. I don't pay to call here. A girl I know taught me how to call in for free by calling in collect. I just have to use a certain long distance access code where they aren't able to tell that this line doesn't accept collect calls. Then I instruct the operator to hit the buttons that get me into one of the rooms and she asks whoever is in the room if they'll accept the charges. Even if nobody is in the room I can accept the charges myself by using a different voice and she can't even tell the difference."

"That's wild, so you're one of the people that call in for free. I'm not paying either. All I do is third party bill the call to another number through AT&T. They use an automated system now that doesn't even require verification from the person I'm billing the call to. It's so stupid."

"But doesn't the phone company have your number when you do that? People on here have done that and gotten into trouble for it," he said.

"Yeah, but those people probably stayed on all day and they probably kept billing it to the same number. I only use that method for short calls and I never bill to the same number twice. That way most people won't even notice the charge on their bill. Some people will notice it and since it's such a small amount they'll just ignore it. Others will report it as fraud and it'll end up getting charged back to my phone bill. Since it's a small amount I really doubt they even investigate it. They probably figure I made a mistake or something. And I've got a lot of other different ways to call in for free too. So I doubt I'll be using this method to call in very often."

"Like what kind of other methods?"

"Well, I could probably go on all night," I said. "There's calling cards, of course. I'm sure people on here must use those."

"Not too often," he replied, "since those would be traced back to the person's home and they'd probably end up in big trouble for using them. I have heard of people using them on here though."

"Well, I'd just go sit at a pay phone if I used a calling card. Or I could use my next door neighbor's phone line. I live in an apartment and I've tapped into his phone lines through the wall dividing our bedrooms. But that's probably risky since I never know when he would pick up his line. And he's a big guy so he'd probably come over and kill me if he figured out what I was doing. Then there's beige boxing. Don't suppose you've ever heard of that, have you?"

"Nope."

"That's when you open up the phone box on the outside of someone's house and you hook up your own phone into their line. Or you open up one of those green telco cans and hook your phone into one of the lines in there. I've done that plenty of times but I usually don't like to sit around chatting out in the open for too long. Too risky."

"Yeah, not too many of the users on here call from the outdoors as far as I know."

Just then a girl popped in and said, "You guys are awful, stealing your phone calls. Why don't you just get a job and pay like we do?"

"We get a lot of people on here who don't like phone thieves," he told me. "They think that if we commit too much toll fraud on this line that they'll shut it down. Which I guess is possible, but I've been calling here for nearly a year now and there's always at least a few people who'll admit to calling in for free. We even get phone calls here from inmates who've figured out how to call in collect from jail. I doubt they ever shut us down. I bet they make plenty of money from legitimate callers."

I began spending all of my free time on these lines and after a while I stopped setting up the free teleconferences for my friends and told them all to call the party lines instead. Since very few of them knew how to call for free, I didn't hear from many of them. Not only did the party lines keep me entertained with new and interesting people, but there wasn't as much effort in calling into them as there was in setting up my own AT&T conferences.

For awhile the party lines turned me into a total hermit. I'd stay inside for days at a time, rarely leaving the couch. To call in for free, I'd ordered call forwarding for a local gas station's credit card phone line. Then I walked up to the station, hooked my phone into their box and forwarded their calls to my favorite party line. Then I just had to go home and dial the local phone number to reach the party line. Since their credit card line was only used for outgoing credit card authorization calls, the forwarding would sometimes last for a month. And by the time they figured out what was going on and shut off the call forwarding, I had already set up another one at another gas station which would last me another month or two.

Nearly a half a year later, after the newness of the party lines had finally started wearing off, I started looking for something else to entertain myself with. So I began listening to the phone calls of some of my neighbors. I'd punched a hole in the wall months earlier, and tapped into my neighbor's phone lines, but he didn't talk on the phone nearly enough.

It turned out that one of the vacant storefront spaces which I lived on top of had once been a business that used a lot of phone lines. So even though the shop downstairs from me was empty, it was wired for at least 50 phone lines. I decided to call my landlord and tell him that I was interested in leasing the business space from him so I could get a closer look at the lines. I looked in the phone book and found that he owned a small realty company just a few blocks away from me. A lady answered the phone when I called and I ended up getting more than I even hoped for.

"Barker Realty, this is Stacy. How can I help you?"

"Is this the company that has some downtown business property for rent?" I asked.

"Yes it is," she replied.

"Well I think I might be interested in renting it for a few years if the price sounds good. How soon would I be able to take a look around inside the building?"

"My boss is out of town until next week and since I'm the only one in the office I wouldn't be able to show it to you. But if you'd like to stop by, I can give you a key and let you take a look for yourself."

"That'd be great!"

I finished up my breakfast, watched a little TV, and sprinted over to her office around noon. She had the key waiting for me and said to take my time looking around and just to bring the key back when I was finished. I told her thanks and ran back to my apartment. I got on my bike and rode as quickly as I could to Wal-Mart to make a copy of the key. When I got back I took a quick look through the vacant office, noting the location of the phone lines coming into the phone closet, then I hurried back to the realty office and returned the key. I told Stacy that I'd definitely be in touch soon about renting, thanked her and hurried back home. Lucky for me, she had never met me before and didn't recognize me as one of the tenants living upstairs.

From what I could tell during my quick tour of the office downstairs, there was once some kind of PBX system hooked up inside a phone closet. Most of it had been removed but the wires were still coming in from outside and they were lying all over the floor of the phone closet in a tangled mess. After a few days of revisiting the office and figuring out where my apartment was from down there, I was able to drill a few holes in my bedroom closet and run my own phone lines across the top of the drop ceiling into the offices phone closet. From there, I just had to open up the phone box in the alley and wire the lines running into my closet onto some other tenants' existing phone lines.

By the time I was finished, I had access to eight different phone lines. Five of them were businesses and the other three were tenants living in the upstairs apartments. Between these eight new lines, my own phone line, and my next door neighbor's line, which I'd accessed through our wall, I now had a total of ten working phone lines coming into my bedroom. I hooked up my Radio Shack phone tap to my stereo and started trying it out on different lines, waiting for someone to use their phone so I could listen in.

The best line I gained access to by far had to be the Domino's Pizza. They probably had several different lines working there, but I only gave myself access to the first line, which was the line that everyone called in on to order their pizzas. I sat and listened as customers called in for nearly an hour. In between calls, the Domino's guy answering the phone would call up his girlfriend and bitch about the idiotic customers he had to deal with. He probably called her three or four times per hour, so to entertain myself, I hooked up an extension phone to the line and each time he picked up the phone and started dialing her number, I would pick up and dial an extra digit which caused him to reach a wrong number. He would apologize, hang up and try again. I would try to hit the same number in the same spot so he'd get the same wrong number each time. The old man who he kept reaching started to get really pissed off after a few times.

"Look kid, you've got the wrong number!" he screamed at one point. "Stop calling my number because it's obviously not the right one."

"I'm really sorry, sir," the Domino's guy apologized. "There must be something wrong with my phone because I'm not dialing you."

"Well, you need to do something about it before I call the phone company on you!" the old man barked and hung up.

Inspiration struck as I used my own phone line to call the old man back. I'd been recording the calls just in case anything funny happened that I wanted to keep on tape. By rewinding the tape and playing the touch tones into the mouthpiece of my phone, I was able to dial the old man back without actually knowing what his phone number was.

"Hello," he said sharply.

"Hello, this is the manager over at Domino's Pizza in downtown," I said. "One of our employees says that he was trying to call his girlfriend and reached you a few times by mistake and that you yelled and cursed at him. I'd just like to say that you've really upset him and he's in the break room crying his eyes out right now. And I sure hope you don't ever want to order a pizza from us because we'll probably do something nasty to it before it reaches you."

"WHAT THE HELL IS YOUR PROBLEM?" he screamed. "I don't believe this is Domino's. Whoever you are, you better quit calling here because I've called the police and this line is tapped!"

You've got to love people who claim that they have a phone tap on their line. Back in 1994 they didn't even have caller ID in Celina yet so I didn't have a whole lot to worry about. About five minutes later the old man called Domino's back to ask if he was the person who kept reaching him by mistake. When the Domino's employee confirmed that he was, the old man went ballistic on him, demanding to speak with the manager that had called him, and swearing to put Domino's Pizza out of business forever. I was on the floor, laughing so hard that it hurt.

Over the next few weeks I spent all of my free time playing operator. Rigging up a few switches, phones and taps I was able to easily switch in between all the different lines and even bridge certain lines together if I wanted to make a 3-way call. I started setting up teleconferences with friends again and we had hours of fun, screwing with my neighbors in various ways or just listening to their calls and making fun of them. I tried not to dial any direct long distance calls from their lines, fearing they might end up calling the phone company to come out and investigate. I'd hate for them to look in the box outside and discover my rewiring job, even though I'd have plenty of time to disconnect it from the inside if I sensed any trouble. I set up the wiring so all I had to do was pull really hard on the wires from my room and they would disconnect from the phone closet downstairs.

Weeks later, I went back into the phone closet and wired even more lines into my apartment. I ended up having the capacity for 43 lines but there were only about 20 working phone lines coming into our building's phone box. So I called the local phone company's DAC-FAC line, which technicians use to get information on lines that they're installing or repairing. They were able to tell me the location of the telco can which serviced our building and the exact location of every single one of the vacant office's wires in that box, called the cable and pair. They even told me what color each of the wires would be. With that information, I was able to walk down the block and start rewiring their box.

I had precut a bunch of wire into short pieces so it didn't take me long to finish my job. I hooked the wires onto the backside of the terminals in the box, hoping that when a real technician opened the box for routine repairs they wouldn't notice my amateur wiring job. I hooked two wires from each cable and pair out of the vacant office to another random cable and pair in the box. After I was done with everything I ran back home to test it all out and it seemed to work perfectly. I ran into a few empty lines but I figured I could go back and hook those to working lines later. I ended up with around thirty-five working lines in my apartment. Most of them were residential lines, but I got two more business lines, including a florist and a cigar shop.

I mounted a large sheet of plastic at an angle on my desk and started drilling holes into it. Earlier in the day I had gone to Radio Shack and bought fifty toggle switches, fifty LED lights and other various components.

I mounted all fifty switches into the plastic sheet and hooked up a phone line to each one. Then I wired all of the switches into my desktop phone so that I could easily use any of the lines just by flipping a switch on. I mounted an LED above each one of the switches to indicate whether or not that line was in use or free for use. Then I used a marker to scribble the phone number to each line above the corresponding switch. If I knew the name of the business or person the line belonged to, I wrote that there as well.

Whenever I wanted to use a line, I just had to flip the switch into the "on" position. Or if the line was in use, I could flip the switch and either listen in on the conversation with my phone tap or pick up my phone and join in with them. If I wanted to cause some confusion, I would flip two different switches that were in use and they would all be able to hear each other talking. If I wanted to create a massive party line, I just flipped the switches on all of the lines that were in use. Of course I never did that since I didn't need them calling the phone company to report problems on their lines.

I spent a lot of time monitoring various conversations from people who lived up to four blocks away from me. To help spice up the conversations whenever they got too boring for me, I had patched my computer's sound card output into my switchboard so that I could add sound effects, music and other noises into their conversations. The reactions to my interference was fantastic; whenever teenagers were involved they would just blame each other for it, never thinking that some deranged psycho with a telephone switchboard in his bedroom was doing it. And when I did the same thing to adults, they would yell at their kids and tell them to quit playing around on the extension phones.

Late at night, I would use random phone lines to connect my computer to bulletin board systems. I rarely called them directly, though. Instead, I would use calling cards that I'd obtained by ordering them for other people and requesting personalized pin numbers.

I was sort of worried that the phone companies would eventually call these people and question them about the fraudulent charges, so I began keeping detailed logs of which lines I used and which fraudulent method of calling I used each time. And I monitored those lines closely, hoping to catch any unusual phone calls that they might receive from the phone company. I purchased a few in-line telephone recording taps from Radio Shack and some tape recorders so that I wouldn't miss anything while I was away from the apartment. I mounted the three tape recorders above my switchboard.

It was around this time that all of the major phone companies decided on a major change in their policy regarding telephone calling cards. They finally noticed that they were losing lots of money from people like me, who ordered calling cards for random people with a personalized pin number, so they no longer allowed anyone to create personalized pin numbers when they ordered a calling card.

This security flaw had been my major source of calling cards for years now, and suddenly it was taken away from me. I was devastated. Sure, I had an entire switchboard at my disposal, but I was determined not to make any free calls from it since I didn't want investigations happening on their lines. I had a few cards left but they were quickly dying out lately, mostly due to my extensive international calling.

Looking out my window, I began eying the pay phone across the street. It was just outside of the florist's shop and it was being used by a man in a grey suit. Since cellular phones weren't quite a big thing in America yet, pay phones were still used frequently. And I was willing to bet that at least a few of those people used their calling cards instead of pocket change. I began to formulate a plan that would bring that pay phone to my switchboard.

That night, at around 4:00 a.m., I called the direct line to the Celina police department from my cellular phone. I explained to them that I had just seen a few kids jump the fence to the boat yard and break into the office. I listened in on my scanner as the dispatcher sent all available units (All two of them.) to the marina, which was on the far end of town. As soon as I heard that, I ran across the street to the pay phone.

I used my specially cut allen wrench to open the bottom panel of the pay phone stand, then I set the base unit of an old cordless phone inside and plugged the AC cord into the outlet. (Some pay phones have an outlet inside the base, usually to power the light on top of the phone.) I clipped the base unit's wires onto the pay phone line and I wrapped the whole thing in a black garbage bag to help protect it from any water that might leak inside. In less than 5 minutes I was securing the panel back onto the pay phone stand. Meanwhile, the brutal Celina police force were still crawling around the marina with flashlights, far away from me, looking underneath all the boats for those hardened criminal teenagers.

I ran back home and picked up my cordless handset. I pressed the talk button and heard a dial tone. It worked! I dialed the local Wal-Mart and a recording came on, asking me to deposit twenty-five cents. So I tried a number a little further away; Mann's Chinese Theater in Hollywood, California. The cordless pay phone asked me for $2.25, which I deposited using my tone dialer red box. There was some static on the line, since I was so far away from the base unit, which caused some distortion with my "coins" and gave me a live operator.

I decided that I'd better get that fixed. I didn't need GTE dropping a trouble card on my pay phone and discovering my cordless base unit in there. I took the handset apart and hard wired it into my switchboard, assigning it to its own switch on the board. I replaced the rechargeable batteries with an AC adapter and I built a red box into the switchboard, which was wired directly into the cordless phone's microphone. Then I boosted the antenna range by hooking it to the old T.V. antenna which was on top of my apartment building.

The next morning I had my alarm clock set for 10:00 a.m. so I could sit at my window and wait for people to use my new pay phone. My first customer arrived at 10:18; a little kid who tried to use a copper slug to get a free call. Damn him, I should call his parents for this! I got on the line and impersonated the operator, telling him that he was in big trouble and if he didn't put in a real quarter immediately, I would come over there, rip that St. Louis Cardinals hat right off his head and hit him with it. He hung up, looked nervously around, and quickly disappeared into the alley.

At exactly 10:57, while I was in the middle of my Frosted Flakes breakfast, the neighborhood mailman stopped by to use the phone. I looked through my binoculars to see him punch a "zero" first, meaning he would most likely use a calling card. I was so happy that milk came out of my nose! As he tried to enter his calling card number into the automated system, I interfered by hitting some extra numbers. He tried it again and I messed it up again. Then a recording said, "Please hold for operator assistance." An operator came on and asked for his calling card number. He read it off to her as I wrote it down. I was so grateful to him that I didn't even harass him during his call.

I got three calling cards that morning. When people tried to use coins, I would pick up my extension and tell them that the pay phone was malfunctioning and wouldn't take money today. I'd try to talk them into using a calling card instead. If they didn't have a calling card, I would tell them I'd put their call through only if they'd sing a song for me.

The next day, I tried a different method of obtaining the card numbers. As I saw a potential customer walking towards the phone, I quickly used one of the lines from my switchboard to place a call to the pay phone. I would immediately pick up the pay phone line on my own phone so that the customer wouldn't hear it ring. As soon as the guy picked up the phone, I played a tape recording of a dial tone. When he began dialing, I stopped the dial tone recording. And when he finished dialing, I played a recording which said, "AT&T! Please hold for operator assistance..."

"AT&T," I said. "How will you be paying for your call?"

"With my calling card."

"Okay, go ahead and give me your calling card number."

After he read the calling card number to me, I said, "Sir, that calling card isn't working. Do you have another card to try?"

"Um, yeah. That was my GTE phone card. Let me find my AT&T card. Okay, here it is..."

"Okay...yep, that card is okay. Here's your call and fuck you for using AT&T!"

I sat on the line for a second, suddenly realizing that I had no idea what number he had dialed in the first place. So I quickly dialed a toll-free phone sex number on one of the other lines and patched onto his line.

"Hi, this is Tina... Are you ready for a hot time?" The poor guy stood there and tried to talk to her for a minute, before giving up and hanging up the phone. I watched as he walked down the street to use the phone booth on the other end of the block.

Hoping to better aid in my harvesting of calling card numbers, I bought one of those touch tone decoders. It had an LED display that showed me exactly what digits were being dialed on any line I hooked it to. I wired this into my switchboard and not only was it easier for me to get calling card numbers, but I could also see exactly what phone numbers my neighbors were calling. I started keeping files on the neighbors, who they called and the durations of each of their calls.

After a couple months, not much had changed. I still had the same setup and was working on expanding it. I added my old, bulky cellular phone into the switchboard so that I could connect neighbors to the cellular roaming network and I added a couple more desktop telephones so that I could listen in on more than one line at a time without them hearing each other. I'd hooked every sound device I owned into the switchboard, including my computer, tape deck, CD player, voice changer, television, and echo machine. I had the ability to hook every one of their lines up to a single phone, creating a monster party line of confused people. And my list of calling card numbers had reached more than 100 numbers. Life was great.

I began wandering into some of the other yards on my block late at night, thinking I could probably hook their lines into my switchboard too. I would just need to dig a small trench from their house to the office building to lay the wires in.

Then, one Friday, the power bill arrived. I was a month behind on paying it and it seemed to be growing larger each month, probably because of the increasing amount of power that my switchboard was requiring as it continued to grow. It didn't seem fair that I should have to pay so much to them, especially since I stopped going to work as often so I could sit at home and play operator all day. That's when I got the idea of stealing electricity, just as I was stealing phone and cable service.

My neighbors Orvil and Verna had a nice deck attached to their house in the back yard. On their deck was a receptacle which had a bug zapper light and a radio plugged into it. And that's where I decided to get my power from.

At about 3 o'clock in the morning, I removed a portion of the lattice which covered the space underneath their deck and crawled underneath. Using a hacksaw, I was able to cut into the plastic conduit under the deck that supplied their power, then I pulled a few inches of wire out from the side that ran into their basement.

To shut off their power temporarily, I pulled the face off of their power meter, which cut off all the power to their house. It took a few minutes for me to splice my own extension cord into their wiring before turning their power back on. The easy part was finished. Now I just had to use a shovel to dig a trench 2 houses down and then into the alley where my building stood.

By the time I was finished, it was nearly daylight. I ran the electrical wire into the abandoned office building and into the PBX closet where I plugged it into another extension cord that I already had running into my apartment.

I was able to plug my refrigerator, space heater, microwave, television, computer, and all of my switchboard equipment into this extension cord. I even bought a few lamps to use instead of the ceiling lights so I could plug those in too. And I stopped using the built-in wall heaters to heat my apartment, since I could just leave the space heater running all day and night now. Luckily I was able to run everything at once without blowing a fuse at Orvil and Verna's house. The next night I walked to their house to peer into the glass bubble at their electric meter, and noticed that the disk was spinning much more rapidly than it had been the night before. Oh well, they seemed like they could afford it.

The following month, my electric bill was about 1/3 of its usual size. And I'd also decided to cancel my own phone service since I really didn't have much need for it anymore. I made most of my phone calls on the pay phone line across the street, using my list of calling card numbers. I usually sat at the window as I used the phone, so I could quickly hang up if someone else needed to use it.

To further enhance the free lifestyle that I was enjoying so much, I decided that I needed to obtain cable TV service for free too. Once again, I turned to Orvil and Verna's house for my needs. And I didn't just tap into their coax line. Instead I ran two coax lines from their house, one incoming and one outgoing. I rigged the two cable lines in kind of a loop, so that I could control what Orvil and Verna watched on their television.

By the time I finished with it all, I had built a second switchboard in my room, this one for cable television hookups which consisted of a few T.V. monitors, VCRs, a video camera and some video mixing devices. I had the power to monitor the channels they were watching, change their channels, make them watch my home video collection or wipe their T.V. show off the air with a variety of 37 different wiping techniques! And within 2 months, I had the same capabilities with 3 more of my neighbors.

What was left for me to obtain for free? I searched for more ways to reduce my monthly bills so that I could pour more of my spare cash into better television mixing devices. The only thing left was water. So the next night, I began digging a trench from the corner fire hydrant to my apartment building...

Finding a Job

"The PLA stopped being cool once I started having sex." -linear

Throughout the nineties, I worked in more convenience stores and gas stations than one person should ever be subjected to. I dealt with beer runs, gun fights, shoplifters, know-it-all managers, asshole customers, double shifts, insane homeless people and barely above minimum wages. It all started with my first convenience store job at Circle K.

Soon after first arriving in Galveston, Texas, I began looking for employment. I'd worked in fast food before and I knew I didn't want to do that again. I'd done a few hard labor jobs as well and I was hoping to avoid those at all costs. What I really wanted was a cash register job inside one of the many Circle K convenience stores that were spread all over the island. I'd seen the amount of work those clerks got away with not doing and I knew that their jobs paid quite a bit more than a restaurant job. I wanted a piece of that.

I applied at every major convenience store on the island and set up a voicemail box with a local voicemail service so that I could be called back. I had some fairly good references from previous employers and I made myself a couple of years older so that I appeared a little more responsible. I even claimed that I was about to attend Galveston's community college. I had a few interviews and they seemed to go okay, but they would always end up hiring someone else, promising me that I was next in line once another position opened up. That's when I decided to *make* a position open up.

I really wanted to work at the Circle K on 39th Street and Seawall. I liked its central location, its view of the ocean, and I especially liked that there were no security cameras inside the store. After a little research, I found that this particular Circle K had a total of 9 employees. I began writing down their names, types of cars, other stores they worked at and any other information I could find about them. I'd managed to get the home phone numbers of most of them by calling the store and asking other employees for them. All it took was an impersonation of an employee or Circle K's regional manager. My plan was to either get them all fired or make them quit, one at a time.

I started off with Joe. I suspected he would be the easiest since he was slow, rude, unkempt and often showed up late for work. I already had Joe's home phone number, which the store manager, Sonny, had provided me with when I called and impersonated the personnel department from the corporate office. I knew that Joe was supposed to come to work that day at 4:00, so about an hour before that I called his home and did my best to impersonate his manager's voice.

"Joe, this is Sonny. It looks like there was a mistake in scheduling and you don't have to come in today. You have to be here tomorrow instead. Is that okay?"

It worked beautifully. Joe bought every word of it and he even seemed happy that he was getting the evening off. I tried to come up with a way to make Joe leave his house so that Sonny couldn't call him and ask why he hadn't shown up for work, but everything I could think of involved me calling his house and impersonating somebody to get him to leave. I was afraid he would recognize my voice from the previous call so I decided against it. I didn't want him figuring things out and calling Circle K back.

At 4:15 I went to the Circle K to get something to eat and to see if my plan worked. I slowly walked the store, looking for food and listening to the irritated employee and manager. The employee was upset because she couldn't go home until Joe showed up, and Sonny was upset because Joe was late again. Just as I was paying for my burrito and drink, Sonny was trying to reach Joe at home. Apparently he wasn't there because nobody was answering. I stalled a little longer by reading the newspaper on the stand. I thought about asking Sonny if he was hiring any new employees yet, but he was in such a foul mood that I decided against it.

It looked like the daytime employee, Amy, was stuck working a double-shift because of Joe's absence. Hopefully Joe wouldn't decide to stop by Circle K for anything during his evening off. I laughed, imagining Joe's excuse for not being there. "You told me I didn't have to come in, Sonny!" I hoped that excuse alone would get him fired.

The next day I was somewhat disappointed to see Joe working the evening shift again, but not entirely surprised. It looked like I would need to try even harder. I wished that I had come in around 4:00 so that I could witness the confrontation between Joe and Sonny. Since it was fairly busy in the store, Joe didn't notice me wandering into the back room. Taped to the office door was the week's schedule for the employees. I ripped it down and put it in my pocket.

On the wall was a time sheet for employees to sign as they arrived to work each day. Joe's entry for yesterday was empty, since he had missed work. Doing my best to forge his handwriting, I signed his name for his missed day. I wrote his incoming time as 3:58 p.m. and his outgoing time as 12:09 a.m. My hope was that Sonny would now suspect Joe of trying to get paid for the day that he didn't show up. I said nothing to Joe as I paid for my drink and left. I decided that I needed to find out where Joe lived.

It wasn't hard to do. I called Domino's Pizza and told them I needed to order a pizza. I gave them Joe's phone number and they read his address to me for confirmation. I wrote it down and hung up the pay phone. Looking in the front of the phone book, I found the map of the island and located Joe's house, which was about 30 blocks away.

Ten minutes later, my car was parked in front of his house. Joe worked tomorrow and I needed to make him miss work. The best idea I could come up with was to flatten the tires on his car before he left for work. It didn't seem like a very good idea since it would be easy for me to be spotted in his driveway, but it was the best that I could come up with.

The next day I went to a hardware store and purchased a few 4 inch nails. At 2:30, I pulled onto Joe's street, noting that his car was in the driveway. I parked my car on the other side of the block and started walking. There was an alley so I was able to enter Joe's yard from the back. It turned out to be much easier than I expected. I simply walked up to Joe's car, quickly wedged a nail under the back of each of his tires and then walked away. My biggest fear was that Joe might be looking out a window and would recognize me as a regular customer, but as far as I could tell, I wasn't spotted by Joe or any other neighbors.

At 4:00, I started driving towards Joe's house again just to see if his car was there or not. On my way there, I spotted Joe pulled to the side of the road, cursing loudly at his flattened tires. He was about 8 blocks from his home, so I knew it wouldn't be very long before he decided to walk back home and call work.

After two days of not seeing Joe at Circle K, I finally confirmed that he was no longer employed there. You want to know how found this out? THEY HIRED A NEW EMPLOYEE! He turned out to be an employee from another Circle K store, apparently there to help pick up the slack from Joe's absence. Unsure if he was there to stay or not, I decided to focus my efforts on Tia, the daytime employee. I'd already noticed, by watching how she interacted with customers, that she didn't deal with stress very well. So I gave her some stress.

I started spending my mornings on the beach across the street from the store, reading a book and keeping an eye on what was going on. Every time the store started to get really busy, I walked across the street and slipped inside, completely unnoticed by Tia, and I made messes. Not just little messes, but huge messes that I hoped would take Tia hours to clean up, stressing her out to the point of desperately searching for a new place to work.

Not only did I start all the coffee makers at once when they already had full pots of coffee under them, I filled the filters with Pepsi to ensure an extra sticky mess would overflow all the pots. I stuffed the drains on the fountain drink machine full of paper and left a few of spouts running. I even jammed the handle on the slushie machine so the ice cold mush began to pile up and overflow onto the floor.

I would only spend a few minutes in the store at a time but each time I would manage to start several messes. Then I'd walk back to the beach and plan my next attack as I waited for the next rush of customers who would camouflage my vandalism. Within a day, I had just about every surface of the store covered with sticky Pepsi. I'd fill up their 64 ounce cup with Pepsi and walk all over the store, dripping it onto merchandise, food, machines, the magazine display rack, windows and counters.

And I didn't limit myself to just Pepsi-related messes either. I opened a pack of razor blades from the shelf and used them to cut slits in all of the plastic and cardboard milk containers at the cooler door. Not huge slits, but maybe just a few inches long. This would cause a small leak inside the cooler, eventually making a huge mess on the floor. That is, until a customer picked up the container. That's when the slit buckled and sometimes turned into a small hole. Milk would suddenly be pouring out all over the floor in front of the helpless customer. Mopping that store must have been hell after my visits.

The condiments bar was a wreck once I finished with it. I'd lift the containers out of their holders and pour them all over each other. Then I'd repeat with another. Sometimes I'd get really artistic with it, adding ketchup and mustard drawings on top of it all. And, of course, I'd usually spill a little Pepsi into it too. You know the containers that hold the little packets of salt, pepper, BBQ sauce, etc? Yeah, those packets were all floating in Pepsi when I left.

During one visit, I noticed Sonny getting into his car to leave right as I arrived. I wasn't sure where he was going or how long he'd be gone, but I knew that having only one employee in the store guaranteed that I could safely wander around the unauthorized areas of the store. That day I chose the walk-in cooler.

I began by stocking the Pepsi bottles into the racks so that there would be plenty for the customers. Once the Pepsi was fully stocked, I took the glass bottles of Lipton iced tea and put one on the very end of each of the 12 racks for Pepsi. Each glass bottle was right on the edge of the shelf, sure to fall and shatter on the floor the moment that somebody jostled the corresponding rack of Pepsi. Before exiting the cooler, I opened up a couple gallons of chocolate milk and turned them upside down in their crates. Outside of the cooler, I noticed the new employee schedule was up. I took it with me as I left the store.

An hour before Tia's shift ended, I stopped in the store to buy a newspaper. Sonny was working at the counter and I noticed Tia was on the floor next to a shelf, individually wiping off sticky packages of cookies with a washcloth. Tia did not look like a happy employee.

Sure, she seemed a little stressed out, probably from the sudden surge in messes that she was constantly having to clean up, but I noticed that her bad day was all happening inside of this nice, climate controlled store. It was then that I realized that I needed to disable the air conditioning. The only thing that could make her day any worse would be having to repeat it in relative discomfort. Walking out of the store, I smiled as I looked at tomorrow's weather forecast in the paper.

Destroying the air conditioning unit on the roof wasn't a very hard task. The only real challenge was getting on the roof, which

I accomplished by stacking milk crates along the back of the building to form a staircase to the top. I tiptoed over to the large, gray air conditioning cube and simply flipped the power switch into the "off" position, and then applied a padlock, which I'd stolen from the store earlier in the day, to the switch to make sure it stayed off.

I wanted to actually break the air conditioner, though. So I'd brought some tools with me and began removing all the protective panels. I spent nearly 3 hours on the roof that night, completely taking the air conditioner apart. I even sawed off the pipes that came up from the roof, which sprayed Freon all over my pants. I cut all the electrical wiring inside the unit into tiny pieces and I took all the important looking parts with me, such as the fan blade and the giant, heavy part that actually produces the cold air. I threw those in a dumpster on the way home. The temperature that night was in the mid 80's. The next day was expected to get into the upper 90's.

I didn't get to the store the next day until noon, still worn out from my late-night activities on the roof the night before. The temperature was already in the 90's and the store felt like a furnace. Tia and the manager were dripping with sweat and both looked miserable. The doors were propped open but it seemed to do little good. They didn't even have a fan in the store.

"Hey, Sonny, something wrong with the air?" I asked casually as I walked in.

"Yeah, we're not sure what. They're coming to look at it in a few hours."

Perfect. Tia's shift would end at 4:00 and there's no way the air conditioner would be fixed by then. It might even be another day before it could be fixed since the entire unit would probably need to be replaced. And I could just keep breaking them until they hired me. I spent the rest of the afternoon, slipping in unnoticed occasionally and performing my usual acts of vandalism around the store. Every single customer made a comment to Tia about how hot it was, which had to get annoying after awhile.

While still spending my mornings making things miserable for Tia, I began making harassing phone calls from a pay phone to one of the other evening and weekend guys. His name was Keith and he had a temper. It didn't take much effort to get him to yell at me on the phone.

"Circle K, can I help you?"

"Hey, who is this?" I asked him.

"This is Keith." He responded.

"Keith Parker?"

"No, this is Keith Hierman."

"Oh. Well, which Circle K is this?" I asked.

"We're on 39th Street."

"What's your district manager's name?"

"Clyde Conyers. Why?"

"Well, Keith Hierman, I think you should know something. I hate you and your store. You're a piece of shit and I hope you die."

"Who the fuck is this?"

"Don't worry about who I am!" I yelled. "Mind your own business and get back to fucking work!"

"Fuck you!" he yelled and hung up on me.

I used my tape recorder to record every second of our conversation. Before long, after many more conversations with Keith, I had more than an hour of my calls with him on a cassette tape. My goal was to put together a conversation on tape, using only his voice, of him yelling at Circle K's district manager. All I had to do was arrange the various sound bytes I had on the tape, call up the district manager, and hope for the best. After a few hours of editing a tape of a one-sided conversation together, I called the district manager at his home, late in the evening and on a day that Keith wasn't working.

"Hello?" the district manager answered.

"Clyde Conyers." my tape recorded voice said to him.

"Yes?"

"This is Keith Hierman. Circle K. On 39th Street."

"Oh, hello, Keith." Clyde said.

"Fuck you!" Keith's voice yelled at Clyde.

"What?" Clyde asked, seeming to be a little taken aback by an employee calling him at home and cursing at him. I rewound the tape and Keith repeated himself.

"Fuck you!"

"What's wrong, Keith?"

From this point, Keith's voice just ranted randomly and yelled all kinds of expletives at Clyde. Every time Clyde tried to reason with Keith, I would press the play button again and Keith would go into his rant against Clyde. This went on for nearly a minute before ending with Keith yelling, "Fuck you, my job is better than anything you've ever done!" This line came from a conversation where I was telling Keith how useless he was and how he couldn't find a better job than Circle K. I slammed down the phone on Clyde, and then exploded into laughter.

After taking a few minutes to recover, I put in another cassette tape, labeled "Sonny," then I called up Sonny's home so that Keith could yell at him too. The conversation my tape recorded Keith had with Sonny was nearly identical to the conversation with Clyde. Only with Sonny, I was sure he'd be more likely to recognize Keith's voice and would have no doubt it was Keith who called him. I'd give anything to have heard the conversations between Sonny and Clyde regarding the bizarre phone calls they received from Keith.

I never gave up on wrecking the workdays of all the employees, though. I continued with my campaign of terror for weeks against that helpless store. I would constantly sneak into the back room, causing as much damage and confusion as I possibly could. I disconnected the hoses to the soda tanks, causing the soda machine to dispense nothing but carbonated water. I cut the phone lines and hid the excess wire above the ceiling tiles, ensuring that the credit card and lottery machines wouldn't work for the rest of the day, especially since the phone lines were down so they couldn't call anyone for help without leaving the store.

I turned off their main water valve, then unscrewed the knob and threw it in the trash. I repeatedly turned off the power to the gas pumps and the hot water heater. Once I even opened the emergency valve on the hot water heater, causing it to unload a full tank of scalding hot water into the back room's floor.

All of these actions created a constant stream of stress and confusion for the employees. And it cost the store probably thousands of dollars in cleanup, repairs, and lost sales. All because I wanted a job there.

Another evening guy, named Larry, received a call from me as I pretended to be a man named John from the company who provided their credit card machine.

"Circle K, this is Larry," he answered, sounding extremely bored.

"Hi, Larry. This is John from Visa. We've been having some issues with the credit card network tonight. Has your manager told you about this problem yet?"

"No, I don't know anything about it," Larry replied.

"I see," I said. "Well, there's a major computer virus in the network that processes credit cards and I need you to unplug your credit card machine immediately, before the virus reaches you."

"Oh, okay," Larry said as he fumbled around with the wires in the back of the machine. "Okay, it's unplugged. How long 'til I can plug it back in?"

"Oh, you can't plug it back in, Larry. If you do, the virus will infect your machine and then it won't work anymore. In fact, I need you to unplug the phone line and the serial cable running into it too."

"What do I do if a customer needs to use their credit card though?" he asked.

"Just explain to them that there's a computer virus spreading all over the country and that they shouldn't use their credit card anywhere until we've stopped the virus. We should be able to have it fixed by tomorrow."

"Okay, it's all unhooked now," Larry said.

"Okay, now take the credit card machine and set it far away from the phone lines, just to make sure the virus can't get to it. If you have a stainless steel sink there, put it in the sink because that will help shield the machine from an airborne virus attack."

It took a little more convincing, but Larry was able to put the store's only credit card terminal into the sink to protect it from the virus. This store didn't even have an ATM machine inside, so any customer wanting to pay with a credit card would be completely out of luck. And any customer who'd already put gas in their car would probably be pissed if they only had a credit card to pay with. I went into the store the next morning at 9:00 for breakfast, and was thrilled to see that it was still disconnected. The manager had been in there for an hour, so I guess he believed the story about the virus too. It wasn't until around noon that I noticed it was working again.

One morning I was sitting on some stairs leading to the beach, keeping an eye on the store, when I noticed Sonny walk out the store with a bank deposit bag. He got into his car and drove away and I knew it'd have to be at least 20 minutes before he would come back since the bank was several miles away. I walked into the store, unnoticed by Tia who was busy with a line of customers, and walked into the back room and into Sonny's open office door. I searched through his desk until I found a thick stack of job applications.

Flipping through them all, I found mine. I quickly searched through the rest of them, trying to pick out the most unlikely people to be hired. I based my judgment mostly on illegible handwriting and very little previous job experience. I put my application back in the drawer with about ten others that I chose, and I took the rest with me, probably 50 of them in all. I shoved them inside a newspaper, paid Tia for the paper, and then left the store. I tossed them all into a trash can several blocks away. A huge chunk of my competition was eliminated.

I can only assume that Keith lost his job that day, because the next morning a NOW HIRING sign was in the window. My heart sank at this, knowing that they were probably looking for somebody else and still weren't interested in hiring me. Maybe my references weren't as good as I thought they were. Or maybe they just didn't like me. It almost seemed like I should just give up. I walked in and Sonny was at the counter.

"Sonny!" I said smiling. "You're hiring again! That is so perfect because I cannot seem to find a job on this island and I've been looking for weeks now."

And just like that, I got the job that I'd been shooting for. Sonny and I had another small interview that morning and the next day I had an interview with Clyde, the district manager. Shortly after this, I was hired. They started me out in a part time position to replace Keith, but they promised me that a daytime position was opening up soon since Tia had put in her two weeks notice.

After a few days of training and then working part-time in the evenings on my own, I quit. The job sucked and I didn't like it at all.

Curtis the Superhacker

"I'm about one of the best fuckin' top elite fuckin' hackers you'll ever run across, bitch boy." -Curtis

I was introduced to the awesome hacking force known as Curtis the Superhacker when I found a story linked to him from the Fark website. The short story was written by a guy named Heywood on a website called major-losers.com and it described some hilarious events, based around some Yahoo chat room drama. While chat room drama is usually boring to read about, this particular story was awesome because of a man named Curtis, who was terrorizing women that he met in these chat rooms.

Curtis was your typical small town tough guy who wasn't very bright and was easily angered. It didn't take much to set him off, and Heywood seemed to be having a great time exploiting this fact. Curtis repeatedly claimed that he was a computer hacker and that he could send emails that would "fry your computer." He emailed Heywood repeatedly with death threats, as well as anyone else who didn't agree with him.

I can barely remember the original story of Curtis or why he was featured on major-losers.com. All I can remember is that, according to a woman named Wench, he would talk chat room women out of their phone numbers and other personal information and then use it to attack, blackmail, undermine, stalk, extort and threaten them. She claimed that Curtis even drove from his home in Pennsylvania, all the way to Oregon, to meet some of these women and stalk them in person, though I can't imagine Curtis having the money or resources to ever make it more than a few miles outside of his home town. He allegedly created Yahoo profiles in the names of these women and then chatted with random men on the internet, pretending to be them and causing these men to visit their homes for sex. Curtis even called Heywood's web host and threatened the lives of the women working there, causing Heywood to lose his website for a few days.

I didn't care about any of that. I just loved the deranged emails from Curtis that Heywood posted on his site, proving that Curtis had some serious issues. Curtis had an unintentionally hilarious way of communicating with people, calling everyone queer-boy and threatening them with physical harm, computer hacking and even litigation. I was instantly a huge fan of Curtis and I wanted to see the story continue for as long as possible, which is why I decided to help out with their cause.

I emailed Wench and asked her for all the information that she had on Curtis. She didn't trust me at first, but I finally managed to convince her that I just wanted to help her out for my own amusement since I found the whole thing so funny. Besides Curtis' name and the town she suspected he was from, Wench didn't have any information on him. No address, no phone number, and a fairly common last name. It took me a few hours, but I finally found Curtis by calling up a video store in Curtis' town and impersonating him, asking the video store clerk if I had any late fees on "my" account.

"Yes, it looks like you do owe us $6.00 right now," the clerk said after looking Curtis up in his computer.

"That's a lot of money, man," I said in what I imagined Curtis' voice to sound like. "If I come there and rent a video, do you think I could just pay $2.00 towards the late fee and then maybe pay the rest next month when I get my disability check?"

"Sure, I think we can arrange that," he replied happily.

"Okay, great. Oh, hey, also...do you still have our address on the account as 618 Roys Place? We moved last year."

"No, I show the address on here as 515 Fifth Street."

"Oh, well then you probably have our phone number as 528-7347 then."

"No, it looks like we've got 528-6618," he laughed.

The account wasn't even under Curtis' name, but in the name of a female who was either his wife or his mom. The video store clerk knew exactly who Curtis was and that he was authorized on her account. I was worried that it wouldn't be the right guy, but after a few calls to Curtis I was sure it was him. It didn't take him long to start making insane threats to me, calling me a queer boy and telling me to go to the "libarry" and do my homework.

Curtis also told me that he had a business phone line that was running through a "central computer" in his home that could trace any phone call. He claimed that it was impossible to hide my phone number from this amazingly sophisticated system hooked to his phone line. In the middle of one of our conversations, he pretended that his computer had just come up with my true identity and he said to me, "So, Roy...now that I know a little more about you, why are we calling you Roy?"

As much as I loved the way Curtis ranted and threatened people in chat rooms and emails, his style of talking and threatening over the phone was even more hilarious. He sounded like he was high all the time and he could never completely finish a point. One second he would be yelling, "Don't drop the soap, queer boy!" at me and then the next second, without any apparent reason, he'd be ranting about Heywood and Wench or saying something completely random like, "It's too bad you don't have a girlfriend or I'd be having her suck my dick right now!" He was impossible to follow, but said the craziest lines ever.

Not only was Curtis the "biggest fucking god on the internet," (his words) he also really seemed to be into devil worshipping. His phone conversations often contained all kinds of crazy satanic references and he was always referring to himself as the devil, once telling a prank caller in Florida, "I'm strictly 999 out of hell, motherfucker." It was like he never grew out of his high school phase of trying to shock people with talk about his love of satan.

(illustration by Sakerobot)

During one of the first few calls I made to him, he slammed down the phone on me and then picked up a few seconds later, dialing three touch tones that I immediately recognized as *57, which is the universal phone company code to have a harassing call traced. He listened on the line, waiting for the automated message to tell him that my call had been successfully traced, but instead he heard me laughing at him and saying, "Star 57 only works if there's a dial tone first, Curtis!" He slammed down the phone again.

Not long after my initial contact with Curtis, I posted the calls that I'd made to him on the front page of phonelosers.org so that all the readers there could laugh at Curtis with me. Then Heywood made another post on major-losers.com, which happened to include Curtis' home address and phone number, along with his usual lengthy, hilarious tales of Curtis. All of this sudden attention really upset Curtis, and he replied with the expected threats and calls to our web hosts.

It didn't take Curtis long to figure out my real identity since I used my real information on my web sites and had a listed home phone number and address at the time. Curtis began calling me and leaving messages on my machine when I wasn't home, mostly directed at my wife who he assumed had no idea about my online activities, even though she was one of the people who had made calls to him. The calls worked out great for me since I could still make hilarious recordings of Curtis, but didn't even have to bother making phone calls to him or worry about him tracing my calls with his elite hacker abilities or the central computer system hooked to his phone line.

Like so many other people who'd tracked me down in the past and vowed to bring down the PLA forever, Curtis used my home page and phonelosers.org to learn as much as he could about me and then attempted to taunt me with all of his newfound information. I never could understand why people always seemed to think this would bother me since I obviously had those pages up for the public to see.

Soon after we'd forgotten about Curtis and moved on to other things, I assume he began missing the attention because he started making collect calls to my home from a pay phone. I always accepted the calls and tried to talk to him, but he would just hang up on me. A quick call to Verizon told me exactly where the pay phone was located, and I'd hoped it would lead me to where he worked, but it was just an outdoor phone on a random street corner in his town.

After Heywood published Curtis' home phone number, I began receiving regular emails from people who had pranked Curtis and wanted to tell me about it. Some would have mp3 sound files of the pranks to send me while others just had fun stories. I began to amass quite a large collection of Curtis prank calls from all over the country. A guy named Tele constantly called Curtis and chatted with him, and Curtis stayed on the phone, giving him hours of crazy talk. Curtis once told Tele that the only reason he talked to him so much was because, "I'm walking you into the biggest fucking trap of your life."

Curtis really snapped when a guy named Geo called him with a text-to-speech operator and tried to have a conversation with him. After listening to an operator translate a robotic voice for about a minute, curtis began screaming at the operator, "*I've had it with these stupid fucking jackasses!*" and said that Geo was going to have his teeth knocked out in jail.

Curtis wasn't the only one in his family with a gift for spouting bizarre things into the phone at us, though. If you happened to catch his wife on the phone, she would come up with some rather ingenious quotes herself, like the time she said to me, "I wouldn't ask you to a fuckin' hog roast if you was the fuckin' hog roastin', you fuckin' piece of shit!"

It seems like every few years, someone will end up with Curtis' new phone number and I'll start hearing new Curtis calls again, either having them emailed to me or they'll be posted on the PLA forums. Not too long ago, Altalp made a call to Curtis, pretending to be a pizza delivery company that wanted to confirm an order. After insisting that he pay for his pizza, Curtis began making threats at Altalp, saying he would come to her store. He even told her that he knew where she was because his central computer system had traced her call. Eventually he put his teenage son on the phone, who threatened to "dot" Altalp's eyes. Like father, like son.

There's a whole lot more to the Curtis story than I know about and this would probably be better told by someone like Heywood or Wench, since they know more of the details than I do, but Curtis has always been a favorite of mine, simply because of his amazing quotes like, "You imbreeded mother fucker, you are stupid!" and "I'm going to be stomping a mudhole in your fuckin' ass." Sure, Dino had some classic white trash quotes and Big Larry had his alcoholism and his power tools, but Curtis was a master at coming up with the most outrageous and insane nonsense ever. His claims of being a super hacking god and his crazy way of speaking and his inability to ever finish a thought or a sentence truly set him apart from the other people who'd crossed paths with the PLA. You are missed, Curtis, and we will live in perpetual fear of someday bumping to you at a hacker convention.

The Yellow Pages Prank

"I laughed, I cried, I charged a $700 phone bill to my neighbor. So many people out there have philes on phreaking, but you guys go that extra mile and capture the phreak sense of humor to go along with it. I have to say thanx for bringing a tear to my neighbor's eye. Keep up the good work." -Digital Phreak in Florida

Making prank phone calls has always been a favorite pastime of mine. I began making them as early as second grade, when my older brother and I would sneak up to the attic and call random people out of the phone book. I kept lists of the numbers we called hidden at the bottom of a toy box. These lists kept track of which people were the most fun to call and which numbers we should never call again. I also listed the people who had answering machines, which was a rare find in those days. We loved filling up their machine with messages.

By the time I was in Jr. High, I discovered how entertaining it could be to order pizzas for neighbors so that I could crack the window open and listen to the pizza guy and the neighbor argue for a bit. This was back in the good 'ole days when you didn't have to dial *67 on your rotary phone because caller ID hadn't been introduced yet.

My pizza ordering had slowly evolved over the years, and I began ordering large amounts of pizzas to various neighbors from multiple pizza delivery services. I'd even throw in a few bottles of 2 liter sodas, just to give the driver more stuff to carry. A few times, and I know this was so incredibly stupid of me, I would use my BB rifle to blow holes in the 2 liter bottles, just to add more chaos to the situation. Somehow I never got into any trouble for that.

I started adding taxi cabs into the mix, and eventually other delivery services. I called florists, plumbers, cement trucks, roofers and countless others. Anyone that had a prominent ad in the yellow pages was sure to eventually get a phone call from me. One day I wandered into my front yard to watch a confrontation between two taxi cab companies at a house across the street.

My father was in the driveway working on his car. I asked him what was going on and he explained to me that sometimes rivaling taxi companies would listen in on each others radio frequencies and try to steal each others customers away. We both watched in amusement as each of the drivers exchanged harsh words, and as the old lady whose house they'd shown up at stood on the porch and watched it all. It didn't seem to occur to my father that the old couple across the street had their own car and wouldn't have any reason to be calling a taxi.

One day I got the brilliant idea of calling up all of these businesses and setting up appointments with every single one of them, hoping to get them all to show up at one single house at the exact same time of day. I figured I could easily cover half of the yellow pages in no time, setting up appointments with each and every business. I ended up falling a little short, scheduling just 10 or so businesses to show up at one guy's house.

It worked fairly well but didn't exactly cause the tremendous amount of chaos and confusion that I'd pictured. The highlight of that particular prank was that I managed to get a clown to come to the man's house. As this guy was out on his front porch, trying to figure out what was going on with all the service people showing up at his door, a clown came strolling up the sidewalk with a bunch of balloons in his hand. He opened the man's gate, walked up and joined the party of confused men. I was standing at my bedroom window, laughing uncontrollably at the scene when the neighbor suddenly pointed up to my window as he was talking to all the men on his porch. It was pretty obvious that I was his prime suspect.

A couple of decades later I was chatting with some friends and we decided that we should actually do my prank the right way. The way that I originally envisioned it. Not just calling up a few dozen businesses but calling up *all* of them. Having over 1,000 businesses trying to get to one location all at the same time would surely cause some major traffic problems, but just to make it worse, it would have to be a dead end street on one end, but a fairly busy road on the other end. This way not only would the traffic be trapped at the end of a dead end street, but the other service vehicles trying to get onto the street from the busy road would tie up traffic far beyond the location of the prank.

Since I couldn't think of a worthy victim for this kind of prank, I decided that I'd have to do this to several houses in a row, all at once. That way none of them would feel personally victimized by the prank. Or maybe even find a small apartment complex and send the businesses to random apartments. An apartment complex where there's a courtyard or parking lot with just one entrance, so all of the service trucks would be trapped in the parking lot. Or maybe even a trailer park.

My friends and I decided that we'd buy some prepaid cellular phones from a convenience store and spend several days on the phone doing nothing but setting up appointments. We'd each have our own sections of the yellow pages to cover, and our cell phones would have voicemail boxes on them so that the businesses could call us back to verify appointments.

We'd start with businesses that show up with really large trucks. Trucks that are hard to maneuver, and would be more difficult to get themselves off of the street once things started heating up. A few cement trucks would be perfect.

We would document everything on video, from setting it all up, to making the phone calls, to the final outcome on the streets. We would also set up wireless microphones at a few of the victims' front doors so that we could listen to some of their initial confusion. An FM radio microphone would be perfect, or maybe an X10 wireless security camera with a built-in microphone, or maybe some old FRS radios.

We would also call up a few TV stations and tip them off to the really strange event as it was occurring. Adding 2 or 3 news vans to the mix of traffic would be great. And, of course, we'd call and order pizzas and taxis during all of this. We were even prepared to spend a little money on putting advertisements in the local paper. There would be an ad for a huge multi-family yard sale at one of their houses that day. And another ad for a home auction, since those always seem to get lots of traffic. Maybe a few other miscellaneous ads, perhaps for some really good prices on rental property, encouraging people to come and fill out applications.

We would print up several hundred flyers announcing a huge party at the addresses of the victim. These would be posted all over the campus of each of the two nearby colleges. We would offer free beer kegs, clowns, strippers, raves, etc. The timing would have to be critical, so the drunken frats would show about an hour into all the chaos to help compliment the event.

Just out of respect for the hundreds of people trapped on this street for the better part of a day, we'd be sure to schedule a portable toilet company to set up facilities up and down the street. And we'd encourage a few local bands to try and set up, to give a show to the massive crowd. It'd probably be the best crowd that these small bands ever had. People in neighboring streets would begin to swarm towards the street once they heard a band begin to play. In fact, a small-scale riot would eventually ensue and police would arrive from neighboring towns in full riot gear.

There would eventually be such a crowd and traffic jam that we could probably just wander around in it with a camera, videotaping the chaos, and not be noticed by anyone. But I still needed to think of the pre-chaos stage; I needed to be able to sit somewhere, unnoticed, and videotape things happening before it got really big.

Soon after this huge event happened, I would piece together all the bits of audio, video, still pictures and frame grabs from the hidden web cam. It would form one hilarious hour-long escapade, showcasing the entire event, from planning, to the event, to the after effects. I would mix in my own footage with footage from the various network news stations and my hidden microphones.

My completed video would eventually be used in a court of law to convict me on terrorism charges and would put me behind bars for nearly a decade. And that's why we never completed the project. It sure was fun to think about it and plan out all the details with the members of the Cal's Forums, though.

Back

"The PLA has changed the way that I look at everything. That's why I don't leave the house anymore." -David H.

It was just after dusk as I approached a lone pay phone in Albany, Oregon. I'd been searching for a suitable phone for nearly an hour, but all I could find were empty booths or the remnants of what used to be pay phone stands mounted to the ground. Pay phones that I *knew* had existed just a few months before were now gone. Earlier in the day I'd downloaded a red boxing program from WeakNet Labs onto my Android cell phone and wanted to test their claims that red boxing could still work in 2010.

Most of the pay phones I found were independently owned, meaning that red boxing would be impossible on them. The one pay phone left at Heritage Mall probably would have worked, but it didn't have a dial tone. I thought I'd lucked out at Circle K when I found two pay phones in the parking lot that were owned by the local phone company, but they were Millennium pay phones and dialing zero on them transferred me to some other company that Qwest appeared to be outsourcing their call centers to. I began to doubt that Qwest even employed their own operators anymore.

Just two summers ago, I'd biked all over Albany, snapping pictures of every pay phone in the city, figuring they'd probably all be gone someday and it'd be kind of cool to have evidence that they once existed. But I didn't think that so many would disappear in just a few short years, making it such a challenge to find a working, red boxable phone. It was kind of sad to see them disappearing so quickly; pay phones had always been such an active part of my life.

It started in elementary school when my best friend, John Sever, came up with the idea of dialing the number to a pay phone to see if anyone would answer. He promised me that extreme hilarity would ensue if someone passing by were to pick up the phone and talk to us. So we wrote down the number from a phone booth several blocks away at the Wilshire Shopping Center and then called it, letting it ring for hours and occasionally having short conversations with people who picked it up. I can't recall if anything truly remarkable happened, but it was definitely the start of an obsession with collecting pay phone numbers that would last us both for years.

From that moment on, neither of us could pass by a pay phone without writing down the number to it and sharing it with each other. We each kept our own separate lists, each organized in our own ways. Whenever my parents asked if I wanted to go to a store with them, many times my answer depended on whether I had written down that store's pay phone numbers yet. Out-of-state family vacations were especially exciting, because that meant out-of-state pay phone numbers.

My parents, who usually weren't too crazy about my phone antics, always allowed me a quick minute to write down pay phone numbers while we were out. They even put up with me dialing the phone company's free ringback number afterwards, which would cause the pay phone to ring as I walked away. Back then it wasn't hard to find two or three pay phones grouped together at a mall or a grocery store, so it was great to make all of them ring at the same time. Bonus points if I got to see someone walk over and pick up the phone. And even more bonus points if I squirted food coloring on the handset first, so that the person answering would end up with it smeared all over their hand and face.

I remember the night that my parents dropped my brother and I off at Ziggy's Skating Rink and I was thrilled to find a new pay phone there, hidden amongst the arcade machines, but surprised to find that there wasn't a number written on the phone. This was a problem I'd never encountered before and I wasn't sure what to do about it, so I dialed zero and asked the operator if she could tell me what the number was. She told me that she had no way of knowing that information. I hung up and called another operator to ask the same question. This one told me that she wasn't allowed to tell me, which let me know that the first operator was lying to me. When the third operator answered, I began yelling, "You're the stupidest operator ever! You're so dumb! I bet you're so dumb that you don't even know what number I'm calling from and you can't do a thing about me calling you names!"

This operator immediately proved me wrong by saying, "Oh yes I *do* know your number!" and then reading the phone's number to me, thereby proving herself better than a bratty little kid. I told her I was sorry and quickly hung up the phone since I was always afraid that an operator could dispatch the police to a pay phone within seconds of pushing a magic button.

As I entered my teens and received a TRS-80 computer for Christmas, I hardwired its speech card into my home phone so my computer could talk to people who picked up pay phones with its robotic voice. For years, I called the pay phones in front of 7-Eleven and talked to the teenagers who loitered in front all evening, using a program I wrote to quickly say common phrases such as, "Hello, how are you?" and "What is your name?" and "Malfunction…need input!" The teenagers seemed to believe everything that a computer voice told them, including the part about me being a top secret military computer system sitting on a desk in the White House and making calls because I was bored. They passed around the phone for hours sometimes, talking to my computer.

Once I learned about red boxing, my obsession with pay phones was taken to a whole new level. When I left home and went to Texas, I spent hours each evening sitting in my car at a pay phone, making free calls to random phone numbers all over the country. This was in the early nineties when long distance wasn't very cheap yet, so suddenly being able to call any number in the world for free was amazing stuff for me. I would spend half the night at a pay phone, calling phone company news lines, test lines, random businesses and friends. This phase of my pay phone obsession lasted for years and followed me all over the country. Having people come up to me and ask, "Are you going to be much longer? I need to use the phone!" was a regular thing for me.

I began to amass a large collection of the plastic cards on the front of pay phones that identified which phone company they were with. I had large stacks of them from old phone companies that didn't exist anymore such as Pacific Bell, Ameritech and Bell South, as well as the newer phone companies like Verizon and Qwest, the short-lived SBC, and independent companies like Fox Fone and Payphones of America. I carried a suction cup in my backpack to remove the cards that were stuck into their frame too tightly for me to remove with a pocket knife or the edge of a dime. It was my equivalent of collecting stamps or coins.

My pay phone number collection continued to grow for more than a decade and eventually became a part of the PLA-UPL Phone Directoroy. Today, a pay phone list is still maintained in the PLA Forums, where people from all over the world continue to contribute phone numbers.

I would call operators from pay phones and just chat with them, sometimes persuading them to tell me details about their jobs or the phone company. In 1994, an operator in Cincinnati told my friend Shawn and I that we would be seeing drastic improvements in pay phones in the years to come, including pay phones that allowed services like 3-way calling and call waiting. All pay phones would be upgraded with screens that would display all kinds of data for a small fee. She really seemed excited about the upcoming changes we would soon see. She had no idea that cell phones would become commonplace a few years later, completely squashing their plans for futuristic pay phones.

Now here I was, more than twenty-five years since my pay phone obsession began, standing in front of the only remaining outdoor pay phone in downtown Albany. The phone was sitting inside a stand, just outside of the entrance to the post office, and seemed like a perfect candidate for red boxing. At this late hour, nobody was around to hear my Android program blasting red box tones. I picked up the phone and was relieved to hear a dial tone, after finding so many broken phones earlier in the day. I pressed zero and the automated system replied that a Qwest operator would be right with me.

"You don't see too many people using pay phones these days," a voice behind me mused. Great. I'd finally found the perfect pay phone and some guy wanted to have a conversation with me. I ignored him and hoped he would go away.

"Some people might wonder why a man with such a nice wireless phone would even need to use a pay phone," he continued. I looked at the man through the reflection in the front of the phone, unable to make out his features too clearly since it was getting dark out. Thinking he needed to use the phone, I glanced over and said, "I'll be off in just a minute," then turned back to the phone. I was annoyed that, with him so close to me, I wouldn't be able to test the program yet. I'd probably need to leave so he could use the phone and then come back later. I could do that, but what a pain in the ass since I'd finally found the perfect phone after hours of searching.

"*I* know what you're up to, though, Alex," he continued as though he hadn't heard me. "You're trying to find a phone that will accept red box tones. I don't see why you're messing with such an outdated concept though."

I was shaken by how much this man knew. Was he a cop? A phone company employee? FBI, maybe? I managed to calmly hang up the phone and turn around. The man wore a long coat with a scarf and his hair stood up in the wind. His thick beard made it difficult to determine his age, but he didn't look much older than me.

"Who are you?" I asked, impressed with my ability to sound annoyed and completely unnerved by his presence.

"I'm surprised you don't remember me, after all the things we've been through together. Looting Bell trucks and breaking open phone boxes to make free calls and even running from the police a couple of times," he chuckled. "Or that time you saw me thrown into the back of a garbage truck and get crushed alive."

I suddenly felt light headed and put my hand on the pay phone to balance myself. "Doug?" I couldn't believe that he was here. For a split second, I thought that I was having a conversation with a ghost. Doug couldn't be alive. I'd spoken to friends over the past twenty years who'd told me that Doug disappeared at the same time I did. They'd all just assumed we'd run off together. Doug's parents had even contacted my parents, asking if they'd heard from him. I was the only person who knew what really happened to Doug. And now here he was, standing in front of me.

"You look surprised," he laughed.

"I just thought..."

"Thought that I was dead? I didn't think you'd care. It's not like you made much of an effort to save me."

"Doug, I..." I didn't know how to explain anything to him. This isn't a conversation that I thought I'd be having today. Or any day, for that matter. "I thought you'd been crushed after you fell into the truck. I ran after the garbage man, but he didn't see me."

"Lucky for me, that load of trash wasn't compacted. I climbed to the top and jumped off at his next stop. He saw me on the truck and yelled at me, so I ran. I had to hide in some bushes until he left, and when I got back to the phone company building, you were gone. I was afraid that you'd gone to the police so they could rescue me from the garbage truck so I ran to the police station to see if your car was there. Then I made an anonymous call to them, asking if you'd been in there. Finally I gave up on finding you, so I walked to the bus station and took a bus home that morning."

"But people told me you weren't in school that day," I said.

"Yeah, Alex, I was tired. I went to my room and slept all day. Then I found out that *you* weren't in school. I had no idea what happened to you. I biked over to your house and let myself in before your parents were home from work and found all of your shit gone, then found the note you left for your parents. I was a little pissed off that you just left me to die in a garbage truck."

"Doug, I'm sorry. I didn't think there was any chance you could be alive. I didn't know what to do."

"Well, I knew where you went," he continued. "Galveston. It's all you and that girlfriend of yours talked about that year. I went back home and packed up my things, thinking it'd be great to freak you out by just showing up there. I took a Greyhound bus from St. Louis and made it all the way to Oklahoma City before deciding I didn't want to see you. Why would I want to hang out with a so-called friend who would just leave me dead in a garbage truck? Who'd skip town, just to save himself, not even caring if I got a proper burial or not.

"I switched Greyhounds and went west instead. I ended up in Los Angeles the first year, then moved to Bakersfield for a job with the phone company. I faked my resume and job references and took a job as an outside technician with Pacific Bell. I worked there for over a year and then transferred to Fresno, doing the same thing. I even emptied pay phones for a while, something you and I had dreamed of doing when we were younger.

"My original intent was to get a job, just to learn the system so that I could fuck with it more effectively. Maybe steal quarters from pay phones on the side and I'd have the coolest collection of lineman's handsets and hard hats ever. But then I began to obsess over the idea of working my way into a job with telephone security so that I could track you down and have you arrested. I started keeping an eye on Zak's phone records, which told me where you where and which pay phones you hung out at. Imagine my surprise when I found out that you'd just moved to Los Angeles with some girl you met in Galveston.

"I faked a resume under a new name and moved back to Los Angeles. The identity I picked belonged to a phone company security guy in Connecticut. I was able to use his references and reputation with Bell Atlantic to quickly find a job with Pacific Bell's corporate security. I got the job, but you moved back to Texas a few weeks later, so I followed you there and got a job with Southwestern Bell, using the same guy's identity. For eighteen years now, Alex, I've been following you around the country and collecting evidence against you. Listening to your phone calls at your home, watching you at pay phones, digging through your trash, following you everywhere you go. Waiting for the perfect time to take you down."

"Doug, that's kind of...weird of you," I said, thoroughly baffled at what I was hearing. "Seriously, eighteen years? I barely even do anything anymore. The statute of limitations has to have expired on all of the stuff from the 90's by now. I mean-"

"Let me finish," he interrupted. "I was really close when you moved back to Illinois for a few years. I took a job with SBC and began monitoring your phone calls. I listened as you stalked that radio DJ in Ohio and then as you made harassing calls to Curtis for over a year. Finally the day came when I was to turn in all my paperwork on you. Which just happened to be the same day the feds came in and arrested me for identity theft and tax evasion."

"That had to suck," I said.

"By the time I got out of prison, you had moved back here to Albany. So I skipped out on my probation and took a new job with Qwest, under the name of a security guy from Bell South. It had been eleven years since I'd worked at Qwest before, but luckily none my old coworkers were still in my department, so I didn't have to worry about being recognized."

"Doug, this is crazy. You wasted two decades of your life on this. It would have been more productive to just punch me in the face a few times and then be done with it."

I barely even saw his fists coming at me. When I awoke, I was lying in the back of a cargo van. I raised my head and saw Doug sitting at a small desk, typing on a computer terminal. "Pain?" he asked me, looking over and offering me a bottle of aspirin.

"Nah, I'm good," I replied, sitting up. I motioned to the computer screen. "What are you doing there?"

"Remember when I was in the dumpster and I told you I had something you would like?"

"Not really."

"Well, this is it," he said, holding up a Panasonic answering machine that looked like it was manufactured in the 1980's. Running from where the dual cassette tape decks were supposed to be were several dozen wires that seemed to be attached to a computer keyboard.

"What is it?" I asked.

"It's a special microchip that can break the encryption scheme on any phone company computer!" he beamed.

"What are those pins moving up and down by your keyboard?"

"Oh, those. Those are converting the text on the screen to braille, for blind people to read. The chip only seems to work on computer hardware made for blind people. God, it's good to see you, Alex!"

I looked at the computer screen and saw that he was connected to AT&T's billing system. The account information was mine. Doug began, once again, a monologue to me.

"In 2006, you signed up for an account with AT&T wireless, porting your old telephone number from Verizon Wireless. You began with a Blackberry Edge phone and then converted to an iPhone two years later. Just recently you've upgraded again, to an Android phone with the 450 anytime minutes plan for $39.99 with unlimited texting for $20 extra."

"Doug, what are you doing?" I asked.

"Oh, I don't know, Alex," Doug sneered. "I think having anytime rollover minutes and 5,000 nights and weekend minutes is a bit excessive, don't you think? Maybe I should switch your account over to a prepaid calling plan!" and with that, his fingers flew over the keyboard, making the changes to my account.

"Doug, please, don't," I pleaded.

"Oh, it's too late now, Alex. What's done is done. When you get your bill next month, you'll be paying by the minute for your calls and your texts individually."

"Doug, I don't want to have to call up AT&T and switch it back. Their hold times are brutal. I thought you were going to have me arrested for thinking about making a 50 cent red box call from that pay phone."

"I was," Doug said, "until you gave me the idea of punching you in the face instead. Now with this account modification, I think we're just about even. Get out." He pointed towards the sliding door of the van.

"Doug, I-"

"*Out!*" he screamed, jumping up and sliding open the door for me.

I moved to the door and Doug pushed me out, making me fall to the ground as he yelled at me, "You always had to win! Always had to get the girl! Always had to be better than me! Well, I don't see you winning this time, Alex!"

With that, he slid the van's door shut and drove off, leaving me lying in the road in a plume of white exhaust smoke. I watched as his van stalled several blocks away, at the traffic light. He started it up again and continued down the road. I stood up and limped slowly across the street, back to the post office, to test out my Android red box.

Back - 291

Imagine that this wasn't really the end of the Phone Losers of America book. What if it just kept going, for another hundred chapters or so, and the stories were accompanied by pictures, videos, news clippings, songs and sound clips. Not only that, but each story ended with comments, posted by readers who either loved or hated the stories, and there were even forums where you could go to ask questions about them. Well, welcome to the amazing, futuristic world of Web 2.0!

The stories in this book are just a tiny portion of what the PLA is. On the phonelosers.org website, you'll find enough content there to keep you busy for months. Hundreds of prank calls, pictures, videos, tutorials, discussions and pages of reading are waiting for you there. You might even find an entire podcast dedicated to your favorite chapter. Maybe you'll be one of the people dumb enough to fall for our April Fools Day pranks. So call your work and tell them you won't be in for a few days, then visit www.phonelosers.org.

I've also set up a companion page for this book, which will give you some history behind each of the chapters here, sometimes linking you to related websites and audio or video content. If you've enjoyed the stories here, you might enjoy them even more when you read them while listening to accompanying multimedia. The companion site is located here:

www.phonelosers.org/book/companion

You can contact me, the author, by emailing rbcp@phonelosers.org or by visiting my homepage at www.notla.com. Thanks for reading my book.

Cactus cactus,
Brad

Acknowledgements

"*When ya can't harass the ones you want...harass the ones you can*" -Spessa

Lots of thanks goes to lots of people for making the Phone Losers of America awesome. I'm almost afraid to list names, because I'm 100% certain that I'm going to forget loads of people and they'll hate me forever, but I'm going to make an attempt at it anyway. Please don't be too sad if you're not mentioned here, because I'm old and senile and can't be expected to remember everything.

I'll thank the dead people first. Micah, our web host for years, always happily dealt with threatening letters from Tannest, members of the Boulder News Forums and many other people. He was also the person who registered the phonelosers.org domain name at a time when I was thinking about ditching the PLA to move on to other things. Mildred Monday was a fun old lady to prank and she never tired of loudly proclaiming that she was Mildred Monday. Spee was a fun person and a good friend to all of us on IRC, and he taught us all how much Raymond sucked. And Tom Lively, who drove our A-

Team van during the McDonald's sign prank, was a great friend and always loved the PLA shenanigans. Rest in peace, guys!

Thanks, el_jefe, aka Zak, for being a major force in the PLA content and being a great friend to plot evil things with. PLA wouldn't have been PLA without him. Thanks, EvilCal, for supporting us for years with web hosting, forums, a telnet BBS and even having a PLA-themed wedding cake. EvilCal helped with a ton of behind-the-scenes PLA stuff, as well as some classic PLA pranks that aren't mentioned in this book, but can be found on phonelosers.org.

Thanks, Mom and Dad, for putting up with my crazy antics and sometimes having to deal with the fallout from them. Thanks, Ralph Steadman (ralphsteadman.com), for not sending the angels of death after me. AmigaDOS for giving us the cactus. Joe Peacock, for inspiration, guidance, a free book and Mentally Incontinent (mentallyincontinent.com) stickers. Yomama, for free legal counsel about this book and to members of Cal's Forums. Heywood, aka Jeremy Morgan (jeremymorgan.com), for bringing the world the awesomeness that is Curtis the Superhacker. El Gordo, for allowing me to steal some text of his for the ending paragraph in the McDonald's sign prank chapter.

Thanks, Trevelyn (trevelyn.com and weaknetlabs.com), for writing amazing PLA music, making PLA DS games, PLA Android applications and tons of other things. Thanks, Rob Vincent, aka Rob T Firefly (robvincent.net), for PLA songs, PLA art, writing awesome things for the 'zine and speaking at the PLA panels at HOPE.

Thanks, Surbo and henvsnt (i-hacked.com) and everyone at pauldotcom.com for being the shit. Thanks for all the fun Richard C. stuff, Naked Kitchen Podcast. Thanks, Exotic Liability, Hacker Public Radio, and Security Justice, for blowing my fucking mind.

Thanks, murdoc (murdoc.net), for the PLA panels, participating in some of our audio content, and giving sound advice to the youngsters on the PLA forums. Thanks, Roxy (amuseyou.net and omghax.net), Jenn (thisisarecording.com),

RogueClown, altalp, Scott McWilliams (party934.com), Drew Curtis (fark.com), i-ball, and even you, trOn.

Thanks, Spessa for copy editing some of this book and yelling at me for all my dumb mistakes, and Mr. Spessa for always taking our silly phone pranks way too far. Thanks, linear, for bringing your unique perspective on hockey and farts to The Phone Show. Thanks, Jammie (jammie718.com), for all the copyediting work and for being such a fun part of the PLA all these years. Thanks, Jason Heckathorn, for being the most hilarious spaz ever. Thanks, RijilV, Legend, CountyKid, Luvox Phreak, Tombstone, Carlito from Madhouse Radio (madhouselive.com), kcochran, Evie, Evilgold, Spuds, Emmanuel, isotek, sidepocket, Patty, Netmask, hektik, all those 303 guys, Jessica, Anne, Chris Tomkinson, Logic Box, NotKevin, Shonna, Joe and Mike Tankersley. Thanks, sakerobot (3rdworm), for educating the masses about mouths. Thanks, Weird Harold, for being fun to prank and unwittingly funding a few of our flights. Thanks, Kristine, for changing the direction of my life a few times. Thanks, John Sever and Sara Grimes, for being major creative influences during my childhood.

Thanks, all you PLA forum people, like Lordnod, Raptor, MattGSX, liife, judasiscariot, Sidepocket, Gangals, frog, M-26-7, mr_doc, Lestan Gregor, Phish-Phreak, Mr. Anderson, silentneep, ApprenticePhreak, RushPwnsX, Colonel Panic, SpaceBison, nova, splyntor, MIB, mordekai, handl3r, Zazen, afreak, Godot, s1acker, mrpeanut, Arox!, ghostman, CerealKiller, Mr. Cactus, ryanfido, Reverend Greed, z3wb, Dr P4nyk, AmishGangsta, ravenmaddox, vixen, BaconStrips, N3gativ3sanity, nwbell, Copyright, Acidpez, JD716, johnnyhacker, JohnKerry, ErrorLoading, nyphonejacks, gnnr, Robert_, nomadcowatbk, computerwiz_222, Skunkworks, Laugh Track Matt, that other matt, SloFuze, nb7899, Yauch, Jersey, Illuminati, amazing_ned, ataxicwolf, Zerobio, Phrank, z09, spsmckintra, sabrebutt, flamoot, Royal, WhiteSword, purplepla69, DBK, Moose-Alini, HektiK, Big-E, Enamon, Chris Ellerbeck, 14D, Arik Burns and everyone else.

Printed in Dunstable, United Kingdom